I also want to thank my family, and especially my wife, Kristen, for the patience, and love it takes to live with a book in progress. She's put up with countless late nights, most of them lit by nothing but a laptop glow while she tried to sleep. I couldn't have done this without you.

I0418350

# ELVIS IN 55
## *A Detailed Account*

Joe Sins

Anthem and Arrow Media

This book is a work of narrative nonfiction.
Every effort has been made to ensure historical
accuracy. Interpretive analysis reflects the author's
research and perspective.

ISBN: 979-8-9941553-4-9
Published by

Anthem and Arrow Media

Printed in the United States of America

Author's Note on Sources

## ABOUT THE AUTHOR

Joe Sins grew up in Southern California. Elvis records were always in the air around him, and that music stuck. Over time, the curiosity turned into a deep dive: photos, stories, dates, and the people who were there.

A gifted musician, Joe's drive and talent were noticed early. Under the guidance of music mentor Patrick Kercheval, who played an integral role in his musical development, Joe became a first-chair performer in the All-Desert and San Bernardino County Honor Bands. While still a teenager, he received early songwriting interest in California, including offers at age eighteen from Hollywood Records. Rainbow Records, as well as a formal letter inviting him to audition in Nashville for Be a Star. During this formative period, Joe persuaded surf-guitar pioneer Dick Dale to appear with him onstage, playing guitar at his side, an early indication of his confidence and ability to bridge generations of American music.

In high school, Joe was picked for the American Musical Ambassadors, honor earned through his honor-band performances. Rather than touring internationally, he chose to start a demanding residency as a country music singer. Performing seven nights a week, an experience that accelerated his stage discipline, stamina, and command of live audiences at a young age. He later performed with the Commandant's Own United States Marine Corps Band and appeared as a trumpet player in a nationally televised concert with the United States Navy Band.

From the ages of eighteen to twenty, Joe lived in Pioneertown, California, where he was shaped deeply by Harrie Allen at the legendary Pappy & Harriet's. During this period, Joe served as part of the venue's house band, performing regularly, and absorbing the discipline of live music at a formative age. It was there that he met and/or performed alongside artists including Jim Lauderdale, Sheryl Crow, Gene Autry, Johnny Lee, Dale Watson, Dusty Wakeman, Victoria Williams, and Cracker. The venue would later host performances by Paul McCartney, Lorde, and Robert Plant, underscoring its enduring place in American music history.

While performing at Pappy & Harriet's, Joe befriended film producer Matthew Patrick, known for producing Hider in the House starring Gary Busey. The two started collaborating on music for an upcoming film project in the area. During this time, Joe often attended gatherings hosted by Patrick on his property in Joshua Tree, an area that later became widely known as Rock City.

During the same period, Joe spent time writing songs, and playing pool with Mike Massey, a world title holder in 9-ball, 8-ball, and one-pocket. Billiards Digest has called Massey one of the greatest trick-shot artists of all time. He is a member of the Billiard Congress of America Hall of Fame and a many-time ESPN Trick Shot Magic champion. Between sessions, Joe, and Massey played often, and Joe even won a couple of games. It was an unlikely but formative influence on that desert period.

At the urging of Jim Lauderdale, Joe moved to Nashville at the age of twenty-one. In a move that showed both belief and practicality, Lauderdale left an envelope of cash for him at his management company, Fitzgerald-Hartley, to help him get started. It was an early vote of confidence that launched Joe into the Nashville songwriting scene.

For the first year and a half in Nashville, Joe slept in the front seat of his 1965 Chrysler Imperial-large enough to stretch out in-parking at KOA campgrounds and outside truck stops. He woke early each morning to look for opportunities, spending his days writing, knocking on doors, and learning the city from the ground up.

After arriving in Nashville, Joe was noticed as a songwriter by Johnny Russell, who helped set up a meeting with one of the city's most established publishing firms, Tom Collins Music. It was there that Joe met Cris Lacy, now Chair, and President of Warner Records Nashville, and worked closely with songwriter Chris DuBois, son of Arista Records founder Tim DuBois, to hone his craft.

Joe's Nashville years were full of songwriting and publishing work. He got an early publishing deal with country music legend Merle Kilgore, whose catalog included "Ring of Fire" (recorded by Johnny Cash) and "Burning Memories" (recorded by Ray Price). Joe also co-wrote with respected writers like Hal Bynum, Ron Hellard, Wayne Carson, David Chamberlain, Mark Alan Springer, Karen Staley, Vern Gosdin, Sammy Lyons, Toni Dae, and Barry Paul Jackson. Songs connected to that circle were cut by artists such as Johnny Cash, Ray Price, Kenny Rogers, Keith Whitley, Willie Nelson, Elvis Presley, George Strait, Tanya Tucker, Tracy Byrd, Alan Jackson, George Jones, and Tammy Wynette.

At just twenty-four, Joe served as publishing manager for Paris Landing Music, building, and pitching songs for artists including Joe Stampley, Tony Stampley, Toni Dae, Tom Botkin, Lew Rawls, and Kelly Lovelace. He also served as administrator for Vern Gosdin's publishing catalog and maintained an office at Merle Kilgore Management. He later served as a pallbearer at Vern Gosdin's funeral and was seated with the family at Merle Kilgore's funeral at the Ryman Auditorium.

He runs the Joe Sins Rare Elvis Photos community and shares rare images, stories, and history for fans who want the details. His goal is simple: keep the record straight and keep Elvis's story alive.

In addition to Elvis in '55, Joe is the author of The Night Elvis Saved Christmas, which remained on Amazon's bestseller and top seller lists throughout the 2025 Christmas season.

Joe's interest in Elvis Presley, and in the human forces that shaped him, fuels his work as a writer, researcher, and storyteller. As an author, songwriter, videographer, and lifelong creative, he keeps digging for the details that define American music and culture. He also writes and performs with his wife, Kristen, as one half of the country duo The Sins Country.

This book is written as narrative nonfiction. When I tell you where Elvis was, who he played with, what he recorded, and what the trade papers, and local papers reported, I lean on published timelines, contemporary reporting, and major biographies. I list those sources in the notes.

When the paper trail is thin, I treat memories like memories. They can add color, but they are not the whole case. I try to back them up with dates, newspapers, recordings, or trusted research. If I can't confirm a detail and it doesn't change the point, I say so.

You'll see a few secondary reference sites in the notes. I use them as signposts (not as the final word), and I lean on primary documents, trade press, and established scholarship when the stakes are high.

# Table of Contents

Chapter 1, January 1955 ........................................1

Chapter 2, February 1955 ................................. 27

Chapter 3, March 1955.................................... 56

Chapter 4, April 1955 ...................................... 77

Chapter 5, May 1955 ........................................92

Chapter 6, June 1955 ...................................... 115

Chapter 7, July 1955....................................... 138

Chapter 8, August 1955...................................155

Chapter 9, September 1955 .............................175

Chapter 10, October 1955 .............................. 194

Chapter 11, November 1955 ........................... 212

Chapter 12, December 1955............................224

FULL KNOWN RECORD OF ALL 1955

PERFORMANCE DATES......................................232

Sources & Notes .............................................247

# Introduction

By January 1955, Elvis Presley isn't a whisper outside of Memphis. Radio has started to carry his voice and his special stage presence across the South. Crowds have reacted in ways that surprise them. His name is starting to arrive in towns before he does on posters, in radio patter and in the kind of arguments people have at kitchen tables and in high school hallways when something new feels both thrilling and slightly unsafe.

What changed between 1954 and now isn't just that more people know his name. It's a weight that all involved with Elvis feel. The schedule gets tighter. What started with few occasional shows here and there in mid-1954 turns into a well-oiled machine in 1955 due to a suddenly booked calendar: drive, arrive, play, leave, and do it again before the adrenaline even has a chance to settle in Elvis's legs. The halls start to blur. The roads stretch longer. And the live performances, show after show after show, keep teaching the same lesson: this isn't a normal moment in time. It's the start of something nobody could put a finger on, but they knew was coming and coming fast.

As the year moves on, Elvis's life splits into five clear parts that keep intersecting and running into each other: his personal life (family and girlfriends), his music, his management and promotion team (Bob Neal and Colonel Tom Parker's growing influence and expanding ambitions) his health, and physical stamina, and the widening circle of people who start to gather around him: old friends, new friends, musicians, DJs, promoters, and recognizable names who sense something building and want to be near it. None of these parts stay separate for long. They collide with each other to grow tension. That is what you will feel as you read these pages.

This book follows 1955 day by day and month by month because it is a year not studied like this ever before. These details help us stay grounded and stop us from looking back and turning the year into legend. Around those dates is detail: the towns that host him, the halls that carry him. The songs in rotation on the radio when Elvis steps onstage, and how it all works together: travel, scheduling, routine that decides whether a live act will succeed or fall apart. You will feel exhausted for Elvis as he crosses from town to town and state to state.

Now, you won't find one single turning point. You'll see buildup of them: crowd reactions in one town turning into expectation in the next. The expectations growing into demand, and demand starts to outrun the obstacles society put in place to contain it. The ticket windows stretch longer, the tight hallways feel smaller and smaller when teenage girls gravitate and congregate into them. Trying to catch even a glimpse of their idol and the few hired hands trying to handle a thousand surging bodies. The year doesn't stop to explain itself. It doesn't have time to. It just keeps moving. Moving to the music of Elvis.

# Chapter 1, January 1955

## JANUARY 1 TO JANUARY 8: TEXAS HEAT AND A SHREVEPORT ANCHOR

### Key Dates

Jan 1 (Sat): Grand Prize Saturday Night, Jamboree, Eagles Hall, Houston, Texas. Radio hosted package show.

Jan 2-4 (Sun-Tue), Houston area. Additional appearances reported in period listings.

Jan 5 (Wed): City Auditorium, San Angelo, Texas. Crowd reaction becomes part of the story.

Jan 6 (Thu): Fair Park, Lubbock, Texas. Radio promotion recorded at KDAV is documented in day-by-day accounts.

Jan 7 (Fri): High School Auditorium, Midland, Texas. Large crowd reported in period reporting.

Jan 8 (Sat): Louisiana Hayride, Municipal Auditorium, Shreveport, Louisiana. Radio barn dance broadcast from Municipal Auditorium.

Houston is a fitting place to open the year because a city like Houston understands large scale. It is a growing Gulf Coast big city, connected to shipping, industry, and the wealth, and labor of the oil economy. A Saturday night show in a city like this isn't a small local gathering. It is part of a larger entertainment machine driven by radio, show planners, and the after World War II hunger for noise and something new. Elvis walks into Houston as a name that has started to move through the

South. But in January he is showing that his name can cash out in real bodies in real seats.

A 1955 package show has its own rules. There is an host who warms the audience. There are quick transitions between acts. There is a sense that the attendees are being managed, kept entertained while equipment is shifted and performers rotate. In that environment, the opener doesn't win by being small. He wins by landing a strong reaction, keeping the pace, and leaving the crowd slightly shocked that the time is over. Elvis learns to handle every appearance like a short story. Hook, heat, release, exit.

On that opening Saturday night in Houston, what was important was just not that Elvis appeared, it was who stood beside his name. The bill mixed rising young faces and established radio personalities, and it carried the feeling of a traveling show that knew how to turn a city's attention into noise. Tommy Sands was there, still a teenager but already familiar to the Colonel's circle. And George Jones was on the same lineup, a reminder that the country world was full of sharp talent even before Elvis broke national boundaries. The radio host, Biff Collie, kept the evening moving with the practiced rhythm of radio broadcast entertainment. This meant Elvis's set was recognized as a public event and not a local curiosity.

Behind the scenes, the business side also clicked into a more formal gear. Elvis's managerial contract with Bob Neal went into effect at the start of the year. And in the weeks that followed, photographs of Elvis with Neal, and Sam Phillips spread in trade and fan publications like quiet proof that a serious team was forming around the singer. It did not change the miles he had to drive, but it changed the way his name started to look on paper: less like a kid getting booked, more like an act being managed, set up, and prepared for larger rooms.

Music in this period is built on the Sun Records breakthrough. The sound is lean: a guitar that snaps and drives, a bass that pushes, and thumps. A singer who can bend a blues note into a country line and make it feel like a new language. Elvis isn't yet singing in a polished, major label way. His strength is that he does not sound trained. His voice sounds urgent. In a hall full of teenagers and their parents, urgency is an attention getter. People may disagree about whether they like it, but they can't ignore it.

His personal life in early 1955 is defined by movement and loyalty. He is still rooted in the circle of his parents and the Memphis home base. He is also still close enough to his old life and to his old world that friends and girlfriends can treat him like someone they know. When he has the time to even see them, which is sparingly as you will see as the pages turn into his history. At the same time, the road is teaching him a new kind of loneliness. Even when he is surrounded by fans, he is alone in the sense that no one can carry his load for him. Every mile is a choice that his body has to endure. There are girls at every show that want to be with him, to get to know him, to capture a piece of him, but Elvis is on to the next city and performance barely after his lips can brush those of another beauty.

After Houston the route turns into West Texas, and this is where the location really matters. San Angelo isn't a suburb of a larger city. It is a local center. Here, the venue is a center for town life. When a touring act arrives, the town treats it as a shared experience, something they will talk about for days, weeks and perhaps even months. The crowd here has a stronger collective sense of who they are than a big city house does. People recognize each other. Parents know whose kid is in the front row. That makes the audience's very strong reaction to Elvis feel even more charged, because it turns into a public demonstration of youthful and female energy in a room that is used to being in control. When Ernest Tubb traveled through, the parents were well in control, when Elvis appeared, not so much.

San Angelo turned the momentum that was building on paper into something physical, they could see with their own eyes and hear with their own ears. The City Auditorium held roughly eighteen hundred seats, and the room's size mattered because it gave the frenzied atmosphere in the town somewhere to gather. One advertisement even misspelled his name as "Alvis Presley," a small, nearly comic mistake that still captured the truth: the public was learning him faster than the show planners could spell him. The lineup around him, Hayride names like Billy Walker and the duo Jimmy and Johnny, plus the country comic Peach Seed Jones, made the night feel like a full variety package, but the teenagers in the house treated

Elvis like the headline. He was who most had come to see anyhow.

Reports from dates like this describe girls rushing the front for autographs and pushing toward the stage with a kind of urgency that didn't match the usual polite town behavior. That mismatch is the story of early 1955: respectable rooms trying to behave like respectable rooms, while a young singer made them behave like something wilder. The adults could sense the danger in it, not danger in the violent sense, but danger as in loss of control, and the kids understood that loss of control as a new kind of freedom.

Lubbock adds radio detail to the story. The South Plains are wide, agricultural, and wind driven. In a region like this, radio isn't background. It is transportation. It carries music across miles of farmland and connects small towns to a shared weekend pulse. When Elvis attends radio promotions, he is learning to sell himself in a different medium than the stage. He learns that his voice can be packaged into a few sentences and still trigger a crowd later when the turnout hears that same voice in person.

Lubbock carried its own myth even in memory. Waylon Jennings, who would later become a star in his own right. Recalled talk the young "hillbilly cat" around this run. What stands out in that recollection isn't a pose but a listening habit: Elvis talking like a man with his ear pressed to the rhythm-and-blues world, telling people his next record might be LaVern Baker's "Tweedlee Dee" just as it was start to catch fire on the R&B charts. It is a small moment, but it shows how his imagination was already crossing boundaries that radio programmers still treated as fences. Waylon worked as a performer and DJ on KVOW, KDAV, KYTI in Texas and Arizona, and was 18 in 1955.

The KDAV radio promotion tied that boundary-crossing directly to the microphone. Local accounts place Elvis at the station with his guitar singing quick, raw performances from that times R&B material: "Fool. Fool, Fool," popularized by the Clovers, and "Shake, Rattle, and Roll," the Big Joe Turner stomper that was ripping through jukeboxes as a way to prime the evening's crowd. He was doing what young artists do when they are hungry: taking whatever room the town gives them. Turning it into a radio broadcast, turning whatever song is in the air into another proof that he can command it.

Midland brings a new kind of audience mix. In the Permian Basin, the economy is shaped by oil booms and the labor that supports them. A hall or school auditorium crowd there includes teenagers, oil workers, business owners, and families who have learned to live with sudden growth. Elvis learns to hold that mixed crowd's attention. He can't perform only for the kids, because the adults are there, and they control the money at the door. He also can't dilute his energy to satisfy adults, because the kids will turn away. That balancing act becomes one of his most important skills he learns in early 1955.

Then Shreveport on the 8th. The Louisiana Hayride isn't just another booking. It is a radio broadcast important show with a disciplined format and a history of launching talent. A Hayride appearance gives Elvis a wider audience than any single hall can provide, and it also forces him to perform inside a professional framework. The stage is shared. The time is limited. The band has to be ready. What the room expects polishes his set of songs. It teaches him how to be explosive on a clock.

By the time the Hayride radio broadcast rolled around, even the introductions sounded like branding. Announcer Frank Page billed him as the "Memphis Flash," and on at least one night he described Elvis to the radio audience in quick visual strokes, crocodile-skin shoes, bright socks, as if the clothes were part of the sound. Elvis moved through a tight set list that paired his core Sun sense of who they are with crowd-pleasers: "That's All Right." "Hearts of Stone," "Blue Moon of Kentucky," and the R&B-leaning "Fool, Fool, Fool." The bill also included rising country acts such as Johnny Horton. This mattered because it placed Elvis inside a world of future stars, not outside it.

If January 1955 has a single lesson, it is that the road isn't a detour from the career. The road *is* the career. In January he is building a reputation the only way a working singer can build it in 1955: by showing up, sounding good, and leaving behind the kind of story that spreads through school hallways, diners, barbershops, and radio request lines.

## JANUARY 11 TO JANUARY 22: THE SMALL TOWN CIRCUIT ACROSS FOUR STATES

Promoter "Colonel" Tom Parker was still an outsider to Elvis's small circle, but by mid-January his ears were already bending toward the noise., DJ "Uncle Dudley" sent word of the crowd frenzy after Elvis's January 11th show. Describing the kind of screaming, pushing, and sudden devotion that could not be explained by radio play alone. Parker did not yet know the boy, but he knew the signs: a name that moved tickets, a name that made adults uneasy, a name that made a room behave like weather. Something everybody could talk about.

### Key Dates

Jan 11 (Tue): High School Gym, New Boston, Texas. Small town touring run begins.

Jan 12 (Wed): City Auditorium, Clarksdale, Mississippi. Delta stop on the circuit.

Jan 13 (Thu): Catholic Club, Helena, Arkansas. River town booking.

Jan 14 (Fri): Futrell High School Gym, Marianna, Arkansas. Listed in regional schedules.

Jan 15 (Sat): Louisiana Hayride, Municipal Auditorium, Shreveport, Louisiana. Regular broadcast work continues.

Jan 17 (Mon): Junior College Auditorium, Booneville, Mississippi. Listed in local reporting.

Jan 18 (Tue): Alcorn County Courthouse, Corinth, Mississippi. Listed in reference day-by-day sources.

Jan 19 (Wed): Community Center, Sheffield, Alabama. Reported as a successful community date.

Jan 20 (Thu): Leachville High School Gym, Leachville, Arkansas. Listed in touring schedules.

Jan 21 (Fri): National Guard Armory, Sikeston, Missouri. Armory date on the Bootheel edge.

Jan 22 (Sat): Louisiana Hayride, Municipal Auditorium, Shreveport, Louisiana. Broadcast work continues.

From this point through the end of the month, the road band itself could expand adding another member and contract back to the original 3 -piece as the circuit demanded. Day-by-day accounts note the lineup being augmented by pianist Leon Post and steel guitarist Sonny Trammell at times, both tied to the Hayride's working musician network. Just as important, Bob Neal's booking work put Elvis alongside polished touring professionals, including Jim Ed and Maxine Brown. This meant some crowds arrived already loyal to the Brown act. Elvis had to win those rooms over anyway. That pressure is part of what hardens his stage instincts early: he learns how to take a crowd that did not come to worship him and make it lean forward with jaws dropped and ask themselves what they had just seen.

In print, even his name would not settle yet. Just as one billed him as "Alvis Presley," the kind of small typo that tells you the world had not learned the spelling, another may bill him as "The Memphis flash."

Shreveport sharpened Parker's focus. When Parker and Tom Diskin came into town for the Hayride, they checked into the Captain Shreve

Hotel. Watched the big system of local fame at work: radio, dressing rooms, after-show conversations, the way a Saturday night could ripple into Monday talk. Announcer Frank Page could describe the outfit down to color and socks. The turnout could repeat it like scripture by the next town. Parker didn't need a contract on Elvis yet. He needed proof that the same reaction could be carried from room to room and reproduced on command. January started supplying that proof.

After the first Hayride Saturday Jan 15th, the month turns into the kind of touring that makes artists either burn up like coal or slowly form into a diamond. The distance between towns isn't just measured in miles. It is a chain of different rooms to play. Junior college auditoriums, scene centers, gym floors, armories, and clubs that smell like cigarette smoke before the first song starts. Each room has its own sound and its own rules. Elvis doesn't get to bring a huge production with him. He brings a guitar, an amp, a bass, a drummer, and a voice that has to adjust to whatever the hall gives back.

New Boston sits in a corner of Northeast Texas where wartime and after World War II military industry left a lasting footprint on the psyche. In a town like this, a junior college auditorium is a badge of pride. It is a place where graduation happens, where scene meetings happen, where an out of town singer can briefly make the town feel connected to a larger world. Connected to a dream. Elvis has to win a crowd over that may not see national acts often. He learns to handle the night as something the house has been waiting for, not something they have stumbled into. He shakes hands leaving a polite, good ol boy impression with the adults, and communicates with the youth from the stage in his own special way.

Clarksdale pushes the story into the Mississippi Delta, where the blues isn't a genre label but part of local air. Home to Muddy Waters, Sam Cooke, Son House, Charley Patton and Jackie Brenston, Known for Rocket 88, it must have injected some extra energy into Elvis's vocals while he stood on stage in the middle of the Delta Blues. Even if the audience comes for a country package show, they live in a region where blues phrasing, and guitar lines are familiar. Elvis does not arrive as an academic admirer of the blues. He arrives as a young singer who grew up hearing it and singing around it. That difference matters. It makes his influence from it feel natural, and it makes the boundary between country and blues feel less like a blocked entrance and more like a shared street.

Helena, Arkansas sits on the river, and carries the layered history of Delta life, cotton, commerce, and cultural exchange. A social club booking such as a Catholic Club date reminds you that Elvis is climbing through a mixed network of organizations. It may seem odd by today's standards, but it was the norm in the 1950s. In January 1955 he isn't marketed as a national icon. He is marketed as the exciting new act you can book for your local event. That marketing pushes him into rooms where the listeners is close enough to touch him, where the distance between performer and listener is nearly gone.

There is also a sharp little irony buried in the paperwork of Helena. Around this same window, Scotty Moore's efforts to solicit dates outside the region were met with a form-letter rejection from Tom Diskin's Chicago office, noting that there were "few places" in that area for hillbilly performers. The letter reads like a door closing: and then, nearly immediately, Diskin and the Colonel are in Shreveport watching Elvis and thinking the opposite. That is how fast the story turns in January 1955: the industry can dismiss him on Tuesday and chase him by Saturday.

## Something Was Happening to the Girls

Show planners and auditorium workers who encountered Elvis Presley during Southern Dance-hall appearances in early 1955 later recalled reactions they had not seen before. Girls screamed during the songs rather than waiting until the end, rushed toward the stage during faster numbers, and required ushers to restrain them even in small venues.

As Peter Guralnick notes, the reactions emerged before Presley even had a national hit record, suggesting that his physical presence and performance style, rather than radio exposure, were already driving audience responses. It wasn't the music making the man, it was the man making the music.

Marianna is another Delta town shaped by river routes and the economics of agriculture. A high school gym show has a specific charge. The building is designed for sports, for rules, for whistles, and lines on the floor. Control and order. When Elvis plays in that space, the beat turns the gym into something else. Teenagers who are used to being crowd-controlled in school suddenly have a moment that feels like freedom. Chaperones can feel the shift, and they respond with caution or anger. That tension is one of the earliest engines of the Elvis story: young people sensing a doorway, adults trying to keep it shut. You can nearly hear the excited talk that surely occurred the next day in the halls and the classes. About the boy with the funny sounding name, the Crazy hair, and the shaking leg.

The return to Shreveport on the 15th kept him on the Hayride stage, and it also kept him inside a professional world. Shreveport is a place where managers, show planners, and industry scouts can see him work. It is also a place where he can learn from the discipline of the show. The Hayride isn't built around one performer. It is built around the idea of a rotating group and a consistent audience. The Hayride operated like one big family, all pulling its weight to entertain "out of town guests". Elvis learns to be part of that family while also a star inside a system. Which will matter later when he turns into a star inside the larger systems of RCA, television, and film, and ultimately the head of those much larger families. Elvis performs "That's All Right," "Hearts of Stone" and "Tweedle Dee." Some accounts have this where Colonel Tom Parker first saw Elvis perform.

Booneville and Corinth pull the route eastward again. Booneville is a small town county sea where a junior college auditorium date is both entertainment and a sign that the town can host something modern. Corinth has long been a transportation junction by history, and in 1955 that translates into a town used to movement and visitors. A courthouse appearance isn't a glamorous tour date, but it is revealing to those who attend. It places Elvis in the center of a town, making him both a spectacle, and a local event.

Booneville, in particular, shows how local media could inflate him into a headline. The Booneville Banner ran a front-page notice calling him one of the fastest-rising stars in the country. And Elvis even stopped at radio station WBIP for an interview with DJ Lynn McDowell to encourage airplay. These small station visits rarely read as glamorous on a map, but they are the invisible architecture of fame in 1955, the short handshake that turns a record into a town conversation. Elvis was turning strangers into friends in every town.

Behind the curtain, Bob Neal was already writing like a man who felt the ground shifting. In correspondence to Dallas promoter Ed McLemore of the Big "D" Jamboree. Neal emphasized that Colonel Parker would be doing bookings "just like MCA or William Morris." and he hinted that Parker was pursuing resort-level work in Nevada while negotiating something "terrific." Even if the details were wishful, the posture was real: they were no longer thinking in terms of one more gym date. They were thinking in terms of agencies, hotels, bigger markets, the next ladder up.

Sheffield, Alabama places him along the Tennessee River in the Muscle Shoals region. This area will later become famous for recording, but in January 1955 it is still a sequence of rooms and dance nights. The point isn't that history is waiting in the wall, the point is that the South is full of stages that look ordinary until you realize how many careers were built on stages exactly like them. How many legends were born. None quite like Elvis though.

Leachville, Arkansas, in the Arkansas Delta, is another example of how this tour lives in places that national maps ignore. An audience here is often practical. They work. They raise families. They measure the value of a night out. The cost is real to them. Elvis has to deliver value quickly. He does it by giving the crowd a new kind of rhythm and a new kind of physicality. While keeping one foot in familiar country songs so adults don't feel entirely abandoned.

Sikeston, Missouri on the 21st, puts the story on the edge of the Missouri Bootheel. This region was reshaped by drainage work that turned swamp land into rich farmland. The National Guard Armory adds a sense of rules and seriousness. Its high ceilings and hard walls can swallow a singer. Elvis answers by pushing the rhythm and making the set more physical. In a room like this, movement isn't decoration. It helps the sound stay alive as it bounces around the space.

Then the circuit snaps back to Shreveport again, and the Hayride keeps supplying proof to Elvis.

Proof to Bob Neal. Proof to Colonel Tom Parker and Tom Diskin. On the January 22 radio broadcast, Elvis was heard doing "Money Honey" and "I don't Care If the Sun don't Shine" alongside staples like "Blue Moon of Kentucky" and "That's All Right," reminding the radio audience that his set could pull from many worlds. In the same stretch, Parker formalized the next step by booking Elvis onto the Hank Snow Tour, February 14-18, and sending a $425 check as a fifty-percent advance. In today's currency (2025) that is approximately $5000.00. It is a concrete moment: not just excitement in a room, but paper, contracts, and money moving in response to that excitement. For a 20 year old kid, this was the beginning of a dream. A dream the he always had. That he just might be able to take care of his mama and daddy.

This week closes with another Hayride Saturday. By now the pattern is clear. Elvis is building his reputation in full public view. The schedule is relentless, but it is doing its job. Every show is a new advertisement for the next one. Every town produces a story that travels on like lightning ahead of him. That is how his fame spreads in 1955, one night at a time.

### JANUARY 24 TO JANUARY 29: EAST TEXAS NIGHTS AND THE MONTH END SIGNATURE DATE

#### Key Dates

Jan 24 (Mon): Humble Oil Company Camp, Hawkins, Texas. Oil camp booking listed in schedules.

Jan 25 (Tue): Mayfair Building, Tyler, Texas.

Jan 26 (Wed): REA (Rural Electric Administration) Building, Gilmer, Texas. East Texas community date.

Jan 27 (Thu): Reo Palm Isle Club, Longview, Texas. Club date noted in day-by-day accounts.

Jan 28 (Fri): High School, Gaston, Texas. Listed in regional schedules.

Jan 29 (Sat): Louisiana Hayride, Municipal Auditorium, Shreveport, Louisiana. Month end broadcast.

Late January swings back into Texas, into oil camps, town buildings, and clubs. Across the piney woods and the edge of the East Texas oil world. The scenery changes from the wide South Plains to thicker trees and smaller back roads. The rhythm of life changes too. In many of these towns, the week is built around work, and church, and entertainment is concentrated into a few nights, if any at all. Elvis arrives as a disruption, a temporary storm, a distraction from a daily life of arduous work.

Hawkins is tied to the history of East Texas oil, and an oil camp booking reminds you how directly his career is connected to labor. Hawkins OIL Field, a major discovery in the 1940s, was still driving the local economy and population. What was once just a humble lumber and cotton town had now helped Texas solidify its dominance in oil production. But just as the rich get richer, the workers work harder. Sometimes the kids come in work clothes. Sometimes they come tired, hungry, and ready for something that makes the day feel less heavy. Elvis's sound works for them because it has drive that gives them extra energy. It isn't just background music like their parents and the radio played. It is forward motion, and forward motion is what people crave when they feel stuck.

These East Texas oil-field dates were not random stops. They were often packaged and promoted by the region's DJ power brokers. Gladewater radio man Tom Perryman presented several of the week's shows, the kind of DJ-promoter who could turn record spins into ticket lines. In towns built around shift work and rough schedules, a familiar radio voice could function like a guarantee: if Perryman said the boy was worth seeing, the crowd showed up to test it. Perryman did indeed bring them in.

Tyler carries a different kind of East Texas sense of who they are, with stronger scene pride, and a sense of downtown pecking order. A Mayfair Building show is a negotiation with respectability. Elvis is provocative without being obscene. He is modern without being chaotic. That edge is part of his power. He gives young people permission to feel, and he gives adults just enough familiarity to keep listening. This isn't something history seems to remember. Elvis was one part "hillbilly cat" and one part "good ol' boy" and he knew when to turn each part on and off. By the end of the month, Elvis knew how to work a crowd. He is learning from all the professionals around him.

Gilmer, a smaller scene in the same region, shows how the tour in January 1955 functions at the level of local life. A building like an REA hall is often used for meetings, dances, and events that hold the residents together. When Elvis plays there, the building briefly turns into a portal. People who may not travel far suddenly feel connected to something larger. The band learns to read the hall instantly, to sense whether the crowd wants more rock, more country, more humor, more tenderness. They do this through instant feedback. People are so close they can hear them breathe. They can hear them whisper. They learn to change directions quickly.

Longview pushes the month into a club setting. The Reo Palm Isle Club. A club crowd is different from a gym full of fans. Teenagers may still be present, but the hall belongs more to adults who have come to socialize. Elvis can't rely only on teenage frenzy. He has to carry the club with musical command, with the ability to turn a simple progression into a moment that feels personal. This crowd is a little more sophisticated than others.

A school show in Gaston returns him to the gym floor dynamic, the chaperone suspense, the closeness that can turn excitement into chaos. Energy becomes part of the story. In January he isn't a headline about poor health as he may have been later in life, but the physical cost of travel is still real. Sleep is broken. Food is irregular. Voices can go hoarse. Equipment fails. The professionalism is that he sets up anyway and finds a way to make the night feel like an event.

The final Saturday on the 29th returns him to Shreveport again. The Hayride closes the month the way it started for him, with a radio broadcast platform, and a professional clock. If you want a straightforward way to describe what January does, it does this: it teaches Elvis and his representatives that excitement can be built, repeated, and doled on schedule. That is the skill that turns a talented good looking kid into an tower of industry. Of course, this was not an ordinary kid and he had more than looks and talent. He had a PRESENCE.

By the end of January, the five parts of Elvis life are still colliding. Personal life is increasingly compressed into phone calls and brief visits with family and friends. Music is shifting from a local rumor into something that will soon become national frenzy. Movies and television are still ahead, but the big system that will pull him toward moving picture cameras is starting to gather. The month ends with him not as a local sensation, but as a local big deal with real proof start to pile up behind him.

The Colonel's partner, Tom Diskin, is also started seeding Elvis's name outward through show-business contacts. In letters seeking television exposure, Diskin pitched Elvis as a "new boy" who could make girls react the way Frank Sinatra once had. And he did not hesitate to sell the visual, calling him "as good looking as all heck." The language is blunt, nearly carnival in its confidence, but it reveals the real strategy forming make the big deal legible to gatekeepers who only understand crowds, camera appeal, and repeatable profit.

The profit, while still small by later standards, was already measurable. Scotty Moore kept meticulous accounts that show the trio grossing $2,083.63, (approx. $25,000 in 2025), over the prior month of touring. With the split landing half to Elvis and a quarter each to Scotty and Bill Black after expenses. In a single paragraph of numbers, you can see the entire year start to take shape: the road generating cash. Elvis who was making $40-50 per week, had now made five times as much. The cash was attracting management attention, and the attention giving the next booking a little more power than the last.

January is also where you can see the deeper truth of his appeal. He isn't only singing. He is offering a new posture for young people in the South. He is showing them that a voice can be both country and blues. That a body can move to a beat without apology, and that a working class kid can walk into a room and become the center of it. The calendar *looks* like dates and towns, but the calendar is really a map of a culture learning a new language. That language was ELVIS.

His personal life in January 1955 is also changing. There is love and family, but it has to fit inside short windows between bookings. A young performer in this period doesn't have a tour bus with privacy and staff. He has a car, a few companions, and the steady pull of the next town. Most of the time Elvis didn't even have a hotel. They took turns driving and slept when and where they could. That kind of life turns small moments into big ones. Phone calls carry real weight because in-person time is rare. Brief visits feel enormous. Kisses feel stolen, and the road leaves behind a trail of "what could have beens." It also teaches discipline: protect the voice, protect the hands, and protect focus, even when everything around you is pulling at you hard.

Music in January is for all intents and purposes practice in public setting. When people say he changed music, they often imagine a single song or a single recording. The truth is a song that feels electric in a studio has to survive a gym with bad sound. An armory with echo. A hall with a cheap sound system, and a crowd that may be hostile before the first chorus begins to be belted out. Night after night, Elvis and the band learn what grooves hold together and what tempos make the audience move. They learn how to shape dynamics in a room where they can't people control volume. They learn how to end a song cleanly when the kids are screaming. Elvis sings a line differently one night, changes his phrasing, and notices a reaction. That isn't theory. That is craft.

Movies are not yet a scheduled item, but the future is present in the way he is watched. Show planners and managers look at him and ask a question that isn't purely musical: can this kid hold attention the way a screen actor holds attention? Part of the answer is his face, part is his movement, part is his timing. The stage teaches timing. A performer learns where to pause, where to smile, where to let the sustained screaming of a vocal hit before start the next line. Those are film skills before a film career arrives.

Elvis is 20 in January and has plenty of energy. Even though the schedule forces irregular sleep and long drives from show to date, he bounces back quickly. The food is whatever is available along the highway. Diners, quick meals, and whatever his companions can find or bring along. His body turns into an instrument that has to be managed. A sore throat isn't a minor hassle. It can mean a weaker night, a weaker night can mean fewer bookings, a bad review, and fewer bookings and bad reviews can mean an end to a tour. January teaches him to protect the instrument, and it teaches his companions to protect him even when the house wants more than the night can safely hold. It also teaches Elvis that he can survive a stretch of 29 days of nonstop dates of travel and performance. That builds confidence.

Elvis also builds relationships with bandmates, local DJs, radio hosts, show planners, and the people who run the halls and the theaters. People like Merle Kilgore, Tom Perryman, Frank Page. These are not glamorous relationships, but they are essential. A DJ who likes you can change your success level on a particular tour. A promoter who trusts you can book you again and pay you better next time. A hall manager who believes you can fill a room and leave the audience happy may take another risk on you. January shows how a career is built through these relationships long before the world truly knows your name. Elvis was smarter than he was given credit for. At 20, he understood this. He was also humble enough to learn from those around him, and he was willing, and eager to ask questions.

If you want another targeted picture of January, it is that he becomes reliable. A reliable performer at 20. A performer who can make a big city hall vibrate and then make a small town gym erupt is a performer who can sell tickets. Reliability is what transforms talent into power. And power is what will later allow bigger recording deals, national television, and ultimately the film contracts that follow.

## TOWN AND VENUE VIGNETTES: WHY THESE ROOMS MATTER

Houston isn't just a city on the itinerary. It is an early lesson in media gravity. A young singer could be a rumor in one neighborhood and a headliner across town because radio stitches the city together. In the mid-1950s, teenagers are forming sense of who they are through the radio dial. Adults are forming opinion through the same dial. When Elvis succeeds in Houston, it signals that his appeal isn't limited to one county or one school system. One age group or another. It can travel inside a large urban space.

San Angelo represents the local town where entertainment functions as a town ritual. A City Auditorium booking means the town has invested in a shared space for gatherings. In such a space, the performer isn't only an entertainer, but he is also a temporary town figure. He is given the stage that normally hosts speeches and ceremonies, and he turns it into a place of rhythm and reaction. That contrast is part of the thrill. It makes his appearance memorable.

Lubbock is a reminder that much of the South and Southwest experiences culture through distance. A long drive separates towns. Radio closes the gap. A performance is the payoff of a radio relationship. The house arrives carrying a version of the singer in their head. The singer must match or exceed that version. Elvis learns to do that early.

Midland shows the link between music and the boom economy. Oil towns attract young workers and young families. They build new schools and new auditoriums quickly. They also carry a sense of risk and money. That energy is similar to the energy of rockabilly. Forward moving, impatient, hungry. Elvis fits the mood of a place that is expanding faster than tradition can keep up.

Shreveport, through the Hayride, is the month's most important show each time it occurs. It is not just a stage. It is a regional radio platform, a network, and a training ground. Both in the hall and across the airwaves. A singer learns not only to play to the front row, but to imagine performing to the listeners he can not see, but knows are there. That imagination is one of the early bridges to television and film.

Delta towns such as Clarksdale, Helena, Marianna, and Leachville place him inside landscapes shaped by agriculture and river systems. In those places, the week can feel repetitive, and entertainment can feel rare. That rarity makes the crowd response stronger. It also makes the social stakes higher. People remember what happened because there are fewer distractions to blur the memory.

Sikeston and the Bootheel region add the layer of transformed land. The region's history includes the engineering and labor that turned wet land into farm land. That history leaves behind a culture that values work and practicality. A performance in an armory in that environment isn't an upper class setting. It is a working class night out, and Elvis's sound is working class in its bones.

East Texas towns such as Hawkins, Tyler, Gilmer, and Longview show the shift in late January from big town halls into more intimate, sometimes more adult rooms. The same singer has to function in all of them. The tour does not let him specialize, but it does force him to become versatile, and that versatility is a major reason the year will explode later.

Why is this important? A performer who could navigate through all of these special landscapes was someone a larger entity could and would invest in. A larger record company, a movie studio, a manager with more connections. Elvis was probably not thinking specifically about this while he rushed from town to town and stage to stage, but he was setting the table for future success unknowingly.

## ON THE BILL: WHAT THESE 1955 NIGHTS LOOKED LIKE

Most January bookings in 1955 don't operate like a modern concert. They are closer to a variety night. A promoter rents a hall or a gym, sells tickets through local places, and then stacks the evening with a few performers so the crowd feels it is getting major value. There is usually an host, often a radio man, because radio is the best advertisement a small town has. The host does more than introduce. He keeps the audience warm while equipment is moved, he fills time if a performer is late, and he frames the headliner as an event.

For Elvis, this setup is perfect training. It teaches him to enter a room that is in motion and seize the attention quickly. It also teaches him to share space. He is learning to be a star without the privilege of an entire evening loyal to him. That means he can't afford dead air. He learns to keep talk short. He learns to tune fast. He learns to follow a previous act without losing heat, and he learns to leave the stage at the peak, so the audience carries the electricity out the door.

The other acts on a given bill vary by town. In some places the bill is heavy on country singers who fit the local taste. In others it leans toward the new rock and roll flavor that is start to surface. What is consistent is the mix of familiar and unfamiliar. The promoter gives the crowd something they recognize and also offers them something a little riskier. In January, Elvis is usually the risky part, even when he is a local favorite, because his style forces people to choose a side.

This variety format also explains why the towns matter. A big city can support niche entertainment. A small town needs an event that can pull different social groups into the same room. A package show does that. Teenagers come for the excitement. Adults come because it is a respectable night out. Local musicians come to study. Town leaders come because the tickets keep the lights on. That mixture creates the friction that makes an Elvis appearance feel dangerous. He isn't playing for one tribe. He is playing for a whole scene, and the scene has to decide what it thinks about him right then.

When the room is a gym, the physical layout shapes the drama. There is rarely a raised stage as high as a theater stage. The front row can be close enough to touch a guitar. The sound bounces off hard walls. The kids can surge forward in a way that makes adults fearful. When the venue is an armory or a scene center, the hall's stature sits in the air. Those rooms are built for formal gatherings, and music that makes bodies move can feel like a challenge. Elvis learns to ride that tension without breaking it. He makes the fans feel free while keeping the show inside the boundaries of what the promoter and the venue can handle.

The Hayride nights are a special case. Those are radio broadcast shows with a fixed pecking order and a professional stage crew. Elvis has to be efficient. He has to hit his mark. He has to finish on time. He is performing with other stars so he may not stand out quite as much in terms of audience reaction, just yet. If a gym booking teaches him how to handle chaos, the Hayride teaches him how to handle a system. The combination is powerful. By the end of January, he has rehearsed both kinds of performance, the raw local night, and the disciplined radio broadcast night, and he has learned that he can deliver in either.

If January 1955 has a single set of threads, all five run together. Personal life tightens and is nearly nonexistent because the road is relentless. Music sharpens through routine and creative changes. The management future is hinted at by Parker and Diskins entrance. Health appears as replenished energy, because the body has to do this night after night. Friends and famous interactions start at the local level, with the DJs, and emcees who hold the microphone before he does and who can change the crowd's temperature with a sentence. Merle Kilgore, writer of the Webb Pierce Million seller "More and More" was on the scene in 1955. As a DJ and a songwriter as well as a guitar player at the Hayride once told me in his Nashville office. "Nobody wanted to follow Elvis on stage, it was death sentence, it started early in 55."

### SONGS IN ROTATION: THE JANUARY TOOLKIT

In January 1955, Elvis isn't yet defined by an extensive list of chart hits. His toolkit is built from the songs that survived the first wave of attention in 1954 and the songs that will soon become part of his signature. The set is designed to work in noisy rooms. It favors strong rhythms and clear hooks. He leans on blues and country material that can be shaped into his fresh style, and he mixes ballads sparingly, so the hall doesn't cool.

A typical night in this period often includes fast numbers that let Scotty Moore's guitar lead. Bill

Black's bass push the tempo, with Elvis's vocal riding the groove in lieu of floating above it. He uses familiar country material so adults can find a foothold, then he twists it with phrasing and movement that signals the future. The result is that the people feels both comfort and shock. That blend is one reason the stories spread. People can describe what they saw even if they can't classify it, as it is something had not experienced before. It was something new and shiny.

The January set of songs is a set of tools built for survival on the road. If a song does not hold the crowd, it may get replaced in the next similar setting. If a tempo doesn't move bodies, it gets adjusted. If a joke does not land, it is dropped. January is when the act starts to learn how to shift when needed.

## BUSINESS SHIFT: MONEY, MANAGEMENT, AND THE FIRST BIG TURN

January also contains the first visible shift in business. A young singer can have talent and still stall if the bookings are weak or the pay is small. The road teaches him quickly that the show is only half the fight. The other half is the deal: the terms, the guarantees, the travel costs, the percentage splits. And the relationships that determine whether he gets better rooms next month or repeats the same small circuit forever. Colonel Parker start to performance receipts of his value.

At this stage he is surrounded by working professionals, bandmates, local show planners, and managers who have seen talent come and go. They recognize that the crowd reaction is unusual. That kid's appetite. People want to be attached to the big deal. They want to represent him, promote him, book him, handle him. January is full of conversations in back rooms, in hotel lobbies, in car rides between towns. The audience doesn't see those conversations, but the shape of the year depends on them.

The Louisiana Hayride is central here because it is both a stage and a marketplace. It is where local industry people can watch him under crowd-controlled conditions. It is where introductions happen. It is where a manager can say, with credibility, that he has seen the act deliver in front of a live radio audience. The Hayride gives power. Every time he returns to Shreveport and performs well, the power increases.

This is also where you can feel the start of the tug of war between different visions for his career. One vision is to keep him as a local touring attraction with strong local draws. Another is to position him for national recording and national media. January does not resolve the tug of war, but it makes it impossible to ignore. The schedule is bigger than the old world he came from. If the business part catches up to the demand part, the year will accelerate. If it fails, the year could stall. January ends with the sense that acceleration is coming.

**Here's a January Road montage, shaped by the month's familiar rhythm.**

Scene one: To the car before dawn or in the middle of the night to beat traffic. The day starts before the sun, with breath in the air, and the quiet clatter of cases being dragged across gravel. Somebody checks the trunk twice and roof tie downs because one loose latch, or improperly tied down Bass can ruin a night. Cords get coiled. A spare string pack goes in a pocket, not a bag, because you don't want to dig for it later. Coffee comes in a paper cup that burns your hand. Breakfast is whatever travels, crackers, a sandwich, a piece of pie wrapped in wax paper. There is no warm-up room, no dressing room, no reset. The road is the schedule, and the schedule always wins.

Scene two: The room manager. The venue is a gym or a scene hall that still smells like floor wax and last night's basketball game. Folding chairs are set too tight. A plywood platform has been built as a stage, and everyone is pretending it is sturdy. The manager walks the space like a referee. He points at the exits. He points at the stage edge. He points at the rope line that is supposed to hold back teenagers who don't believe in rope. Elvis doesn't argue. He listens, nods, keeps the smile easy, and signs whatever needs signing, if anything needs signing at all. The show starts with permission before it starts with music.

Scene three: The radio man. At a small station, the studio is cramped, the walls are thin, and the microphone looks older than the building. The DJ is working at the speed of a man spinning plates. He is reading sponsor copy, cueing a record, taking a request, and selling the night's show all in the same breath. Elvis waits in the doorway until he is waved in. He gives the DJ a clean name drop, a short hello for the listeners, and a line that makes the event feel local, not imported. Then he shakes hands like it matters, because in towns like these, it does.

Scene four: The front row. The house does not sit the way a people sits in a theater. They lean. They edge forward. They test the boundary. Flash bulbs pop. A girl is gripping the rope line with both hands like it is the last thing holding her to the ground. Boys watch the girls more than they watch the band. A deputy or an usher stands in the aisle, pretending he isn't worried. Elvis clocks all of it without turning it into panic. He gives them a look, a grin, a small move that raises the temperature, then he goes back to the mic, and sings like the room is still under control.

Scene five: The band as a unit. The sound is never perfect. The amp hums. The cord crackles when someone shifts their foot. Scotty tests a lick and hears it bounce back from the far wall. Bill checks his tuning by feel because the room noise eats the subtleties. D. J. Taps a stick on the snare, listening for the point where the hall turns it into thunder. Elvis's rhythm guitar is the glue. He keeps it strumming so everybody else can take risks. They communicate in small signals, a nod, a glance, a half step, because there is no time for long conversations once the first song hits.

Scene six: The motel after the show, when they don't hit the road immediately. The hallway smells like cigarette smoke and passion. Somebody is laughing too loud in the next room, and then, suddenly, everything goes quiet. Elvis sits on the edge of the bed with his tie loosened, still buzzing, while the others are already dropping toward sleep. He wipes sweat from his hands, checks his guitar, flips through a few folded notes or letters, then stares at the phone like it is a lifeline. A quick call home is never long enough. The road gives him noise all night and loneliness the moment the door shuts.

Scene seven: The adult audience member. Somewhere in the room is a man who did not come to be entertained. He came to measure the damage. He sits with his arms folded, watching the crowd more than the stage. He is listening for vulgarity, looking for chaos, waiting for proof that the rumors were right. Then Elvis hits a line clean, holds a note the right way, and the doubter's face changes before he can stop it. Respect arrives in small increments. Afterward, that same man might not clap like a teenager, but he will nod, and he may even ask for an autograph for someone at home. There may be another adult that can not be convinced that Elvis is NOT a danger. He plans to write the paper or complain to the police.

Scene eight: The backstage conversations. Backstage isn't glamorous. It is a corner, a hallway, a coat room, and a space behind a curtain. A promoter counts the gate with his thumb, fast, practiced, serious. Someone argues about gas money. Someone is trying to lock in the next date before the chairs are even folded. Names get traded like currency. A phone number is written on the back of a ticket stub. Elvis stands close enough to hear it all, not saying much, taking it in. This is where you learn the real shape of the business, in the minutes between the noise and the drive.

Scene nine: The returns to Shreveport. When they roll back into Shreveport, the atmosphere tightens. There is a clock on the wall that actually means something. There are cues. There are people who point where you stand and when you stand there. The backstage area feels more formal, more crowded, more controlled. You can hear the murmur of a larger audience before you see them. Then the moment comes, the walk to the mic, the light, the first chord, and the realization that this stage is both a home base and a showing ground. The month has taught him how to survive the small rooms. Shreveport shows whether that survival can look like momentum.

## THE OTHER ACTS: WHY THE BILL MATTERED MORE THAN ANY HEADLINER.

It is tempting to tell the story of January as if every room held only Elvis and the crowd. In reality, most of these nights are shared nights. The bill matters because it frames how the audience hears him. A town that expects a straight country show will hear his rhythm as a provocation. A town that expects a mixed variety night will hear him as the sharpest edge of the program. The bill also determines the social mix. If the bill includes performers older audiences trust, adults will attend. If the bill signals teenage excitement, teenagers will attend in larger numbers and adults will stay home. Elvis benefits from the mixed bill because it puts him in front of people who might not buy a ticket for a pure rock and roll night yet. One night in January Elvis may be on a bill with Sonny Curtis and the next with Billy Walker. A later set in the month would find him opening for Jim Reeves or Johnny Horton. Jim Ed and Maxine Brown were often paired with Elvis. Regional Artists like Merle Kilgore share the stage and sometimes the hotel room as well. Some nights Elvis was the attraction. Other nights he was the guest performer.

On the road, shared bills create a small moving scene. Performers see each other in dressing rooms, on stage wings, in the same diners, and sometimes in the same cars if the bookings are chained tight. The social part starts to widen. The friendships and rivalries that form in these conditions are not glamorous, but they are formative. A singer learns tricks by watching another singer. A band learns pacing by listening from the back of the hall. Elvis learns how different performers handle a hostile crowd, how they recover from a broken string, how they keep the audience with them when the sound system fails. Those are skills that can't be learned in a studio. They are learned in the live world of a shared bill.

The bill also shapes the story towns tell afterward. A scene may remember the whole night as a package event. But the entertainer who is the talk of the town is the one who produces the strongest emotional reaction for days and weeks afterward. Elvis was often that figure. That matters because word of mouth is the strongest marketing in 1955. A teenager tells a friend that the singer at the start or the end was different. A parent tells another parent that the kids went wild. A radio man mentions that the turnout response was like nothing he has seen, or the crowd was dead for him/her.

Those stories travel faster than the car, bus train and telegraph. They arrive long ahead of him. They turn the next night into a bigger night.

## WHAT JANUARY PROMISES FOR THE REST OF 1955

By late January, the shape of the year is visible even if no one has the language for it yet. A local schedule is turning into a local movement. The band is tightening. The stories are traveling. The radio nights are amplifying the live nights. Each time Elvis returns to Shreveport, he isn't just repeating an appearance, he is reinforcing a narrative: this is the act that makes the hall tilt.

The month also reveals how fast the culture is changing. Teenagers are becoming a market with their own tastes and their own power. Adults are becoming uneasy about that power. Elvis stands in the middle. He isn't the cause of every change, but he is the most visible symbol of the change. That visibility creates conflict, and conflict creates attention. Attention is fuel.

One more note belongs here because it explains why January feels so alive on the page. In later years, when Elvis is surrounded by layers of security, schedules, and publicists, the story can turn abstract. In January 1955, everything is still close to the ground. The audience is close enough to see sweat and to hear the guitar amp crackle if it misbehaves. The band is close enough to feel every change in tempo, to trade glances, and to correct a drift before the song collapses. The towns are small enough that a single wild night turns into a local legend that will be retold for decades. That closeness produces sharper detail: the smell of a gym floor, the echo in an armory. The quick backstage hallway talk about money, the long drive where the radio is the only company. It also produces a clearer sense of risk. If something goes wrong, there is no buffer. If the venue turns against him, he has to win it back himself.

So, when February arrives in the next chapter, carry one simple expectation forward: the schedule will keep growing, and the exposure will keep widening. The pressure will keep building. January proves the act can travel. The rest of the year shows what happens when a local traveling act with a once in a lifetime talent like Elvis meets a national appetite.

### JANUARY 1955 RADIO

Radio in January still sounds like order: clean vocals, safe endings, the kind of songs that can play while supper is on the stove. But on jukeboxes and the late-night dial, Black R&B is already carrying the heat the wider country will soon pretend is new: "Pledging My Love", Johnny Ace, "I've Got a Woman", Ray Charles, "Hearts of Stone", The Charms, "Earth Angel", The Penguins,. And "Sincerely", The Moonglows,. You can feel two Americas sharing one speaker: one smoothing the edges, one sharpening them. Elvis is coming up inside that split, learning which rooms want the polished sound, and which rooms want the rock n roll truth.

*Pop radio in January leaned heavily toward warmth and familiarity:*

Frank Sinatra "Young at Heart" Optimism given through maturity. Hope framed as reflection rather than urgency., Billboard year-end ranking: #11 (1954, in 1954)

Doris Day "If I Give My Heart to You" Careful romance, offered slowly. Emotion presented as responsibility, not impulse., Billboard year-end ranking: #20 (1954, in 1954)

Dean Martin "That's Amore" something new wrapped in charm. Rhythm softened by humor and familiarity.

Jo Stafford "Make Love to Me" Controlled intimacy, carefully phrased, and emotionally held back., Billboard year-end ranking: #5 (1954, in 1954)

*Country radio reinforced stability and moral clarity:*

Hank Williams "How Can You Refuse Him Now", receiving airplay following his death, Spiritual urgency framed through repentance and warning, not rebellion., Issued in 1954. A Hank Williams gospel/demo release charting is inconsistently recorded,

Webb Pierce "More and More" Heartbreak given through routine and restraint., Billboard year-end country: 6 in 1954,

Carl Smith "Loose Talk" Narrative caution. Social bill placement reinforced through story., Billboard country chart: 1 in 1955,

## What Was Playing in Movie Theaters January 1955

On the Waterfront Moral conflict resolved through internal struggle rather than action. Masculinity framed as restraint.

White Christmas the Christmas Movie was still playing in early January. Nostalgia as comfort. Harmony presented as emotional safety.

The Country Girl Fame examined through fatigue and responsibility, not excitement.

The year has just started to move. But the conditions that will force it to explode are all present.

## FULL KNOWN JANUARY 1955 PERFORMANCE RECORD

January 29: Louisiana Hayride, Municipal Auditorium, Shreveport, Louisiana.

January 28: High School, Gaston, Texas.

January 27: Reo Palm Isle Club, Longview, Texas.

January 26: REA, Rural Electric Administration, Building, Gilmer, Texas.

January 25: Mayfair Building, Tyler, Texas.

January 24: Humble Oil Company Camp, Hawkins, Texas.

January 22: Louisiana Hayride, Municipal Auditorium, Shreveport, Louisiana.

January 21: National Guard Armory, Sikeston, Missouri.

January 20: Leachville High School Gym, Leachville, Arkansas.

January 19: Community Center, Sheffield, Alabama.

January 18: Alcorn County Courthouse, Corinth, Mississippi.

January 17: Junior College Auditorium, Booneville, Mississippi.

January 15: Louisiana Hayride, Municipal Auditorium, Shreveport, Louisiana.

January 14: Futrell High School Gym, Marianna, Arkansas.

January 13: Catholic Club, Helena, Arkansas.

January 12: City Auditorium, Clarksdale, Mississippi.

January 11: High School Gym, New Boston, Texas.

January 8: Louisiana Hayride, Municipal Auditorium, Shreveport, Louisiana.

January 7: High School Auditorium, Midland, Texas.

January 6: Fair Park, Lubbock, Texas.

January 5: City Auditorium, San Angelo, Texas.

January 1: Grand Prize Saturday Night, Jamboree, Eagles Hall, Houston, Texas.

## Chapter 2, February 1955

February brought more touring, and with it familiarity with each other. By now Elvis and the Blue Moon Boys were stacking mileage in the Lincoln - leaning on it far past comfort - and filling the gaps with borrowed cars whenever the schedule or need demanded it.

One night in February looks like the next on paper, but it doesn't feel that way in the venues. Posters go up earlier. Kids show up sooner. Adults linger longer at the back, watching to see whether the sustained screaming turns into a problem. The same circuit towns start to recognize the pattern, and that honor changes the atmospheric buildup and dynamics.

The five parts keep crossing. The personal part is the one most people forget, because a young singer can look fearless onstage and still be a teenage son trying to stay grounded. A boyfriend feeling insecure about his gal back home. The music part is relentless: new songs in the set, new arrangements, new ways to pace a show. The movies part is quieter for now, but the influence is everywhere in the way he carries himself and the way audiences read him. Health is the part that hides in plain sight, because travel is stress even when you feel invincible. No matter how young and healthy you appear on the outside, the road takes it's piece of you, even if not seen. And the friends and famous interactions part expands quickly, because February includes moments when the industry starts to reach back.

Keep those parts in mind as the month and year unfolds. The dates below are the spine, but the real story is what happens when the spine is forced to flex. A stop in a small Delta town can change the way Elvis, Scott, and Bill approach sound checks. A night in Shreveport can change who is now watching the young boy sensation. A school show can teach a lesson about chaos that will be useful later on national television. February 1955 is still early, but it is early in the way a storm front is early.

## FEBRUARY 1 TO FEBRUARY 8: HOME BASE AND THE FIRST HINGE DATE
### Key Dates

Feb 1 (Tue), Randolph, Mississippi. Small-town booking that keeps the week moving.

Feb 2 (Wed), Augusta, Arkansas. High School.

Feb 3 (Thu), Memphis, Tennessee. Most likely a midweek studio and rehearsal window at Sun during this stretch, as the act resets and prepares for the next run.

Feb 4 (Fri): Jesuit High School, New Orleans, Louisiana. A school auditorium turns into a proving ground.

Feb 5 (Sat), Shreveport, Louisiana. Louisiana Hayride, Municipal Auditorium; a KWKH photo appears on this date.

Feb 6 (Sun), Memphis, Tennessee. Ellis Auditorium package show at 3:00 and 8:00 p.m., between sets, a meeting at Palumbo's with Colonel Parker, Sam Phillips, and RCA's Steve Sholes.

Feb 7 (Mon), Ripley, Mississippi. Ripley High School Gym (sponsored by senior class).

Randolph, Mississippi sits in the Delta world where farms, small businesses, and county roads shape the tempo of everyday life. A booking like this isn't about glamour. It is about testing and saturation: loading in, sound check, play, pack up, and drive again. Testing the temperature of the crowd. For a twenty year old singer, the work is also a kind of training in emotional audience control. If the hall is restless, you have to deliver a set with focus. If the microphone is weak, you have to project. These early stops harden the show into something that can survive imperfect conditions.

In Randolph, it wasn't just Elvis carrying the night. Bob Neal's bookings often paired him with a local name, so the town felt ownership of the bill. This week he shared the stage with Mississippi singer Bud Deckelman, remembered locally for "Daydreamin'", and that pairing matters. It shows how Elvis's act was still moving through the same school-gym circuits as local talent. Even as the kids response was already breaking the old scale of what a high-school date was supposed to be.

The personal part shows up in small ways on nights like Randolph. Traveling in early 1955 isn't comfortable. Meals are grabbed between drives, sleep happens while taking turns driving, and privacy is rare even before national fame. A quick phone call back home to his mother Gladys, then maybe another to a girlfriend. Yet the band is still close enough to feel like a small family: jokes in the car. Shared frustrations, and the steady process of learning what keeps the singer in a good headspace. Make no doubt about it, Elvis was the one that mattered, but scotty, and bill knew they were an important part of the growing success. That bond matters because the house can sense confidence. When the group moves as one, the house believes the act is bigger than it really is. Bill Black clowned around. Scotty played the recognizable licks and Elvis was... Elvis.

Augusta, Arkansas adds another layer. Towns along the Arkansas River and the Delta region have deep musical traditions, gospel, blues, and country carried through churches, juke joints, and radio. When a new sound arrives, the crowd listens through those older filters. Elvis isn't arriving as a polished star. He is arriving as an experiment that seems to work on teenagers and unsettle adults. That charge is part of the electricity. The show isn't just music. It is a social event where people test the limits to what they can express in public.

Augusta's senior-class sponsorship also preserved an image that was already aging out. Newspaper ads still pictured Elvis, Scotty, and Bill as "The Blue Moon Boys" in western shirts. A carryover look from the Starlite Wrangler days, even though Scotty and Bill had largely abandoned the cowboy styling by this point. The mismatch is useful: 1955 is moving so fast that the photograph can't keep up with the sound, and the towns keep advertising yesterday's costume while the stage is already tomorrow. This also may have felt like a safer way to present Elvis in advance, who was start to leave a trail of distraught parents in his wake.

A midweek return to Memphis is more than a break. It is a chance to sharpen the recordings. Sun Records is a small studio. But it is a place where songs have started to take a permanent place on radio late 1954 and Early 1955 with artists such as Malcolm Yelvington's- "Drinking Wine Spodee-o-dee," Billy "the kid" Emerson's- "Move Baby Move"/"When It Rains It Really Pours" and Carl Perkins- "Movie Magg/ "Turn Around" which was released in February on the Flip Records Inc Label. Session work forces decisions: tempo, phrasing. This guitar figure carries the hook, and where the vocal should sit against the slapback echo. The February session period includes recordings that will help define the early catalog, including 'Baby Let's Play House' and other titles tracked at Sun. Even if the road is the primary classroom, the studio is where Elvis history is preserved.

Around this Memphis pause, local coverage started to narrate the transformation right then. A posed photo run in the Memphis Press-Scimitar placed Elvis, Scotty, and Bill inside Sun with Sam Phillips at the console, turning a cramped room into a stage of its own. The paper framed the something new plainly: a white singer leaning hard into Black rhythm patterns, then dragging them through rural rhythm until they sounded like something new. In that same window they cut "Baby Let's Play House" for the next single. And they also worked on titles that didn't see immediate release, early takes of Ray

Charles's "I Got a Woman", later reported lost, and a first pass at "Tryin' to Get to You."

New Orleans on February 4 brings Elvis into a city with its own powerful music sense of who they are. The room is a high school auditorium, but the cultural weight of New Orleans doesn't disappear just because the hall has folding seats. This is a place that has been shaping rhythm and blues for decades. A young performer stepping into that environment has to be convincing, because a New Orleans crowd knows when a singer is only copying. The set leans into the hybrid that is starting to define him: country framework, blues phrasing, and a vocal urgency that feels modern.

That New Orleans stop carried a small, telling scramble. Elvis was late for a radio appearance at WWEZ meant to plug the show, the kind of quick. Street-level promotion that kept the calendar alive, then rushed into the building with the night already humming. He also appeared on the bill with Ann Raye, the daughter of Biloxi promoter Yankie Barhanovich. A reminder that the 1955 circuit was still built on family ties, local hustlers, and borrowed favors even as the crowds started behaving like something closer to a national big deal. Elvis was not becoming famous by accident, or because of one "lucky" song, he was earning it. And along the way there was an endless amount of people helping push him to the top.

Shreveport on February 5 is the centerpiece of the week. The Louisiana Hayride isn't a casual appearance. It is a local radio broadcast machine that can turn a rumor into a name. By this point, Elvis isn't just another act passing through. He is now a recurring event. The kind of performer teenagers talk about all week. The Hayride setup also teaches discipline. There is a schedule, a live radio broadcast feel, and a lineup with other artists who are also fighting for attention.

On the Hayride that week, details survive and feel nearly cinematic because the rest of the year moves so quickly. Elvis walked out in pink pants and a matching tie under a darker jacket. Then ran a set that stitched his worlds together: "That's All Right," "Blue Moon of Kentucky," "Tweedlee Dee," and "Money Honey" among them. Behind the curtain, the business part tightened as well: Colonel Parker sent another deposit check for $550 toward upcoming package dates, treating the road like inventory that could be purchased, scheduled, and scaled. This allowed Elvis, Scotty, and Bill to really focus on the music in a way a struggling act would not have been able to do. They KNEW more money was coming, so they had to get it right.

February 6 in Memphis is a hinge day. The booked stop is Ellis Auditorium, with package-show sets at 3:00 and 8:00 p.m., and it forces Elvis to learn how to switch gears quickly - soundcheck, crowd, backstage, and back again. Between those two sets, he meets with Colonel Parker, Sam Phillips, and RCA's Steve Sholes at Palumbo's, a small business huddle tucked inside a public day.

This stretch also shows how fast the operation is professionalizing. Beyond the headline booking, the week includes school programs at Messick High School and Messick Junior High. And the schedule starts to feel less like a string of favors and more like a routed enterprise, with drivers, show planners, radio, and Parker's instincts tightening around the calendar.

Movies remain a quiet but steady influence. In cities like Memphis, where theaters and radio shape what people imagine stardom looks like, Elvis is learning how to carry the same sense of who they are from a school gym to an auditorium stage without losing the thread of who he is.

At nineteen, it's easy to ignore the health side of the road. Yet February's pace is already a warning: long drives, uneven meals, quick wardrobe changes, and the stress of performance nights stacked too close together. Even without a formal tour bus, the act is starting to live like professionals.

A useful way to picture early 1955 is to imagine how information moves. A single radio mention, a newspaper blurb, or a KWKH cue on a weekend radio broadcast can ripple across states, turning a local show into a huge event before the posters ever fully go up.

That reach also explains why a weekly obligation can become a creative discipline. A show that returns to the same stage forces you to refine. You can't repeat the exact same performance forever, because regular listeners compare notes and are always listening for something new. You also learn how to perform for many audiences at once: the people in the hall and the people at home. A singer who understands microphone technique, pacing, and timing is thinking like a broadcaster. In February 1955, Elvis is learning that skill nearly by accident, because the Hayride contract demands the routine.

Memphis is where the personal and professional parts tangle. At Sun, Sam Phillips isn't building a mainstream country product. He is chasing a feeling. The studio is small enough that every mistake is obvious. That is why the band's chemistry matters. Scotty Moore has to anticipate the vocal. Bill Black has to keep the rhythm alive without drowning out the guitar. When 'Baby Let's Play House' is recorded in early February, it grows more than a song, it becomes proof that the sound can live on vinyl, not just in noisy rooms. The act is learning how to translate stage electricity into a record that can travel without them. They had their next "That's alright mama"

The February 6 Memphis date shows how quickly the big deal is moving into youth culture. Graceland's Memphis Stages article notes that Elvis performed at Messick High School and Messick Junior High School in early February 1955 to support promoter Bob Neal's son in a student council campaign. That detail is easy to gloss over, but it matters. The performance isn't only entertainment. It is a social force powerful enough to be used in a school election. It also explains why adults in the business start to watch closely. When teenagers respond this intensely, money and influence usually follow.

One practical reason the day ran tight is nearly comically ordinary. Before the Ellis Auditorium show, the group made a stop at Messick High. Messick Junior High to help promoter Sonny Neal with a student-council campaign: quick handshakes, hallway chatter, the kind of local politicking that kept a young promoter connected. The detour put Elvis behind schedule. And that lateness itself became part of the lore: the people had already worked itself into a pitch, and he walked into a room that had been waiting too long to stay calm.

The room adds another layer of symbolism. The same Graceland article points out that Elvis's own Humes High School graduation ceremony took place at the venue and only a few years later he is back on that stage as a young rock star. That kind of return is emotionally loaded. It collapses time. The boy who sat in the audience is, by this point, the one creating the sustained screaming. It is a reminder that the rise isn't abstract. It is happening in familiar places, in the same city blocks where ordinary life continues while Elvis's own life changes.

The business part turns more visible in that same the building window. Promoter Bob Neal arranged a talk across the street involving Sun Records president Sam Phillips, Colonel Tom Parker, and Tom Diskin, all interested in Elvis. This is one of those moments that looks small right then and enormous in hindsight. A performer's world is about to expand from clubs and radio to contracts, long term planning, and national ambition. Even if

February is still mostly about playing shows, it includes the first clear shadow of what comes next.

By mid-month, even RCA's internal correspondence starts to show the push-and-pull. A&R man Steve Sholes wrote in surprise that Elvis was still tied to Sun, he'd been hearing Parker talk as if the changeover was already a matter of paperwork, while Parker continued floating other names like Tommy Sands as cover and power. The letters are mundane on the page, but they reveal the strategy: keep the room filled with options, then steer the decision back to Elvis when the moment is right.

One of the quieter turning points happened between those Memphis shows, not under spotlights but across the street at Palumbo's Restaurant. Neal brought Sam Phillips into the room with Parker and Tom Diskin under the polite cover of "planning the future." Parker did not soften his point: Sun could not carry Elvis where he intended to take him. RCA had already been approached about buying the contract. Phillips, proud of the sound he'd captured and protective of the label's stake, didn't take kindly to hearing his artist described as a man already halfway out the door. The talk ended with no public rupture, but the temperature had changed in the relationship. From that moment forward, Parker revised his strategy in silence, pushing harder without announcing the push.

New Orleans deserves more than a passing mention because it represents a different musical temperature. In 1955, the city's rhythm, and blues scene does not have a minor impact on music. It is a living industry, with bandstands, and record shops that are shaping national tastes. A performer coming out of Memphis can feel both at home and challenged here. When Elvis sings, he is drawing from black musical sources that audiences recognize as local, even if they don't say it out loud. That honor can create a complicated response. Some listeners embrace the blend because it feels honest. Others resist because it blurs social lines that the era tries to keep rigid. In a high school auditorium, that cultural tension gets compressed into one question: does the crowd move or does it sit still. The fact that Elvis keeps getting booked suggests the house is moving.

A practical detail that matters in February is amplification. In the mid-1950s, many venues are not built for electric bands. High schools and courthouses are designed for speeches and assemblies. Rockabilly depends on rhythm, attack, and presence, and that means microphones, small amplifiers, and quick problem solving. Scotty Moore's guitar lines have to cut without tearing. Bill Black's bass has to thump without turning into a muddy roar. When you read a schedule of small town shows, it is easy to miss that each night involves technical improvisation. That improvisation shapes the sound. The rawness that later turns into a signature is partly the result of making electric music work in rooms that were never meant for it. This was the genius of Elvis, Scotty, and Bill.

The February 3 studio window in Memphis also matters because it is where the band can experiment without fighting a screaming audience. A live show teaches what gets a reaction. A studio session teaches what holds up on repeated listening. Elvis's early Sun recordings are marked by immediacy, but they are also carefully framed by Phillips's production choices. The slapback echo, the placement of the vocal, and the balance between guitar, and bass create a sense of motion even at lower volume. For the reader, the key point is that the road, and the studio are feeding each other. New songs are tested in front of audiences, refined in the studio, and then brought back to the road with new confidence.

If you want a snapshot of what an early 1955 set could feel like, think in terms of contrast. A show might open with a fast number that announces energy, then pivot into a slower ballad that lets the listeners breathe, then return to an up tempo rhythm and blues cover that encourages movement. Elvis's gift isn't only in voice. It is in sequencing. Even before he has a massive catalog of hits, he understands how to ride the wave of a crowd's attention. The listeners might not remember every title, but they remember the arc: excitement, intimacy, and then a final push that leaves the hall louder than it started.

The money details in early 1955 help ground the story. Graceland's Hayride history notes that Elvis's pay was $18 per show when he started as a regular, with Scotty Moore, and Bill Black each receiving $12 per set. Those numbers explain why the schedule is relentless. No one is getting rich yet. The act is financing its future through sheer volume of work. A week of appearances isn't optional, it is the way rent is paid, and car repairs are covered. How fuel and food is purchased. It also means that every canceled date matters. A blown tire or a bad promoter isn't a minor hassle. It is a direct hit to the fragile economy of the group.

The family part also stays close in February, even when the calendar looks impossible. Elvis's parents are part of the early story not as celebrities, but as anchors. When a twenty year old starts to draw screaming crowds, the grounding influence of home can be the difference between confidence and chaos. The Memphis returns, even short ones, provide chances to sleep in familiar places, eat real meals, and reconnect with people who knew him before the spotlight. That emotional reset is one reason the act can survive the travel. It is also why the later story of fame and isolation feels so tragic. In early 1955, the roots are still reachable.

### FEBRUARY 7 TO FEBRUARY 16: THE WESTERN SWING AND NEW PEERS
#### Key Dates
Feb 7 (Mon): Ripley High School Gym, Ripley, Mississippi.

Feb 10 (Thu), Alpine, Texas. The road bends southwest into thin air and long distances.

Feb 11 (Fri): Sports Arena, Carlsbad, New Mexico (4:00 p.m.); Hobbs, New Mexico (evening).

Feb 12 (Sat): Legion Hut, Carlsbad, New Mexico.

Feb 13 (Sun), Lubbock, Texas. Buddy Holly is on the same bill as 'Buddy and Bob.'

Feb 14 (Mon), Roswell, New Mexico. A stop remembered as much for the mythic name as the music.

Feb 15 (Tue), Abilene, Texas. A college, and military town where the stage is learning to contain him.

Feb 16 (Thu), Odessa, Texas. Oilfield rhythm, late-night travel, and more songs learned by repetition.

Tour calendars for this western swing sometimes slide by a day because the band was grabbing school bookings, matinees, and late-night drives where the paperwork lagged behind the wheels. What stays consistent is the pattern: Mississippi and Shreveport fall away, then the route runs through West Texas into New Mexico and back, with two-show nights, and long gaps of highway in between. When the record differs by twenty-four hours, the house reaction does not.

On February 7 the Monday show in Ripley, Mississippi is reported as a courthouse appearance, a continued reminder of how improvised early touring can be. It is the start of a workweek and seems odd to host a date by today's standards. A courthouse isn't designed for amplified music, and that mismatch creates its own drama. For the audience, the unusual setting adds to the legend. People remember where they were when they heard something new, especially when the new thing arrives in a place that was never meant to host it.

Industry ears were pricking up too. Around this stretch, William Morris agent Harry Kalcheim wrote to Neal with a small but revealing admission: he'd misplaced a photograph Neal had sent, but he didn't lose interest in the voice. Notes like that are easy to overlook, yet they show Elvis's name starting to circulate in rooms where bookings were brokered on stationery rather than posters.

Then the map stretches. Alpine, Texas on February 10 is a gateway into the Big Bend region, where distance turns into a physical sensation. Alpine grew as a rail and local center in far West Texas, and by the mid-century it served travelers and local ranching economies. Driving into Alpine means driving into open space. For a touring act, that space can feel both liberating and punishing. There are fewer stops, fewer familiar landmarks, and a stronger sense that the show is a traveling island.

Trade press treated the growth as something you could track like a business opening. Cash Box noted that Neal had established a booking office at 160 Union Avenue in Memphis, putting a formal address on what had been a rolling operation. That detail matters: it is the moment the touring hustle starts to look like a company, and Elvis is the asset at the center of it.

The health part becomes practical. Long drives through sparse country demand alertness. Weather can shift, roads can be rough, and a late arrival can mean a rushed setup. One tire slightly off the road can cause calamity, so they need to take turns driving and sleeping. The band's routine tightens instruments checked, cables packed the same way every time, and a focus on doing the job even when the body wants sleep. You can also see how leadership emerges. Someone has to decide when to push on and when to stop. In early 1955, those decisions are often made on instinct and necessity.

Carlsbad, New Mexico on February 11, and 12 sits in a region shaped by resource extraction and the rhythms of working families. A crowd in a town like this isn't impressed by hype alone. They respond to energy, to clear rhythm, and to a singer who looks like he means every word. Elvis's stage style, a mix of confidence, and raw nerves, plays well in these environments. He isn't offering a polished nightclub act. He is offering a jolt, and that jolt cuts through the usual entertainment options. Elvis stood out from the other performers who shared the show with him. Nancy Jones and Bill Robertson were talented, but they were no Elvis Presley.

February 13 in Lubbock, Texas is one of the month's most fascinating intersections. The bill includes 'Buddy and Bob,' a reference to Buddy Holly's early performing sense of who they are before national success. Two young artists, both learning their voices, share space in the same local ecosystem. Lubbock's musical culture is shaped by West Texas influences and radio promotion, and it produces performers who understand how to blend country roots with a modern edge. Seeing Elvis on the same circuit highlights how quickly the mid-

1950s are changing. Multiple futures are being born in the same small rooms.

Roswell, New Mexico on February 14 carries a towns name that later becomes shorthand for mystery and U.F.O. sightings, but in 1955 it is simply a town on the route. That is part of the charm of historical detail. Places that later acquire myth were once practical stops where people bought groceries and attended shows on weeknights. Elvis's music, at this stage, is also something practical. It is a way to earn money, to build a reputation, and to prove that the act can travel. The myth will come later. February is still about work.

Roswell also exposes how Parker and Diskin started treating the day as a managed sequence rather than a simple arrival-and-sing routine. They instructed Elvis to report to Diskin at the leading hotel by mid-afternoon, then move through radio promotion before curtain. That night's show was staged at North Junior High School Auditorium with two times, roughly 7:30 and 9:30, under a sponsorship as ordinary as the city's fire department. In a year where mythology would eventually attach itself to nearly everything. This is the grounding detail: the big system of fame still ran on school auditoriums, town sponsors, and men watching their watches. Hank Snow and his Rainbow Ranch Boys, The Duke of Paducah, Charlene Arthur, and Jimmy Rogers Snow are part of the bookings that evening.

Abilene, Texas on February 15 is a larger city environment compared to some earlier stops, with institutions, and military ties that influence local culture. Bigger towns bring bigger expectations. The stage is higher, the sound system may be better, and the seats can include more skeptics. A performer who relies on something new is exposed quickly. Elvis survives because there is musical truth under his movement. The band's groove, the combination of rhythm, and blues feel with country framing, gives the show a foundation that doesn't fall apart under scrutiny. The boy can sing, and the music is real.

Odessa, Texas on February 16 places the act in the heart of oil country. Odessa's growth and sense of who they are are tied to the Permian Basin and the oil and gas economy, and that boom, and bust mentality can shape a crowd. People who work hard tend to expect entertainment that feels alive. Elvis's intensity fits that expectation. The personal part also flickers here, because the road can make a young man feel older than his years. He is carrying adult responsibilities: money, reputation, turnout's appetite of being the engine that keeps everyone employed. This is the beginning of one of the larger lesser known talked about curses of Elvis. He became responsible for everyone. With Colonel Parkers continued deposits for future package shows comes the realization that he can't just quit if he feels worn down or lonely. If he quits, everyone around him suffers.

Throughout this middle stretch of this month, the musical part is evolving. The set isn't static. Songs are adjusted for audience reaction. If a number triggers a bigger response, it moves earlier if needed to get the joint jumping. If a ballad loses attention, it is trimmed or reframed. The band also learns the importance of dynamics. A loud show turns louder if there is no contrast. Elvis starts to understand that a quieter moment can create space for the next explosion.

Movies and pop culture remain present as a kind of background fuel. On the road, performers often kill time by talking about films, radio programs, and the stars everyone recognizes. Elvis's own tastes in movies are well recorded in other periods, and in 1955 the influence is visible in the way he performs masculinity. The hair, the posture, and the timing of a glance are not accidents. They are part of a young man assembling a public image out of the materials his generation shares. The beginning of his Movie Career, before a movie camera was pointing at him.

Friends and famous interactions in February are not common as the later era of Hollywood parties show. They are the practical relationships of touring: talk veteran artists, being watched by show planners, being introduced to radio people, and learning which adults in the business can open doors. The most consequential door will involve management, but even before that, every handshake on a package tour can change where the act is booked next month. In 1955, networking isn't a buzzword. It is survival.

The health part shows its teeth when the schedule tightens. A voice is a muscle, and muscles can fail when abused. Elvis's vocal style includes grit and intensity, and that can be risky if he isn't careful. By mid-February the act is learning how to protect the instrument: not every note needs to be pushed, not every scream needs to be real. The illusion of effort is sometimes as powerful as the effort itself.

By the time February 16 ends in Odessa, the tour has covered a remarkable range of geography and audience type. Delta towns, major cities, oil towns, and college towns have all heard the same young singer. That spread matters. It means the music isn't trapped in one local scene. February 1955 is showing that the big deal can cross borders, both state lines, and cultural lines. The next question is who will guide it, and how fast it will grow.

The Hank Snow touring package that carries Elvis through Texas and New Mexico in mid-February is a lesson in hierarchy. On a package bill, there is a running order. Veteran names expect respect, and the schedule is often brutal: show, travel, appearance again. Elvis is younger than many of the people around him, but his effect on crowds can be bigger. That creates suspense and opportunity. If the headliner sees you as an asset, you get better slots, and better towns. If the headliner sees you as a threat, you have to keep winning without provoking open conflict. Either way, Elvis, as a young performer, learns diplomacy quickly. It didn't hurt that he was naturally a respectful young man.

The other acts on the bills are not background characters. They are part of the education. Comedians and emcees like the Duke of Paducah understand pacing and crowd control. Family acts like Mother Maybelle Carter and the Carter Sisters carry an old-school respect that audiences trust. Standing next to that tradition forces Elvis to be honest about what he is doing. He isn't replacing country music. He's colliding with it, blending influences, and daring the world to follow. In February 1955, that collision is still the main event.

Lubbock deserves a closer look because it illustrates how the mid-1950s are a crossroads. The day-by-day record places Elvis on a bill where Buddy Holly appears as 'Buddy and Bob.' That small detail captures a moment before fame locks names into permanent forms. Both artists are still in the phase where sense of who they are is flexible, and local scenes are incubating future national culture. This is one of the best examples of why a day by day approach matters. History often only remembers outcomes. Lost in the details is how it someone got there.

Period ads around Lubbock give the show a sharper outline than memory usually allows. One notice billed Elvis as a "Be-Bop Western Star" returning to Fair Park Coliseum, a phrase that sounds half-dismissive and half-afraid. The bill itself was a snapshot of a changing South: Charlene Arthur and Jimmie Rodgers Snow carried the established part. While a young Buddy Holly appeared low on the card as "Buddy and Bob." Neal later treated this date as a milestone because it was among the first got directly through Parker's booking muscle. And the fee, about $350 for the group on a matinee, showed both how small, though growing, the guarantees still were and how loud the reaction was becoming.

Odessa and the Permian Basin region also provide a lesson about audience psychology. Resource towns can be intense. Work is physical, the days schedules are long, and entertainment is the release valve of all the pressure that was growing in their personal life. A performer who is timid will not break through. Elvis breaks through because the performance is physical. His energy is relentless. When the band locks into a groove, the people responds as if it has been given an order to move. The new music is more than a sound. It turns into behavior. Teenagers imitate it, some adults fear it and show planners sense that they are watching a new kind of market. A market made up of dollar signs.

Odessa's numbers hint at how far the live show was pulling ahead of the records. Reports put the crowd above 4,000, too big to describe as a local something new, and performers who followed him felt the shift in the room. Roy Orbison who attended, still early in his own path, later described the experience in simple terms: the energy was incredible, Elvis instinct astonishing. The audience behaved as if they'd been waiting all day to erupt. That kind of testimony matters because it comes from another working musician, not a headline writer.

The health part across this long swing isn't only about the voice. It is also about nerves. Performing in a new town every night is stressful. The band walks into a room without knowing what the crowd will be like, what the local promoter will demand, or whether the sound equipment will even function. A performer learns coping strategies. Some are healthy, like routines, and rest. Some are less healthy, like pushing through exhaustion with sheer rush, or leaning on a bottle or pills. In February 1955, the rush of success for Elvis is the obvious fuel, and the long miles make that fuel feel necessary.

Movies and radio meet with the touring life in practical ways. Radio stations in these towns are often the local kingmakers. A short interview or a quick station visit can turn a quiet afternoon into a packed night. At the same time, the movie theater is still one of the main gathering places in many communities, and its imagery helps audiences interpret new stars. When Elvis appears on stage, he isn't only heard. He is seen, and the way he looks from the turnout is judged by the same standards people apply to screen idols. February 1955 is building the visual vocabulary that later television cameras will carry. He is a live MOVING PICTURE.

The western routing also changes the emotional tone of the month. When you travel through wide open landscapes, the silence between towns becomes part of the experience. A southern tour can feel like an adventure. Elvis Scotty and Bill watched many westerns growing up. Now they were living it. But with an expansive setting comes a reality. A

West Texas and New Mexico run can feel like a chain of islands separated by distance. That isolation can intensify relationships within the band. Small disagreements feel bigger when there is no escape. At the same time, shared hardship can build loyalty. When you follow the schedule, this is the month where the band starts to look less like a casual trio and more like a seasoned unit.

It is also worth pausing back to the idea of the package show itself. In this era, a concert is rarely often a single artist event. It is a traveling variety bill. That format means Elvis is learning from every act on the stage. When a comedian works a hostile room into laughter, that is a lesson in timing. When a veteran singer adjusts the key to protect the voice, that is a lesson in longevity. When a family act maintains dignity under chaos, that is a lesson in image management. Elvis's later mastery of stagecraft does not come from nowhere. February 1955 is one of the months where the classroom is the bill itself.

The Buddy Holly overlap in Lubbock invites another thought. Teen culture in 1955 is hungry for sense of who they are. The war years are over, prosperity is rising, and young people start to demand music that feels like their own language. Both Elvis and Holly are tapping into that hunger, each in a different way. Elvis brings a visibly physical style that shocks older audiences. Holly brings songwriting and a cleaner public persona that will later appeal to broader markets. In February, none of that is guaranteed. It is simply two young men on the same circuit, each taking notes on what works. The future is sitting in the wings, waiting for a microphone.

A final musical note for this stretch is how Elvis's vocal approach starts to broaden. The earliest Sun sides show a youthful, nearly playful vocal. On the road, especially on a demanding tour, the voice can darken. Late nights and steady performance can roughen the tone, but they can also add the building's stature. A listener in Odessa might hear a slightly different singer than a listener in Memphis, not because the songs changed, but because the body changed. That is one of the benefits of a month by month narrative. It captures how sound evolves right then, shaped by miles, rooms, and fatigue.

A reader can also watch the sound system of American culture changing right then. Country audiences are used to polished crooners and clean stage manners. Rhythm and blues audiences are used to intensity and swing. Elvis carries both languages, and on the Hank Snow circuit he is effectively translating between them. That translation sometimes creates confusion. Some adults hear the rhythm and fear it. Teenagers hear the rhythm and recognize themselves, a voice for them. In February 1955, you can see the generational divide widening in each town, because the same songs are interpreted as either entertainment or rebellion.

Even when the records don't preserve every set list, certain anchors are likely present because they were associated with Elvis by this time. Early Sun sides like 'That's All Right' and 'Blue Moon of Kentucky' are foundational, and by February the act is also introducing newer material being cut in the studio such as Baby let's Play house. The key point is to understand how routine creates mastery. When you sing the same core songs night after night in different rooms, you learn how to work a crowd through them. You learn where to stretch a phrase, where to pause for the audience, and where to push the band harder. That is how a local act like Elvis could turn into a national act. Not by something new alone, but by craft sharpened through routine.

## FEBRUARY 17 TO FEBRUARY 28: RETURN ROUTES AND A NORTHERN LEAP
### Key Dates

Feb 17 (Thu): City Auditorium, San Angelo, Texas (7:30 and 9:30 p.m.). Final confirmed date in the Hank Snow package-show run.

Feb 18 (Fri): West Monroe High School Auditorium, Monroe, Louisiana (7:30 and 9:30 p.m.). End of the Hank Snow run.

Feb 19 (Sat): Louisiana Hayride, Municipal Auditorium, Shreveport, Louisiana.

Feb 20 (Sun): Robinson Auditorium, Little Rock, Arkansas (3:00 and 8:15 p.m.). Return to a familiar Arkansas circuit.

Feb 21 (Mon): City Auditorium, Camden, Arkansas.

Feb 22 (Tue): City Hall, Hope, Arkansas.

Feb 23 (Wed): High School Auditorium, Pine Bluff, Arkansas (7:30 and 9:30 p.m.).

Feb 24 (Thu): South Side Elementary School, Bastrop, Louisiana (7:30 and 9:30 p.m.).

A fast northern leap follows, setting up the month's close with a booking in Ohio.

Feb 26 (Sat): Hillbilly Jamboree, Circle Theater, Cleveland, Ohio (7:30 and 10:30 p.m.).

The High School Auditorium on February 18 in West Monroe is the end of the Hank Snow tour. One recorded song rundown had Elvis performing "Milk Cow Blues Boogie," "Good Rockin' Tonight," "You're A Heartbreaker," "Baby let's Play House," "That's alright mama," "Breakin' the Rules," and "Blue Moon of Kentucky"

The Louisiana Hayride on February 19 functions like a weekly report card. It is where the region can compare notes: is the act growing, is the crowd's bodily response still wild, is the singer still unpredictable? For Elvis, the Hayride is a place where the professional part and the personal part run into. He can be cheered like a star and then be back in Memphis the next day like a local kid, if the schedule allowed as it was only 5 hours away. That tension can be disorienting, but it also keeps him hungry. There is no illusion that the work is finished.

Little Rock, Arkansas on February 20 introduces a larger city energy, and city energy changes the stakes. Urban audiences include more mixed groups: older listeners, couples on dates, working people, and teenagers who have planned for weeks. The hall and the press environment can make the show feel more formal. Elvis's music holds up because it is rooted in recognizable forms. Even when the style feels new, the bones are older: blues patterns, gospel intensity, and country storytelling.

Camden, Arkansas on February 21 and Hope, Arkansas on February 22 are reminders that Arkansas towns are connected by rivers and rail, and the long memory of trade routes. Camden's history is tied to the Ouachita River and earlier trading eras, and Hope sits in southwest Arkansas with rail lines and a sense of being on the way to somewhere else. For a touring act, that geography matters. These are places used to travelers passing through. A good show becomes another story added to a town's collection of passing events.

Even while the tour doubled back through smaller Arkansas rooms, Parker was testing the edges of the map. In correspondence from late February, California promoter Bam Bamford was contacted about Elvis and his response captured both the promise and the caution of the moment: the boy was a sensation, but a West Coast push would need buildup and the right timing. Parker absorbed that kind of feedback as strategy. He didn't chase the first available door. He measured which door would open widest once Elvis became impossible to ignore.

Pine Bluff, Arkansas on February 23 brings a river town history that includes its role as a cotton center and port. Industrial and agricultural economies produce crowds that can be tough in a special way. They have seen traveling entertainment before, and they are not automatically impressed.

Winning Pine Bluff means earning attention with rhythm and presence, not with reputation. Elvis's stage approach, direct, and physical, is built for that challenge. He doesn't ask politely for attention. He takes it.

The Bastrop, Louisiana Southside Elementary shows are the last booking of the 2nd Jamboree Attractions tour. The tour had less draw than the Hank Snow tour and it loses money.

Now the month makes a sudden leap. Elvis, Scotty, and Bill load up with Bob Neal, and point the car toward Cleveland, their first real date outside the South. It's a long pull north, the kind of drive where the heater barely keeps up and the miles feel louder than the conversation. They don't just go straight there, either. They detour into radio stations along the way, quick handshakes, a few words, a record passed across a desk, anything that might turn into airplay after the show. In 1955, a spinning turntable can matter as much as the stage. Sometimes more.

Back in the paper trail, Colonel Parker is working his angle again. He writes Harry Kalcheim at the William Morris Agency in New York and, true to form. And closes by asking what Kalcheim thinks of "this ELVIS PRESLEY BOY." Then he adds his own verdict: Elvis can make it, if he's "exploited properly." In Parker's vocabulary, that word isn't a slur. It's his trade. Exploitation means exposure, power, headlines, turning momentum into money, and attention before anyone else can. That's how the Colonel thinks, and that's how he sells the future.

After that long drive to Cleveland, Ohio on February 26 this places Elvis in a northern hall, the Hillbilly Jamboree, hosted by singer Tommy Edwards. This isn't a simple extension of the southern circuit. It is a signal that the act is becoming interesting to people outside the immediate region of the south. Cleveland also matters because of radio. DJ Bill Randle is associated with this stop in day-by-day accounts, and radio personalities are gatekeepers. If a key DJ is interested, the music can travel even further and faster than before.

The famous interactions part starts to look like a ladder. In the South, Elvis is becoming a headline. In the North, he is a curiosity with potential. A single influential person can bridge those worlds. The music industry in 1955 is still heavily local, and radio remains one of the fastest ways to break that local barrier. Talk the right broadcaster can change the scale of distribution, bookings, and publicity. February plants seeds that will sprout later in the year.

The personal part in late February is defined as much by absence as by presence. When the schedule is this heavy, relationships at home survive through small windows and quick visits. Elvis is known to have dated Dixie Locke during this period, a Memphis relationship that overlaps with the first major touring push. That matters because it reminds you that the performer is still a teenager balancing private life and public attention. Even if February does not provide a headline romance story, the suspense between home and road is part of the month's emotional detail.

Health in the final stretch isn't just about illness. It is about stress and recovery. A young body can outrun fatigue for a while, but the mind keeps a ledger. Long drives, screaming crowds, and steady performance can create a kind of numbness if there is no rest. By the end of February, the act has survived a schedule that would challenge older performers. The survival itself is a statement: the show isn't a fluke, and the energy is real.

The movies part stays in the background, but it continues to shape what the audience believes it is seeing. In 1955, America is saturated with screen images of cowboys, rebels, and romantic leads. Elvis carries pieces of that imagery without needing to name it. When he pauses, when he smiles, when he turns his head at the right moment, the crowd reacts as if the stage has become a movie screen. That reaction is part of what makes the big deal feel larger than the songs themselves.

If February 1955 has a single lesson, it is that crowd hunger is built by ordinary nights performed with extraordinary commitment. The month isn't remembered for a single famous television appearance or a single record breaking headline. It is remembered, in the detailed accounts, as a chain of rooms and towns that taught Elvis how to become what the people expects. Consistency is what lets talent scale. By the last dates of February, the calendar isn't just a record of where he went. It is evidence that the machine has started.

The Arkansas run in late February is a reminder that the South isn't one uniform audience. Each town has its own mix of church influence, working class rhythms, and local pride. In Hope, Camden, and Pine Bluff, people know each other. A show is a scene event. When the teenagers scream, their parents often know exactly whose child is screaming. That closeness can raise the stakes for everyone. For Elvis, it means that the surge of noise isn't anonymous. It is personal, and that can make a young performer feel both powerful and exposed.

The personal part in these towns also includes the reality of temptation and rumor. Elvis's fame at this stage creates a new kind of attention that follows him from the stage door to the street. If there are girls waiting, they are often ordinary local teenagers, not celebrities, though those will come in the near future. The key point for February isn't a single named romance. It is the pattern: attention arrives faster than emotional maturity can process it. This is why family, bandmates, and trusted friends matter. They create boundaries, even when the world is trying to erase them.

Cleveland's significance grows when you think in terms of distribution. A southern act traveling north has to overcome stereotypes. Some audiences expect country music, some expect rhythm, and blues, and some don't know what to expect at all. A DJ like Bill Randle has the power to frame the artist for listeners: as a something new, as a rebel, or as the next big thing. The day-by-day accounts connect Elvis with Randle around the Hillbilly Jamboree date. That is a sign that the northern radio world is start to pay attention, and once radio pays attention, the calendar changes.

When February ends, we can now see the outline of the year ahead. The weekly Hayride obligation, the expanding tour circuits, the studio sessions, and the first serious business meetings are all in motion. The five parts are not separate. They are merging. Personal life is being shaped by touring, or rather strained by touring. Music is being shaped by audience reaction. Movies and pop culture imagery are shaping perception. Health is being tested by pace. Friends and famous interactions are opening doors that can't be closed again. February 1955 isn't a climax. It is a takeoff. It's a runway, and Elvis is the jet.

When the route swings back toward Shreveport and Arkansas, you can feel how the Hayride serves as a center of gravity. Graceland's Hayride history notes that Elvis appeared weekly through 1954 and 1955, initially for modest pay. And that the program helped launch many stars by broadcasting from Shreveport and touring regulars through Louisiana, Texas, and Arkansas. Those touring loops are exactly what February illustrates. The Hayride isn't only a stage. It is an organizing principle for the entire early career. It dictates geography, it keeps the act visible, and it provides a consistent context where growth can be measured week to week.

*We should also notate what isn't happening yet*. There are no Hollywood contracts, no movie scripts in hand, and no national television spotlight. Those things will arrive later, and when they do, it can be tempting to pretend the leap was sure. February 1955 argues against certainty. A career can still be derailed by a bad contract, a blown voice, or a single promoter who turns hostile. The reason Elvis breaks through is that the fundamentals are being built in months like this: reliable performances. Expanding reach, and the early alignment of business forces that will eventually carry him beyond the local circuit.

Cleveland also hints at how quickly Elvis's story will outgrow the South. Once northern radio starts to pay attention, the logic of the career changes. A performer can't rely on being a local big deal amplified by a local program. Now the audience includes people who have never seen the act live but feel like they know it through radio. That shift in crowd puts pressure on 45s. A live reputation can carry a tour, but national awareness requires records that can stand on their own. February 1955 contains both worlds: the live circuit that built the legend and the business relationships that will demand broader distribution.

Because the goal here is to stay anchored to reliable documentation, it is worth naming the limits I come up against in documenting this. Day-by-day timelines preserve dates, venues, and key meetings, but they don't always preserve the private conversations that make history feel intimate. When an account does not document a detail, the responsible move is to describe the pattern without inventing a scene. In February 1955, the pattern is clear: a young performer is being pulled outward by opportunity. That pull affects friendships, romance, and family life, even when the month doesn't hand you many headline moments to quote. We can still feel the human cost, because the calendar itself is exhausting to look at. Every date is a demand, and every demand leaves less space for a normal teenage life.

The recorded women in Elvis's early life are often discussed in broad strokes, but their presence matters for understanding the personal part in his life. Dixie Locke, for example, is remembered in interviews, and later coverage as a Memphis girlfriend in early 1955. A relationship that overlaps with the period when local fame starts to turn into local fame. There are other girlfriends of this year that were recorded later as well, although some scrutinized and questioned. That overlap is huge even if February doesn't provide a dramatic public episode. It suggests that Elvis's private sense of who they are is tied to ordinary hometown life, even while the stage sense of who they are is becoming larger than any one city. This helps keep the story balanced. The month is full of screaming crowds and expanding miles, but it is also full of small personal choices. The kind that decide whether a young man stays grounded or drifts into a public persona with no private center.

As we move into March, remember what February accomplished. It proved that he could repeat success without losing intensity. It stretched the geography from Mississippi and Louisiana to Texas, New Mexico, and then as far as Ohio. It placed Elvis on bills with established names, where professionalism was required, and it kept him tied to the Hayride, where weekly performance sharpened the edge. It also introduced the early business forces circling the big deal, hinting that management, and national strategy were not optional. When people later describe 1955 it should always be as the year the fuse was lit. February is where you can hear it crackling. Not in one explosion, but in dozens of rooms where a teenager stepped into the lights and left the hall louder than it was before.

One last note: every date in February is a rehearsal for the national stage. The crowds are training him to handle hysteria. The miles are training him to endure. The bills are training him to share space with legends. By the time the year reaches its bigger headlines, the foundation has been laid night after night.

## FEBRUARY 1955 RADIO, CINEMA, AND A COUNTRY HOLDING THE LINE

February keeps its public face, ballads, harmony, a steady hand on the wheel. But the records that change a room's temperature are coming from Black artists who know how to make rhythm feel like a decision. In the same month you can hear sweetness and defiance sitting back-to-back: "Only You, And You Alone,", The Platters,. "The Wallflower, Dance with Me, Henry,", Etta James & The Peaches, "My Babe", Little Walter, "Tweedle Dee", LaVern Baker, and "Every Day I Have the Blues", Count Basie Orchestra with Joe Williams,. It's not just music, it's a new way of carrying yourself, and the country is starting to pick it up by accident.

*What America Was Hearing on the Radio
February 1955*

In February of 1955, American radio leaned even more heavily toward familiarity than it would a month later. Winter programming favored emotional steadiness. The goal was comfort, not confrontation.

Pop radio during February was dominated by songs that lingered without demanding movement:

Doris Day "If I Give My Heart to You" Warm, reassuring, and deliberately unhurried. Romance framed as careful promise as an alternative to risk., Billboard pop chart peak: 8 in 1954,

Rosemary Clooney "Mambo Italiano" Playful something new wrapped in polish. Rhythm presented as flirtation, not threat., Billboard Honor Roll of Hits peak: 7. Cash Box peak: 8, 1954-55,

Eddie Fisher "Hearts of Stone" A warning song given gently. Emotion held back inside conventional phrasing., Billboard year-end pop: 15 in 1955,

Frank Sinatra "Learnin' the Blues" A veteran voice reflecting in lieu of reacting. Experience replacing urgency., Billboard year-end pop: 14 in 1955,

Country radio carried a different kind of the room's stature, rooted in tradition rather than experimentation:

Hank Snow "I don't Hurt Anymore" Controlled heartbreak. Pain expressed cleanly, without disruption.

Webb Pierce "Even Tho" Direct storytelling with emotional restraint. Familiar forms reinforced., Billboard year-end country: 4 in 1954,

Kitty Wells "Making Believe" Domestic sorrow framed, reinforcing stability rather than rebellion., Billboard year-end pop: 16 in 1955,

Across formats, February radio favored reflection over release. Songs settled into listeners' homes like furniture. They stayed in place.

What radio avoided was instability.

That avoidance mattered.

*What Was Playing in Movie Theaters February 1955*

Cinema continued to reinforce restraint, even as it flirted with restlessness.

Films in circulation during February included: On the Waterfront, still widely playing,: Masculinity shown through inner struggle and moral weight, not speed. The Caine Mutiny, continuing its run,: Authority, discipline.

Christmas movies were still appearing in some theaters,: Nostalgia, harmony, and emotional safety served up as spectacle.

Rear Window, still booking in plenty of towns,: Suspicion as entertainment-every glance a clue, every body a message. 20,000 Leagues Under the Sea, a newer holdover drawing crowds,: The future dressed as adventure-machines, depth, and danger made beautiful. A Star Is Born, released in 1954, still pulling big audiences where it landed,: Fame as romance and warning at the same time-lights bright enough to burn. Battle Cry, new in the circuit,: Young men shaped by discipline and belonging, learning what the world expects them to become. The Country Girl, still circulating,: Respectability with cracks in it-quiet rooms where love and damage live side by side. The High and the Mighty, still showing in some houses,: Fear and courage in tight quarters-men trying to hold themselves together under pressure.

Movie houses remained social centers in the towns Elvis passed through. Marquees glowed nightly. Audiences learned how to read bodies-posture, move, stillness-long before they questioned music.

In February, cinema still taught America how to sit still.

*Where Elvis Fit and Did Not Fit into That Landscape*

By February 1955, Elvis Presley was not yet a radio fixture. In many towns, he was being heard first in person, not through a speaker.

That distinction mattered.

Radio presented voices that stayed in place. Elvis presented a live physical voice and body that moved.

Where radio singers resolved emotion, Elvis sustained it. Where films portrayed tension internally, Elvis externalized it.

Audiences did not need to analyze the difference. They felt it.

By February, the pattern isn't isolated enough to dismiss. Teenagers arrive primed, as if word-of-mouth has written the first chorus. Adults arrive watchful, not always opposed, but wary of how quickly the hall can tip from entertainment into weather.

February is the month where this gap becomes consistent.

## What Elvis Sounded Like Against February Radio

Elvis's Sun recordings were circulating unevenly, often trailing behind his physical presence. Many audiences encountered his voice without preparation.

Radio offered:

Calm

Closure

Predictability

Elvis offered:

Motion

Suspended tension

Physical urgency

The contrast did not require explanation.

In towns where audiences spent the afternoon hearing Perry Como or Patti Page, Elvis's rhythm arrived like a disturbance. Not a rejection of tradition, but a refusal to remain still inside it.

This is why February reactions escalated so quickly in high school gyms and package shows. They were discovering a new relationship between sound and body.

The economics followed the noise. By late February, routing notes. And accounting summaries put the month's earnings above four thousand dollars, more than double what the early winter weeks were yielding, despite the modest guarantees on many school and town dates. The split was still the old touring arithmetic, expenses first, then shares, but the direction was unmistakable. The rooms were getting bigger, the hysteria louder, and the money was start to behave like the start of an industry rather than the end of a hustle.

Why February 1955 Matters Culturally

February isn't the month of explosion. It is the month of acceleration.

The schedule gets tighter. The miles lengthen. The crowds grow louder.

What changes isn't Elvis's sound, but the frequency of reaction. Night after night, town after town, the kids' very strong response repeats often enough to become undeniable.

Radio has not yet caught up. Cinema has not yet adapted.

But the audience has started to.

Radio and film still move in measured steps, but the live circuit is accelerating. The institutions aren't wrong, they're simply slower, built for gradual change. February is where the appetite starts to outrun the infrastructure.


## FULL KNOWN FEBRUARY 1955 PERFORMANCE RECORD

February 26: Hillbilly Jamboree, Circle Theater, Cleveland, Ohio, 7:30 and 10:30 p.m.,.

February 24: South Side Elementary School, Bastrop, Louisiana, 7:30 and 9:30 p.m.,.

February 23: High School Auditorium, Pine Bluff, Arkansas, 7:30 and 9:30 p.m.,.

February 22: City Hall, Hope, Arkansas.

February 21: City Auditorium, Camden, Arkansas.

February 20: Robinson Auditorium, Little Rock, Arkansas, 3:00 and 8:15 p.m.,.

February 19: Louisiana Hayride, Municipal Auditorium, Shreveport, Louisiana.

February 18: West Monroe High School Auditorium, Monroe, Louisiana, 7:30 and 9:30 p.m.,.

February 17: City Auditorium, San Angelo, Texas, 7:30 and 9:30 p.m.,.

February 16: Odessa Senior High School Field House, Odessa, Texas, 7:30 and 9:30 p.m.,.

February 15: Fairpark Auditorium, Abilene, Texas, 7:00 and 9:00 p.m.,.

February 14: North Junior High School Auditorium, Roswell, New Mexico, 7:30 and 9:30 p.m.,.

February 13: Fair Park Coliseum, Lubbock, Texas, 4:00 p.m.,.

February 12: Legion Hut, Carlsbad, New Mexico.

February 11: Sports Arena, Carlsbad, New Mexico, 4:00 p.m.,. Hobbs, New Mexico, evening,.

February 10: High School, Alpine, Texas.

February 7: Ripley High School Gym, Ripley, Mississippi.

February 6: Ellis Auditorium, Memphis, Tennessee, 3:00 and 8:00 p.m.,.

February 5: Louisiana Hayride, Municipal Auditorium, Shreveport, Louisiana.

February 4: Jesuit High School, New Orleans, Louisiana.

February 2: High School, Augusta, Arkansas.

February 1: High School, Randolph, Mississippi.

# Chapter 3, March 1955

March 1955 opens on the road and on the clock as we race towards fame. The month's traceable itinerary runs from two shows in Newport, Arkansas, March 2,. To a string of Southern dates and larger-package appearances, then to a New York television audition, March 23, before dropping back into the Deep South and the Louisiana Hayride, March 26,.

Recorded stops this month include Newport, Arkansas, U. S. Armory, and Porky's Rooftop Club, Covington, Tennessee, Ruffin Theater, Austin, Texas, Dessau Hall, Houston's Grand Prize Jamboree. Dermott, Arkansas, Shreveport for the Hayride, and a late-month run through Big Creek and Tocopola, Mississippi, El Dorado, Arkansas, and Longview, Texas.

Elvis is traveling mostly in the Lincoln through these March runs, driving hard miles between towns, loading in fast, playing, and leaving. When the Lincoln can't take the beating, borrowed cars bridge the gap - but the pace of the road never slows.

Somewhere in these early March miles, the road makes its own history. Bill Black wrecks the Lincoln. Reports place it under the lift of a hay truck in Arkansas, and the band's sense of certainty snaps into plain hassle. For a brief Texas swing, Elvis borrows the family car from Jim Ed and Maxine Brown. The kind of favor that only happens when people love and respect you. It's a small detail with a large meaning: the act is growing faster than the big system meant to carry it, and the calendar keeps moving even when the wheels don't. Yet you still need support from friends to keep you moving.

The month opens with Elvis living inside motion. Travel isn't an event between shows. It is the condition under which the performances exist. The car is as familiar as the stage. Distance is measured not in miles, but in how quickly equipment can be packed and unpacked and how quick you find your way to the next town. Speed limits get broken.

On March 2, Elvis performs twice in Newport, Arkansas. The first show takes place at the U. S. Armory. The second, later that evening, at Porky's Rooftop Club.

These two rooms could not be more different, and the contrast matters.

An armory is a town building. It carries expectations of supervision, pecking order, and restraint. It is designed to contain bodies and sound. Performances in armories are public events in the strictest sense. Parents attend. Local officials attend. Behavior is observed, and reaction is judged as much as the performer. Elvis would play this show a little more reserved as he would play to the audience.

Porky's Rooftop Club belongs to the opposite end of the social clock. It exists for the late hour. The listeners arrives loosened, willing to react. Where the armory demands crowd control, the club invites release, and release it did.

Elvis performs in both spaces on the same night.

This isn't a detail to skim past. It reveals something essential about his working life in early 1955. He isn't changing who he is from room to room. He is learning how to release himself differently without losing coherence. The songs remain largely the same. The tempo remains recognizable. What shifts is emphasis.

In an armory, Elvis establishes permission. He proves he belongs on the stage before he pushes against its boundaries. In a club, he pushes sooner, trusting the audience to follow.

That trust is earned.

Newport itself isn't an accidental stop. As a river town and local crossroads, it was accustomed to passing influences. Traveling musicians, variety revues, and radio promoted acts had been moving through towns like Newport for decades before Elvis arrived.

Music in Newport was not rare. What was rare was the intensity Elvis brought.

Before Elvis, audiences in places like Newport were familiar with country performers, blues musicians traveling the Delta corridor, and acts that balanced humor with song. These performers brought professionalism and familiarity.

That urgency mattered because Newport understood entertainment as movement. People came and went. Acts passed through. What stayed were the nights that felt different from the others. March 2, 1955, becomes one of those nights not because Elvis was unknown, but because the surge of the crowd was unmistakable.

The town did not need to be educated about music. It needed to be ignited.

Musically, the opening days of March are defined by the crowd's expectation. Elvis is already headlining often enough that he must satisfy many expectations in a single performance. show planners want reassurance. Parents want decorum. Teenagers want ignition.

The solution isn't compromise, but sequencing.

Country material establishes stability. Rhythm driven material creates release. This approach is tested nightly. A song that settles a room earns Elvis time. A song that excites a room earns him loyalty. By March, Elvis understands that both are necessary, and he orders his sets accordingly.

This ability to handle a mixed audience becomes one of his most reliable professional assets. It keeps him bookable in conservative towns while allowing his reputation among younger listeners to grow unchecked.

The personal record of early March is thin, and that thinness is itself revealing. There is little recorded leisure, little recorded romance, little recorded pause. The rhythm of the month leaves limited space for sustained private life outside the touring circle.

This does not suggest isolation. Elvis is constantly surrounded by people. But intimacy, in this phase of his life, is structured by work. The band, the car, the show planners, and the managers occupy most available space. March rewards endurance more than reflection.

Physically, the month demands quiet discipline. Two shows in one night require vocal stamina and crowd control. Long drives require energy. Loud rooms demand projection without recklessness. Nothing in March suggests crisis, but it does suggest the start of pattern. Elvis would work himself to death if necessary. The schedule assumes durability. It doesn't ask whether durability can be maintained indefinitely. It demands and Elvis has no choice but to deliver.

Meanwhile, the business atmosphere has started to shift. Elvis isn't operating in uncertainty. The crowds have proven consistent enough that money can be projected. Projection invites scrutiny into his present representation.

Management. This once existed to secure bookings, now exists to secure strength in the future. Decisions made in March will not resolve immediately, but the tension is present. The road continues to reward Elvis. The people around him start to argue over what that reward should mean and who should be rewarded.

### March leads to a chance meeting and a lifelong connection

By the middle of March, the calendar starts to compress. The distances grow longer, the halls grow larger, and the conversations within the core group of Elvis, Scotty, Bill, and Bob Neal grow more serious. This is the point where touring stops feeling improvised and starts to feel strategic.

That compression shows up clearly on March 7 in Paris, Tennessee. Elvis, Scotty, and Bill are no longer the add-on curiosity inside a larger package: they are the headliners. Carrying the evening's center while lesser-known names fill out the bill: Betty Amos, Onie Wheeler, Jimmy Work. This is the touring life turning a corner. The posters may still look like a scene performance. But the room starts to behave like it came for one thing, and the other acts start to feel like the deep breath before the storm.

Bart Herbison-Executive Director of the Nashville Songwriters Association International in Nashville, Tennessee once shared with me a story over the phone tied to Elvis's March 7th, 1955, show in Paris, Tennessee. His father, Joe Billy Herbison, made it inside that night, and bought an autographed Elvis photo for fifty cents. For a brief moment, in the crush of the evening, he even spoke with Elvis before being pulled back into the current of the people.

Bart's mother, Martha Carol Pullen, wasn't as lucky. She and a friend tried desperately to get into the concert, but the place was packed, and they couldn't get in. Still, the night wasn't finished with either of them. Afterward, they ended up at a local diner counter where the real turning point happened. A conversation between two strangers, Joe and Martha, that started with Elvis as the centerpiece became something larger: a talk that led to marriage. To children, and eventually to Bart Herbison, long before he became a media, and political strategist, and eventually one of the strongest, most effective advocates songwriters have ever had. The story started with a crowded auditorium and ended at a diner table-proof that cultural moments don't just change music. Sometimes they change lives.

On March 16, Elvis appears at the Ruffin Theater in Covington, Tennessee. The choice of armory matters. A theater carries a different expectation than a gymnasium or an armory. It is a place where audiences are trained to sit, to watch, and to judge. Before Elvis, rooms like the Ruffin hosted touring country acts, radio sponsored revues, and film screenings that anchored the town's social calendar. A performer booked into a theater was expected to justify the ticket price.

Most likely, this is also the night Covington remembers as its "small-time Opry" moment. A homegrown Grand Ole Opry imitation promoted by theater owner Jack Sallee and the local radio station, with Elvis as the draw that made the imitation feel dangerous. The setting matters. A theater teaches an audience to sit still, to clap on cue, to behave. Elvis's presence tests that setting. He only has to sing a song with rhythm in it and watch the room decide what it wants to become.

Covington also sits in a region where radio and live performance were deeply intertwined. Local stations did more than advertise shows. They validated them. A performer promoted on the air was understood to be worth seeing in person. When Elvis appears at the Ruffin, he arrives with that validation in place. The surge of noise inside the theater confirms what show planners along the circuit start to accept. Elvis does not need something new to hold a room. He needs crowd's appetite.

That crowd expectation is, by this point, being tracked carefully.

Around this time, Bob Neal formalizes his position by amending his agreement with Elvis to a fifteen percent management fee. The adjustment is modest on paper, but it signals honor. Elvis's earning potential is already clear enough to measure.

The paperwork is blunt. On March 15, Elvis signs an amended one-year agreement with Neal that locks in a 15 percent management fee. That number is both ordinary and explosive: ordinary in an industry that runs on percentages, explosive because it confirms, on paper, that Elvis isn't being handled like a promising act. He is being managed like a commodity with a foreseeable future.

### Measurement attracts competition.

Colonel Tom Parker's presence grows more visible during this period. His concerns are not aesthetic. They are logistical. Distribution limits at Sun Records restrict where show planners can be convinced Elvis is useful and profitable. Parker understands this. If records are not traveling far enough, touring must compensate. If touring proves demand beyond distribution, crowds can not be monetized.

In this same stretch, the letters, and telegrams start to read like pressure, not conversation. William Morris agent Harry Kalcheim telegrams Parker to ask if Elvis can audition for Arthur Godfrey's Talent Scouts, the very part Bill Randle had been urging. It sounds like opportunity, but Parker hears it as negotiation. He replies in his blustering way that he'll pay for the trip to New York only if Neal and Elvis agree to give him the right to represent Elvis on any bookings that might arise from the appearance. The audition isn't just a stage. It is a contract trap, or a contract victory, depending on who signs what.

Every date in March still runs through Bob Neal's hands. He is the one confirming armories, high schools, and auditoriums, and he keeps pressing Parker for another Hank Snow tour. Believing a package run is the cleanest way to widen the map without breaking it. Neal thinks in routes and relationships. Parker thinks in power and a larger picture. March forces them to share the same calendar and space while imagining two different futures for the same boy.

Parker's private tone is sharper. In a note to Tom Diskin, he complains again that they can't waste time and money opening territory for Presley without being assured of exclusive control on certain dates and places. He doesn't want Neal, or any local promoter, benefiting from the expense of doors Parker forces open. This is the core conflict of March: Bob Neal keeps Elvis booked and growing. Parker wants Elvis owned, and open to a larger career, at least in the territories that matter.

Kalcheim cables again with the logistics: an Arthur Godfrey tryout date set for March 23. And the dangling reward that would follow if Elvis won, a spot on Godfrey's morning television program for the next three weeks. Parker agrees to fund the trip only after securing Neal's promise to protect the Colonel's interest in whatever bookings the exposure might generate. Even the word "promise" tells you how unstable the arrangement still is. The future is being negotiated in handshakes, while the present keeps demanding another show in contracts.

In early March, Elvis returns to Sun for another session - cutting three more sides and continuing to build a catalog that radio can lean on while the road schedule keeps accelerating.

That return to Sun in early March also produces one of the month's quiet pivots. Elvis records "I'm Left, You're Right, She's Gone" twice, first as a slow blues, then again in the up-tempo country form in which it was written. Hearing the two takes back-to-back is like watching a face change under different light. The lyric stays put, but the temperature does not. One version leans into ache. The other leans into motion.

The faster take carries another first. Drums enter the room, played by Memphis teenager Jimmie Lott, making him the first musician outside the Blue Moon Boys to appear on an Elvis Presley record. They record a faster version of Blue Moon of Kentucky. It's easy to handle that as trivia, but it signals the broader truth of March: Elvis's sound is already too big for the original container. The group is still the core, yet the edges start to open, one borrowed instrument at a time. Jimmy also attended Humes High School, so the fact Sam Phillips brought him in potentially could have been as an audition for a larger touring group. Ultimately, it was not to be.

On March 17, Elvis performs at Dessau Hall in Austin, Texas. Dessau isn't just a hall. It is an important show. Built for dance and scene gatherings, it belonged to a tradition of rooms where success is measured physically. If the floor fills, the music works.

Elvis's performance style aligns naturally with that expectation. His rhythmic show encourages movement. His pacing allows the hall to breathe and surge in cycles. In a dance hall, there is no illusion to hide behind. The crowd either moves, or it doesn't. Dessau responds.

Two days later, on March 19, Elvis appears at the Grand Prize Jamboree in Houston. The bill places him alongside established entertainment figures, with a master of ceremonies whose job is to frame what the seats is about to see. This isn't a random lineup. It reflects the entertainment world Elvis is entering.

The Grand Prize Jamboree itself is loud enough to leave artifacts. Live recordings of "Good Rockin'

Tonight," "Baby Let's Play House," "Blue Moon of Kentucky." "I Got a Woman." and "That's All Right" have surfaced on bootlegs over the years. And they matter because they capture the thing newspaper language can't: the room's timing, the pause before the scream, the way Elvis rides the audience rather than simply singing at it.

Behind the scenes, the management dynamic continues to shift. Parker presses Neal for information on where records are selling and where show planners might respond. This isn't idle curiosity. It is groundwork. Parker is mapping demand. Neal is maintaining operations unaware of Parkers plans. March reveals both approaches in motion.

Neal's strength lies in stability. He understands the circuit and the people who make it function. Parker's strength lies in power and relationships in the larger industry. He understands that regionality eventually caps growth. March does not resolve this difference. It exposes it.

Late March brings the month's sharpest contrast, not in sound or scale, but in judgment.

On March 23, Elvis travels to New York City for an audition connected to Arthur Godfrey's television program. The audition takes place in an environment built for assessment instead of reaction. There is no crowd to lean into, no room to warm up, no shared energy to shape the performance. The people watching are not show planners measuring ticket sales. They are gatekeepers measuring risk.

It is nearly certainly Elvis's first airplane flight, and the destination feels like a different planet. The audition is set for 2:30 p. M. On the fourteenth floor of 501 Madison Avenue, an office address that sounds sterile even when you say it aloud. There is no stage, no hush of a theater, no gymnasium echo. There is carpet, fluorescent judgment, and strangers trained to handle reaction as unprofessional. Elvis walks into a room that doesn't know how to behave like a normal Elvis crowd, and for once, the reaction is silence before applause. It is a verdict.

The house's reaction is immediate and final. There is no interest.

The rejection isn't dramatic. Elvis does not fail loudly. He fails, in a room where excitement is considered a liability rather than an asset. It is instructive to Elvis because it exposes the distance between local demand and national approval. The halls Elvis dominates in the South reward energy and immediacy. The audition room rewards predictability and containment. The mismatch is purely structural and temporary.

What happens next is more revealing than the audition itself. Elvis does not linger in New York. The schedule doesn't pause to accommodate disappointment. He returns directly to the Southern circuit, where his value isn't theoretical.

On March 25, Elvis performs at Dermott High School in Dermott, Arkansas.

The shift from a Manhattan office to a Delta school auditorium matters only if you miss where Elvis's career actually lives in 1955. School performances aren't fallback options. They are engines. In towns like Dermott, the high school is a social center. Events held there carry real community weight. Students remember them not as concerts, but as memories and milestones.

The following night, March 26, Elvis returns to Shreveport for another appearance on the Louisiana Hayride. By this point, the Hayride functions as a force beneath the chaos of travel. It offers continuity, radio broadcast exposure, and legitimacy. Even as management tensions increase and national gatekeepers decline interest, the Hayride affirms that Elvis belongs on a stage heard across state lines.

On March 28, Elvis appears at Big Creek High School Gym in Mississippi, sponsored by the senior class. On March 29, he performs at a high school in Tocopola, Mississippi, sponsored by the junior class. These sponsorship details matter.

In the mid-1950s, school sponsored shows required organization. Students sold tickets, negotiated with administrators, and assumed financial risk. A performer booked under these conditions was being trusted not only to entertain, but to deliver value. Elvis is already reliable enough that students are willing to stake their class funds on his name.

These gymnasiums are not neutral spaces. They carry sound, magnify movement, and fall apart the distance between performer and audience. When Elvis moves onstage, the surge of noise moves with him. In these rooms, crowd control isn't enforced from the front. It is negotiated collectively. This environment favors performers who can ride chaos without losing command.

Adults notice these shows, but often after the fact. Reports circulate. Complaints follow. Curiosity builds. By the time concern surfaces, the surge of fame has been validated by history. This is how youth culture spreads in 1955, not through headlines, but through buildup.

Parker's insistence on knowing where records sell, and his concern over Sun's reach, point to a coming realignment. Neal holds the formal authority. Parker builds quiet influence. March doesn't resolve that tension. It brings it into the open.

By the last week of March, Parker puts the complaint into plain words. Sun's distribution is too small, he tells Neal. And it is getting harder to convince show planners outside that narrow range to take a chance on a singer they can't reliably hear on their local racks. He pushes Neal to ask Sam Phillips a practical, nearly unromantic question: where, exactly, are the records selling? Parker wants a map. If he can identify the pockets where Elvis is already moving units, he can pursue show planners in those areas with proof instead of persuasion.

March 30 places Elvis at El Dorado High School Auditorium in El Dorado, Arkansas. March 31 closes the month at the Reo Palm Isle in Longview, Texas. These final dates resemble the opening of the month more than its midpoint. Schools. Clubs. Rooms where reaction matters more than reputation.

Yet the context has changed.

By the end of March 1955, the outlines of the year have hardened.

Nothing explosive has happened. There has been no national breakthrough, no decisive contract that transforms Elvis's life overnight. What has happened instead is more durable. The evidence has accumulated. Night after night, town after town, the surge of audiences has repeated itself often enough that it can't be dismissed as coincidence.

Elvis has proven something fundamental. He can enter a room, regardless of its size or purpose, and alter its temperature. He can do it in an armory watched closely by adults. He can do it in a dance hall built for motion. He can do it in a theater accustomed to restraint. He can do it in school gyms where teenagers test the limits of supervision. The environment changes, but the crowd's physical reaction remains consistent. This has never happened before in the history of music, and everyone around sees this.

That consistency is what transforms attention into value.

The failed New York audition sharpens this understanding in preference to undermining it. Elvis does not lose crowd hunger because a gatekeeper says no. He returns to the road and continues producing the same reaction he produced before the trip. The rejection reveals a mismatch between systems fighting with each other, not a weakness in the act.

That gap is the central problem of the year.

Bob Neal continues to provide stability. He keeps the circuit intact, the calendar full, and the logistics functioning. His strength is continuity. Colonel Parker starts to exert influence by identifying limits. His strength is power. Neither man is wrong. Both are operating from the same evidence. What differs is their interpretation of what that evidence demands next.

March doesn't force a decision. It forces a direction.

As April approaches, the question isn't whether Elvis belongs on the road. That has been answered repeatedly. The question is how long the road alone can carry what he has become.

March 1955 ends without resolution, but not without consequence. The machine is running smoothly. The value is real.

Everything that follows in 1955 will be shaped by what March has proven.

Show planners ask more questions than they did in February. Managers speak less casually. Travel decisions start to factor in reputation as an alternative to convenience.

Bob Neal feels this shift immediately. His work has always been grounded in access. He knows which towns will book a young act. He knows which venues will take a chance. He understands the personalities that make local circuits function. In early 1955, that knowledge is still indispensable. Without Neal, the machine stalls.

But March introduces a new problem. The machine is, by this point, producing more demand than it can efficiently serve.

Colonel Parker sees this clearly. He does not question whether Elvis can draw crowds. He questions whether those crowds are being converted into lasting power. A sold out gymnasium in Mississippi proves something locally. It proves far less to a promoter in another region who has never heard a Sun record on his local station.

Distribution grows more than a technical issue. It turns into a ceiling.

Sun Records is effective where it is present. Its recordings provoke reaction where they are heard. What Parker recognizes in March is that the reach is uneven. There are pockets of excitement separated by silence. That silence doesn't mean disinterest. It means absence. Records are not circulating widely enough to announce Elvis's arrival before he reaches a town.

For Neal, the solution is familiar. Keep touring. Let the surge of reaction speak for itself. Build demand town by town.

For Parker, the solution is structural. Touring alone can't carry a national future. It can prove value, but it can't scale it indefinitely. Early on parker understands that touring isn't sustainable and there needs to be a leap in exposure. Not locally or regionally, but nationally.

March is the month where these philosophies start to coexist uncomfortably.

The towns themselves reinforce Parker's concern. Places like Covington, Newport, Dermott, and El Dorado respond instantly to Elvis because they are accustomed to live music as an event. Entertainment in these towns has always arrived in person. Radio supports it, but the hall decides its fate.

Before Elvis, these communities hosted performers who worked the same way. Country singers, western swing bands, blues musicians, and traveling revues built reputations one night at a time. Elvis fits that tradition perfectly. In fact, he exceeds it. His reaction is faster and louder than what many of these rooms are used to.

That speed becomes part of the problem.

A reaction that spreads too quickly through live performance risks outgrowing its infrastructure. March exposes this tension repeatedly. The crowds respond. The stories travel. The records lag behind.

This isn't failure. It is an imbalance.

The school shows carry this imbalance most clearly. When students sponsor a performance, they do more than attend. They promote. They persuade parents. They organize transportation. They create expectation weeks in advance. By the time Elvis arrives, the hall is primed.

These students are not waiting for radio validation. They are validating each other. That is why school gyms become such powerful accelerators. They fall apart the distance between discovery and loyalty.

Adults notice only after the fact. Administrators worry about behavior. Parents worry about influence. By the time concern surfaces, the surge of noise has replicated itself in the next town.

This pattern repeats throughout March.

Elvis does not need press to spread. He needs proximity.

Parker understands that proximity is powerful but temporary. He is thinking about what happens when proximity isn't possible, when the road can't physically carry Elvis to every place where interest has ignited.

Neal is focused on keeping the road intact. Keeping the money flowing. His instincts are not wrong. Without the road, none of this exists.

March doesn't crown a winner between them. It establishes the stakes.

The contrast between proximity and scale becomes sharper as the month progresses. Elvis is reaching more people than ever before, yet the mechanisms that would allow that reach to compound are still incomplete. Each successful night proves demand, but it also exposes the limitations. The road can only carry him so far, so many nights in a row, before it becomes inefficient.

Bob Neal remains focused on what has always worked. He books aggressively. He keeps Elvis visible. He protects relationships with show planners who took early chances. These relationships matter because they are built on trust in lieu of reputation. In March, that trust continues to pay dividends. Venues rebook. Schools request return appearances. The circuit remains intact but keeps Elvis from growing nationally.

At the same time, Neal starts what the turnout expects from a different direction. Parker's questions are precise and persistent. Where are the records selling? Which stations are playing them? Which regions respond without direct exposure? These are not abstract inquiries. They are diagnostic tools. Tom Parker was planning strategically, while Bob Neal was booking a workhorse to keep the money flowing in.

Parker is attempting to map Elvis's future footprint using the limited data available. Touring crowds provide one form of evidence. Record sales provide another. Where the two overlap, Parker sees opportunity. Where they diverge, he sees friction.

The New York audition underscores the urgency of that positioning. Elvis's rejection by Arthur Godfrey's program is treated by Parker as evidence that national platforms will not respond until they are forced to. The path forward will require power, not permission.

The towns Elvis plays late in the month reinforce the lesson. Dermott, Big Creek, Tocopola, El Dorado, and Longview are not cultural centers in the national sense. They are cultural laboratories. Each one reveals how quickly Elvis's presence reshapes local expectation.

Before Elvis, entertainment in these towns followed predictable patterns. Performers arrived, played, and left. Audiences attended politely. Elvis disrupts that rhythm. He provokes reaction strong enough to linger. People talk about the show days later. They compare it to others. They argue about it.

That argument is critical. It signals engagement. Engagement can be monetized.

In El Dorado, the high school auditorium functions as more than a performance space. It is a gathering point for the town. When Elvis appears there, the event is discussed across generations. Students bring stories home. Parents react to secondhand descriptions. The performance travels beyond the hall.

Longview's Reo Palm Isle offers a different test. Club audiences are less forgiving. They are not obligated to attend, and they are not impressed easily. A club demands command. Elvis meets that demand. The surge of noise confirms that his appeal isn't limited to supervised youth environments.

By the final days of March, the pattern is unmistakable. Elvis is effective in every type of room he enters. The variation lies not in reaction, but in amplification.

Neal continues to carry through routine. Parker is preparing to carry through setup.

As the month stretches on, the economics beneath the touring schedule become harder to ignore. Every mile driven carries cost. Fuel, lodging, food, equipment wear, and time itself all accumulate. Early in the year, these costs are accepted as the price of opportunity. By March, opportunity has become reliable enough that cost must be weighed against return.

Show planners don't negotiate from uncertainty. They negotiate from fear of missing out. A show that sells out once isn't a gamble. It is a risk not to book. Neal uses this power carefully, maintaining goodwill while protecting the circuit that has allowed Elvis to grow without national exposure.

Parker approaches the same problem differently. He is less concerned with individual nights and more concerned with trajectory. He understands that touring economics flatten as schedules fill. There are only so many nights in a month. There are only so many towns that can be revisited without saturation. Growth, in Parker's view, requires expansion beyond the road's natural limits.

March provides him with evidence.

The school gym circuit demonstrates how quickly demand can exceed supply. Students organize shows weeks in advance. Word spreads before Elvis arrives. Some towns request dates that can't be accommodated. The calendar turns crowded enough that choices must be made.

Those choices reveal hierarchy.

Towns with proven reaction are prioritized. Venues with reliable show planners are favored. Areas where records show signs of circulation attract Parker's attention. The calendar becomes a strategic document rather than a simple list of opportunities.

Elvis remains focused on the immediate task. He continues to refine his performances. He adjusts pacing. He responds to crowd energy with increasing confidence. The stage remains the only place where all competing theories are tested honestly.

By the final week of March, exhaustion and crowd demand coexist. The schedule is heavy, but the ticket holders' bodily reaction is rewarding. Elvis isn't chasing validation. He is producing it.

March closes without spectacle. There is no announcement, no decisive talk that resolves the tensions introduced. What exists instead is alignment. The evidence points in a single direction even as the path remains contested.

The road has proven Elvis's power. The business has started to reorganize around it.

What distinguishes March from the months before it isn't volume, but certainty. Earlier in the year, success could still be framed as the expectation in the seats that might stall. By the end of March, that framing does not fit the evidence. The surge of noise has repeated itself too consistently, across too many environments, to be dismissed as temporary.

The local musical context matters. Elvis is stepping into a Southern landscape shaped by country, gospel, blues, and radio variety. These traditions have trained audiences to listen closely, to respond physically, and to share experience communally. Elvis's achievement isn't invention, but synthesis. He draws from each tradition without fully belonging to any single one.

This synthesis explains why his performances land differently depending on the hall while producing the same result. In dance halls, the rhythm dominates. In theaters, crowd control and timing take precedence. In school gyms, energy overwhelms restraint. Elvis adapts without losing sense of who they are because his sense of who they are is rooted in response in preference to form.

That adaptability turns critical as touring economics tighten. By March, Elvis's calendar reflects prioritization as an alternative to availability. Nights are chosen not only for pay, but for impact. Return engagements are favored over something new bookings. Regions showing organic growth receive attention. The road becomes a tool in lieu of a test.

Bob Neal's influence is strongest in this phase. His understanding of territory allows Elvis to grow without overexposure. He avoids saturating markets too quickly. He maintains goodwill with show planners by delivering consistency rather than spectacle. This approach preserves crowd's appetite while limiting backlash.

Colonel Parker is thinking beyond preservation. He sees that consistency alone can't support national transformation. His focus remains fixed on scalability. March confirms his belief that Elvis's appeal isn't fragile. It doesn't depend on careful handling to survive. It depends on setup to expand.

Psychologically, March represents a small shift for Elvis. The early anxiety of showing worth starts to fade. In its place emerges confidence rooted in routine. He does not wonder whether a crowd will respond. He wonders how well they will respond.

Confidence of this kind changes performance. It frees attention. It allows risk. It encourages command in preference to request.

March ends without triumph and without defeat. The performances continue. The crowds respond. The arguments remain unresolved.

March 1955 doesn't deliver a breakthrough but it does deliver more proof.

And proof, once established, changes the terms of every argument that comes after it.

## MARCH 1955 RADIO, CINEMA, AND THE SOUND OF A COUNTRY FURTHER SHIFTING

By March, the country is still pretending it wants its music tidy, but the beat under the floorboards is getting louder. The "new" energy people will later pin on one man is already in motion: pianos pushing. Guitars snapping, voices leaning past old manners: "Ain't That a Shame", Fats Domino, "Flip. Flop, and Fly", Big Joe Turner, "Reconsider Baby", Lowell Fulson, "You don't Have to Go", Jimmy Reed, and "It's Love, Baby, 24 Hours a Day,", Louis Brooks,. When Elvis hits a town, he doesn't invent this current, he rides it into places that used to pretend it belonged somewhere else.

*What America Was Hearing on the Radio*
*March 1955*

In March of 1955, American radio sounded orderly on the surface. Programming favored polish, restraint, and emotional clarity. Most stations avoided disruption. Music was expected to reassure instead of provoke.

Pop radio leaned heavily on crooners and vocal groups. Listeners turning the dial during March repeatedly encountered:

Perry Como "Ko Ko Mo, I Love You So," Relaxed, conversational, and rhythmically gentle, the song dominated airplay without demanding attention. Romance was framed as calm and manageable., Billboard DJ chart peak: 2 in 1955,

Eddie Fisher "Heart" Earnest and crowd-controlled, Fisher's vocals showed the ideal of emotional sincerity without danger.

The Four Aces "Love Is a Many-Splendored Thing" Harmonized, orchestral, and emotionally resolved. This was music designed for living rooms, not dance floors., Billboard year-end pop: 7 in 1955,

Patti Page "Cross Over the Bridge" / "Croce di Oro" Exotic suggestion given safely, with no urgency or physical tension., Billboard pop chart peak: 2 in 1954,

*Country radio reinforced similar values:*

Webb Pierce "In the Jailhouse Now" Narrative-driven, traditional, and rooted in familiar storytelling setups., Billboard country charts: 1 for 21 weeks in 1955,

Hank Snow "I'm Movin' On" A song about motion that obeyed the moral hierarchy. Restlessness, but disciplined.

Lefty Frizzell "Mom and Dad's Waltz" Emotional pull without volatility. The past framed as comfort.

March makes the contrast sharper: radio broadcast culture offers polish and containment, while Elvis delivers friction rhythm with edges, emotion with no tidy landing. He doesn't negate what's on the radio. He exposes what it can't express yet.

What was notably absent was physical urgency.

That absence mattered.

## What Was Playing in Movie Theaters March 1955

Cinema reinforced the same emotional hierarchy radio maintained.

Major releases in circulation during March included:

"Blackboard Jungle", released March 25, 1955, Its use of Bill Haley's "Rock Around the Clock" during the opening credits marked a shock to many viewers not because of its melody. But because of its rhythm. This was one of the first moments American audiences heard youth unrest expressed sonically in a mainstream film.

"Guys and Dolls", still in wide release, Technicolor, choreography, and carefully held back rebellion. Energy was stylized, not threatening.

"The Seven Year Itch", premiering later in the spring but heavily advertised, Desire framed as comedy, not confrontation.

Movies in March did not yet belong to youth culture but cracks were forming. Music was start to slip into places where it did not behave politely.

Who Elvis Was Performing with and What They Represented

In March 1955, Elvis Presley was appearing largely on package bills, sharing stages with performers who represented the existing Southern entertainment pecking order.

Among the artists most often associated with his circuit at this time:

Johnny Horton A disciplined country performer known for clear phrasing and command. Horton's music emphasized setup and crowd control everything Elvis was start to destabilize.

Slim Whitman, well known for his falsetto ballads, Whitman's radio presence made him familiar across age groups. His songs offered romantic restraint in lieu of very strong reaction.

Ferlin Husky A seasoned crowd-worker with something new instincts. Husky knew how to entertain, but within understood limits.

The significance of these pairings was not competition, it was contrast.

Audiences could hear the difference immediately.

Where co-billed performers given polish and familiarity, Elvis given tension. Where their songs resolved emotion, his songs left it open.

This contrast made Elvis legible even to listeners who did not yet understand what he *represented*.

*What Elvis Sounded Like Against the Radio*

By March 1955, Elvis Presley's Sun recordings were circulating unevenly. In many towns, audiences had not heard him on the radio before seeing him live.

That gap mattered.

Containment

Predictability

Emotional closure

Elvis offered:

Movement

Uncertainty

Bodily response

Where radio voices asked listeners to relax, Elvis asked them to react.

In towns where Elvis appeared after audiences had spent the day hearing Perry Como or The Four Aces, the difference felt physical, not stylistic. His rhythm landed in rooms that had not prepared for it.

This is why reactions escalated so quickly in school gyms, armories, and clubs. The audience was not being introduced to a new singer. They were being introduced to a new way of responding to a sound.

*Why March 1955 Matters Culturally*

March was not the month Elvis became famous. It was the month his sound became misaligned with the culture broadcasting through radio and film. That misalignment created friction.

By March, the lag becomes visible as a social problem, not a technical one. Bookings, chaperones, and radio men try to frame what's happening in familiar language, but the surge of noise keeps arriving ahead of the explanation.

March 1955 reveals a country broadcasting calm while start to crave motion.

Elvis did not invent that craving. He gave it a voice.


**FULL KNOWN MARCH 1955 PERFORMANCE RECORD**

March 2 Newport, AR, U. S, Armory (8:00 p.m.,. Porky's Rooftop Club, 10:00 p.m.,)

March 31: Reo Palm Isle, Longview, Texas.
March 30: El Dorado High School Auditorium, El Dorado, Arkansas.
March 29: High School, Tocopola, Mississippi.
March 28: Big Creek High School Gym, Big Creek, Mississippi.

March 26: Louisiana Hayride, Municipal Auditorium, Shreveport, Louisiana.

March 25: Dermott High School, Dermott, Arkansas.

March 19: Grand Prize Jamboree, Eagles Hall, Houston, Texas.

March 17: Dessau Hall, Austin, Texas.

March 16: Ruffin Theater, Covington, Tennessee.

March 12: Louisiana Hayride, Municipal Auditorium, Shreveport, Louisiana.

March 11: Jimmie Thompson's Arena, Alexandria, Louisiana.

March 9: Armory, Poplar Bluff, Missouri.

March 8: Catholic Club, Helena, Arkansas.

March 7: City Auditorium, Paris, Tennessee.

March 5: Louisiana Hayride, Municipal Auditorium, Shreveport, Louisiana.

March 4: High School, De Kalb, Texas, unconfirmed,.

March 2: U.S. Armory, Newport, Arkansas, 8:00 p.m.,. Porky's Rooftop Club, Newport, Arkansas, 10:00 p.m.,.

# Chapter 4, April 1955

April 1955 rolls in at the end of an exhilarating March. The uncertainty that defined earlier months has been replaced by movement so steady it barely allows room for a breath. Elvis Presley enters April not testing whether audiences will respond but discovering how far that response can be pushed.

Touring dominates the rhythm of his days and travel the rhythm of his nights. It is routine. Cars replace rooms. Stages replace sleep. The geography of the South becomes familiar not through leisure, but through weekly routine. Each town carries its own rhythm, its own expectations, its own limits. Elvis starts to understand that success does not look the same everywhere, and that adaptability matters as much as consistency.

The shows themselves are tightening. What once felt spontaneous now feels sharp like a blade as they cut through each song. Elvis knows what works, and so does Scotty and Bill. They become a machine most nights playing off of each other and the crowd. In April, his performance is becoming so professional it makes it easier to improvise. When you know the music like the sound of your own heartbeat, it is easy to make a quick casual change to a vocal line. He is learning how to deliver performance reliably, night after night, without exhausting himself or the house, so if he needs to change a vocal line to rest his vocal, he pulls it down a notch. If he feels in full control, he lets it loose.

The crowds respond with increasing intensity. Reactions are not tentative. Screams arrive early and often, often before he begins his first strum. Movement in the audience spreads quickly. Attention concentrates on Elvis even when the bill includes other performers. When Elvis isn't on stage, heads are turning looking for him. This imbalance is not only noticed by fans, but by show planners, and fellow musicians. Elvis isn't just part of a package. He is becoming the center of their world.

The towns they travel to in April themselves matter. Small Southern cities and rural stops are not interchangeable. Each carries its own musical history, its own social boundaries. Some have long traditions of gospel quartets and country acts. Others have been shaped by blues, radio barn dances, or traveling revues. Elvis starts to sense these differences instinctively. He adjusts the shows pacing, emphasis, and demeanor accordingly. This adaptability deepens the listeners response and reinforces his reputation as someone who connects with rather than performs at people.

Behind the scenes, management dynamics are solidifying. Bob Neal remains the visible setup handling planning, bookings, and immediate needs. He travels often on regional tours while maintaining his position on the radio at WHBQ. His role is practical and stabilizing, ensuring that crowd hunger does not fall apart under its own weight. Neal's presence provides continuity, but it also reveals the limits of local management in the face of expanding attention.

Colonel Tom Parker's influence grows more pronounced during this period. His presence isn't always visible on the surface, but its effect is unmistakable. Parker understands crowd expectation as currency. He recognizes that April represents not just opportunity, but power for him personally. Before Elvis ever becomes Elvis, Colonel Tom Parker is already a proven operator, carnival-bred, house-trained, and fluent in the art of making a name feel bigger than the town it's in. He's had his hands on real careers, most famously Eddy Arnold, helping turn a country singer into a national property with bookings, exposure, and the kind of positioning that makes "talent" look like the sure thing.

So, when Parker circles Elvis in 1955, he isn't guessing. He's reading reactions like receipts: the sound of the room, the way the line forms, the way teenagers move as one. Bob Neal may hold the manager title, but Parker starts sliding into the big system. Routing, promotion, power, and taking a share of the steering wheel.

This tension doesn't erupt into conflict yet, but it defines the background of April. Decisions start to carry longer shadows. Where Elvis performs, how often, and under what conditions becomes increasingly consequential. Parker's instinct is to maximize exposure quickly, even at a physical cost. Neal's instinct is to handle growth sustainably. Elvis stands between these approaches, benefiting from both while feeling the strain they create.

Physically, April starts to test limits. Travel is relentless. Sleep is inconsistent. Meals are irregular. Elvis's body absorbs this punishment without immediate breakdown, but the buildup is real. Fatigue does not announce itself loudly. It surfaces in quiet moments, between shows, during long drives. When he finally crashes out in a hotel room. Elvis learns to perform through it, but he isn't yet skilled at recovering from it.

Despite this strain, Elvis health remains outwardly strong. His voice holds. His energy onstage remains explosive. The contrast between private fatigue and public vitality becomes part of the mythology forming around him. Audiences see only the result, not the cost. April teaches Elvis how to compartmentalize, a skill that will later define both his success and vulnerability.

Musically, April reinforces clarity as an alternative to experimentation. Elvis isn't searching for his sound. He is refining it. Songs that elicited strong reaction in March continue to center setlists. Rhythm and phrasing are adjusted subtly as opposed to radically. Elvis is learning how to pace a show emotionally, how to escalate without overwhelming, how to leave audiences wanting more rather than exhausted.

The presence of other artists on the bill in April continue to provide contrasts. Some perform competently and are politely received. Others struggle to command attention once Elvis appears. This dynamic alters relationships backstage in the hallway. Admiration mixes with resentment.

Curiosity mixes with caution. Elvis navigates these interactions without confrontation, because at his core he is a soft spoken, polite, well-mannered young man, and who can stay mad at someone like that? He is aware of the shift and does his best to de-escalate with sincere compliments of their performances. He isn't just another young performer working his way up. He feels lucky to be where he is, but understands he is also earning his way by working diligently at his craft. He does make real friends like Merle Kilgore, who he holds a special connection with. Both of their mothers names were Gladys. Merle Later became Hank Williams Jr manager and my manager and publisher as well. He would later share stories about being on the road with Elvis with me as we would have dinner or sit in his Nashville office late at night. We would also share lunches with DJ Fontana when he was in town.

Personal life during April remains secondary to his career. Where women appear in the documented record of Elvis, the encounters are brief and constrained by the need for travel. There is no sustained relationship shaping his emotional center this month in the documented records, but there was little need to wonder who specifically Elvis was dating. That was never the focus of anyone around. They were focused on his music, his career. This was before Colonel Parker exercised his control on Elvis relationships, but Elvis had very little time for anything serious. He probably had strong feelings for one, or many girls, but Elvis's own focus remained outward, toward achieving his own personal goal of changing his families reality. The pace of April leaves little room for any *new* attachment to develop, other than the girls that were secretly in his heart.

Emotionally, Elvis must have started to feel the pressure of all of the expectations. Success doesn't feel hypothetical anymore. It feels immediate and fragile, like the room is holding its breath between the count-off and the first chord. Each town and crowd brings added pressure, not just to entertain, but to confirm his growing reputation. He senses that attention can vanish as quickly as it appears. He has seen it happen in history. The one hit wonders. This awareness sharpens his discipline. Elvis grows less tolerant of unfocused performances, both from himself, and those around him.

The mid-1950s South is a place of rigid social boundaries and unspoken tensions. There was the focus on communism in Korea, USSR, and China. Elvis's stage presence unsettles these boundaries. His movement, his sound, and his physicality provoke responses that go beyond music. Adults fear his music because Rock 'n' Roll April audiences respond viscerally, and that felt like rebellion. He didn't just worry some parents, he started to worry the institutions of America. Elvis does not fully articulate this yet, but he feels it.

Show planners notice as well. Bookings become more frequent. Venues become larger. Word spreads beyond immediate regions. April represents expansion not just in miles traveled, but in reputation carried ahead of him. Elvis name starts arriving in towns as anticipated as an alternative to being discovered.

This expectation also changes the atmosphere of shows. Crowds arrive primed now. They expect to have a life changing time. Reactions accelerates long before the first strum of the guitar, or vocal note. Elvis must now handle all of these new expectation as opposed to just generate interest. This shift requires confidence and crowd control. He responds instinctively, leaning into energy rather than resisting it. In some ways getting the reaction out of the crowd becomes easier and in others it becomes an impossible stressor.

Behind the scenes, discussions start to hint at broader horizons. Radio exposure beyond local markets turns a topic. Recording opportunities loom as realistic rather than wishful. Parker's presence ensures these possibilities are framed in terms of negotiation as an alternative to gratitude.

April doesn't pause to allow for thought for the young artist, he is a ball of energy, and he is taking that energy as far as it will let him. Momentum continues to build. Each successful performance reinforces demand for the next. The machine around him continues to jostle for position. Elvis isn't moving toward something abstract. He is being carried forward by forces he only partially controls.

On any April night, you could feel the change before the first chord was struck. The line outside formed earlier, the chatter carried farther, and the hall filled with people who knew what they wanted to see. Teenagers pressed toward the front as if the show has a gravity. Adults didn't always intervene. They measured the mood, deciding whether to handle it or let it crest. April didn't announce permission for the teens to react, but it started to feel like the adults had no choice in the matter.

Odessa, April 1, sits at the crossroads of "small" and "impossible." It is the Ector County Auditorium. Sponsored by the Voting Home Owners Club, it pulls 850 paid admissions and later gets treated like a measurable event. The detail that survives is how specific it becomes, tied to a local witness. Record shop owner Cecil Holifield, the kind of name business pages trust when they talk about crowd size and demand. Floyd Cramer is there too, plus a local boy on drums, another quiet clue that the sound is already outgrowing its original frame.

Twenty four hours later, April 2 in Houston confirms what Odessa suggested. The Louisiana Hayride goes on the road for a remote radio broadcast from the City Auditorium. And Elvis shares the bill with Slim Whitman, Hoot, and Curley, Johnny Horton, Tibby Edwards, and Floyd Cramer. On the air he runs "Little Mama," "That's All Right," "You're a Heartbreaker," and "Shake. Rattle and roll." Reporting later says 2,000 people were turned away, with the line that Elvis, and Slim "tore the house down." The noise isn't trapped in one room anymore. It travels through the radio.

April 3 isn't a show date, but it offers a slice of Elvis history. Driving outside Shreveport in his 1954 four door pink and white Cadillac, Elvis is stopped for speeding, and posts a $25 bond, notified to appear for arraignment on Tuesday, April 5. It isn't a scandal, not a headline. It is just the reminder that even the fastest rise still has to stop for a siren now and then.

April 4 carries the road forward, but the real motion is also happening on paper and over phones. Bob Neal tells the Colonel he can't fulfill a request to track where Elvis's records are selling. At the same time, the Colonel, and Tom Diskin keep pushing his name toward show planners across the South, because Parker never treats "later" like a safe place to wait.

The itinerary keeps the momentum tight. Nettleton, Arkansas, April 4, a high school room with borrowed staging and bright light that doesn't flatter anyone. Charleston, Mississippi, April 5, another high school gym, another night where the crowd doesn't bother to sit in their velvet seats, the stand and scream. Sledge, Mississippi, April 6, a date that looks meaningless on paper, but it is nights like these that build the muscle memory and makes the next expansive room possible.

Corinth, Mississippi, April 7, lands in a courthouse, split into two shows at 2:30, and 8:00. A courthouse is built for order, for lines, for consequences. Elvis walks in and the lines dissolve away, not because anyone breaks the law, but because his reaction can not be held in by 4 walls and bars. It has to be free.

April 8 shifts the texture at the B and B Club in Gobler, Missouri. A club compresses everything, the air, the sound, the eyes, the dares of the girls in the front rows. The distance disappears. The show has a personal feel. So close the sweat drops off of Elvis onto the crowd.

Shreveport on April 9 brings him back onto the Louisiana Hayride stage at Municipal Auditorium. The bill includes Johnny Horton, Hoot, and Curley, and Jim Reeves. Elvis leans into the numbers that carry instant voltage, "That's All Right," "I Got a Woman," "Blue Moon of Kentucky." The Hayride had always been a showing ground. By April, it is starting to feel like a launchpad.

April 13 in Breckenridge, Texas, gives a rare inside look because the local paper captures both desire and backlash in the same breath. Elvis sings "That's All Right," "I Don't Care If the Sun Don't Shine," "Tweedlee Dee," and closes with "Blue Moon of Kentucky." The paper reports young women swooning with his every appearance, then records the other current in the room too, men overheard talking about meeting him "out behind the bar," or warning they better not see a girlfriend going up for an autograph. That is the month in an eggshell, the room dividing itself around him right then.

April 14 in Gainesville, Texas, is the honest counterweight that keeps the story of the month from turning into pure legend. Elvis leaves Breckenridge in the morning behind the wheel of the pink and white Cadillac, wearing pink slacks, and an orchid colored shirt, then plays Owl Park and draws only a handful of people. He appears shaken, promises he will return, and make up for it, and the record of time lands the hardest line of all. He never does return. Not that he didn't want to, but Gainesville for whatever reason did not understand Elvis yet or was not given permission to

127

by all the parents. One night the world can't hold him down. The next night the world reminds Elvis that he has not made it just yet. It fans the fire.

April 15 in Stamford stacks the night into two rooms, a 7:00 P.M. High school auditorium and a 9:00 P.M. Round Up Hall. The calendar tells the truth about 1955. The early show, the late set, the same band, the same voice, two different rooms asking for the same miracle. Elvis follows through on both.

April 16 widens the map in Dallas. The Big "D" Jamboree at the Sportatorium places Elvis on a bill that includes Sonny James, Hank Locklin, and Charlene Arthur, with tickets at sixty cents for adults and thirty cents for children. It is a live Saturday night show with a strong local radio signal, the kind of platform that can carry his name even further. Bob Neal lines up four appearances even though it costs him, as he commits Elvis to two Beaumont sets in June with that same promoter. By June Elvis fame would have grown and perhaps the appearance fee would have increased. This was a smart move on the promoters part. Later that night the schedule pushes hard again, a second room at the Round Up Club.

The route drops back into Mississippi for April 19 at the VFW Club in Hernando, April 20 at the American Legion Hut in Grenada, and April 21 at Houlka High School. Those three were built for meetings and respectability, and for dances that stay within the lines. Elvis keeps stepping into them and changing what "order" feels like.

April 22 is Texarkana, Arkansas, Municipal Auditorium, another official sounding room trying to contain Elvis energy. April 23 is Waco, Texas, the Heart O' Texas Arena on another Louisiana Hayride remote. The bill includes Slim Whitman, Jim Reeves, Jim Ed, and Maxine Brown, and Jimmy "C" Newman. Reporting calls the crowd 5,000, one of the largest the venue had ever seen, and the quote that survives singles out Elvis alongside J. E. And Maxine Brown as key to making the night great. That is a shift from something new to becoming a force.

April 24 returns to Houston with two show listings, Magnolia Gardens in the afternoon and Cook's Hoedown in the evening. The record supports the possibility of it with good circumstantial evidence. But without confirming ads or paperwork to go along with it, it is more legend then fact currently.

April 25 begins the TNT Records tour and the road turns into a story with sharp edges. The M B Corral poster in Wichita Falls bills "Elvis 'That's All Right Mama' Prestley" as the headliner, with TNT's Chuck Lee, and Gene Kay, plus Capitol recording artist Dub Dickerson. The tour structure is pure motion, Wichita Falls then Seymour, Texas, the same night. Elvis runs out of gas and money on the way and doesn't arrive in Seymour until after midnight. A hardcore fan, Doug Dixon, describes the moment Elvis finally takes the stage in a fire engine red sport coat, Scotty pretending to wind him up like a toy. And then the release when Elvis grabs the guitar and the show explodes. This is Elvis growing as an Artist. He was not afraid to take risks.

Big Spring, Texas, April 26, comes with advertising that tries to calm the adults before the teenagers even arrive. "LOTS OF CLEAN FUN AND HEAPS OF MUSIC." The line reads like reassurance, because by April reassurance has become part of the pitch anywhere Elvis is booked. The grown ups are worried, and it is a necessity.

April 27 lands in Hobbs, New Mexico, at the American Legion Hall. April 28 bridges through Andrews, Texas, another high school stop that keeps the month rolling. April 29 returns him to Lubbock at the Cotton Club. These are the dates that don't always get mythologized later, yet they are the dates that groomed Elvis to become the international sensation he became shortly after.

April ends on the 30th with another Hayride remote from Gladewater, Texas, staged at the high school there. The detail that survives is a telling one. His performance of "Tweedlee Dee" is recorded. In 1955, recordings like that are not polished releases. They are evidence, proof that the same electricity that rattled a school gym could leap through a microphone and stay alive after the night is over.

By April 1955, the Southern touring circuit Elvis Presley traveled had been shaped by decades of movement, routine, and expectations. These towns were accustomed to seeing performers pass through, often in quick succession, carrying with them variations on familiar sounds. What distinguished Presley's appearances during this month was not just audience enthusiasm, but the way that enthusiasm started to reshape the rhythm of the tour itself.

Many of the venues Presley played in April were municipal auditoriums, converted movie houses, armories, and school gyms. These spaces were designed for getting together rather than sound. Performers learned quickly how to project, how to pace themselves without reliable sound reinforcement. And how to read a room that might hold seated families at one end and restless teenagers at the other. Presley adapted to these conditions rapidly. He learned how to command attention even when amplification was uneven and sightlines imperfect.

The towns themselves varied widely in size and temperament. Some stops were small agricultural centers whose entertainment calendars revolved around fairs, church events, and occasional touring acts. Others were local hubs with established radio stations and a history of hosting traveling country and rhythm-and-blues performers. In both cases, audiences arrived with expectations shaped by what they knew or rather what they heard. Presley's challenge was not just to meet those expectations, but to disrupt them without alienation.

Package tours remained the dominant setup in April. Presley rarely traveled alone. Bills often included country singers, hillbilly comedians, gospel acts, or local favorites who had spent years cultivating local followings. This context matters because it framed Presley's performances not as isolated spectacles, but as part of a shared evening of entertainment. What became increasingly apparent in April was how decisively attention shifted once he appeared. Audience energy concentrated around him, sometimes to the visible discomfort of the other performers, some of whom were very famous at the time.

This imbalance did not occur instantly. In early April, Presley's name might still appear mid-bill in advertisements. By the latter part of the month, surviving promotional materials increasingly highlighted his presence more prominently. This shift was not the result of formal renegotiation so much as promoter response. Ticket sales, crowd behavior, and post-show conversation made clear where interest was consolidating.

Radio exposure played a critical role in this process. Southern radio stations in 1955 operated as scene hubs. DJs were tastemakers with direct relationships to their listeners. Songs spread quickly, sometimes ahead of formal charting. Presley benefited from this world. His 45s and live reputation reinforced each other, creating a feedback loop that intensified throughout April.

The relationship between touring and radio can't be overstated. Performances validated what listeners heard on air, while radio amplified expectation for upcoming shows. In towns with strong radio presence, Presley often arrived to audiences primed for him. In smaller towns without such exposure, his performances *created* that reputation firsthand. Both scenarios contributed to crowd demand.

From a business perspective, April exposed the limits of informal management. Bob Neal handled coordination with care and diligence, but the pace, and scale of touring now demanded strategic foresight. Contracts multiplied. Travel costs increased. Scheduling conflicts became more likely. Neal's role was essential in preventing disarray, but the complexity of operations hinted at the need for broader infrastructure.

Colonel Tom Parker continued to notice this inflection point. His interest lay not in the how it works of daily travel, but in power of controlling it. Parker understood how quickly crowd expectation could dissipate if not converted into opportunity. April represented proof of concept. Presley was not a promising act. He was a demonstrable draw. Parker's involvement during this month showed an effort to shape that reality into long-term strength and to show Elvis what he brought to the table.

This period also clarified the physical demands of sustained performance. Presley's endurance was remarkable, but not infinite. The touring schedule left little room for recovery. Performers of the era often accepted fatigue as part of the profession, but April revealed how quickly strain could accumulate when audience expectations escalated nightly.

Health, in this context, is best understood as energy as an alternative to illness. Presley continued to perform with intensity and crowd control, but the cost was cumulative. Long drives, inconsistent meals, and late nights created a cycle that would become familiar in the years ahead. Whatever you do to your body when you are young affects your later years.

Social dynamics on the road evolved as well. Presley's growing prominence altered relationships with fellow performers. Admiration replaced camaraderie in some cases. In others, distance emerged. Presley did not instigate these changes, but he also could not prevent them. Success, even in its preliminary stages, isolates a person.

Personal relationships during April remained transient. The pace of travel limited continuity. Encounters were brief and shaped by circumstance as opposed to intention. Presley's emotional focus remained directed toward performance and what the room expects rather than intimacy. This pattern was less a choice than a consequence of schedule.

Culturally, April 1955 sits at an intersection. The South was navigating generational shifts in taste and behavior. Presley's performances tapped into that tension. His style challenged established norms without overtly confronting them. Audience reactions showed both excitement and unease, often simultaneously.

April's end did not bring closure. It brought clarity. Presley exited the month with more proof of his viability, awareness of his limits, and the beginnings of a machine forming around him. The decisions that followed would be shaped by what April revealed.

Note on documentation: a few day-by-day itineraries differ in minor details, especially Sundays. Where reputable sources diverge, I flag it once in preference to repeating a disclaimer line after line.

## APRIL 1955 RADIO, CINEMA, AND A COUNTRY BEGINNING TO LOOSEN

April is where the divide starts to feel less permanent. A song can live on an R&B chart and still leak into the white mainstream: sometimes through the original, sometimes through a cleaned-up cover, sometimes through kids who don't care about categories. The pulse is unmistakable: "Ain't That a Shame", Fats Domino, "Only You, And You Alone,", The Platters, "My Babe", Little Walter, "Tweedle Dee", LaVern Baker, and "Most of All", The Moonglows,. This is the ground Elvis is walking on every night: a country trying to keep its music in separate rooms, while the sound keeps slipping under the door.

*What America Was Hearing on the Radio April 1955*

By April 1955, American radio had started to shift subtly, cautiously, but noticeably. Winter's emotional restraint was giving way to spring restlessness. Programming favored familiarity, but rhythm was creeping closer to the surface.

Pop radio in April leaned toward something new, color, and light movement rather than introspection:

Perez Prado "Cherry Pink and Apple Blossom White" A Latin instrumental that flooded the airwaves with rhythm disguised as elegance. Movement allowed but safely abstracted., Billboard year-end pop: #1 in 1955,

The McGuire Sisters "Sincerely" Harmony-driven pop that softened emotional intensity into reassurance. Romantic commitment without friction., Billboard year-end pop: #8 in 1955,

Nat King Cole "A Blossom Fell" Polished heartbreak given with poise. Emotion framed as reflection rather than demand., Billboard pop chart peak: #2 in 1955,

The Chordettes "Mr. Sandman" Playful and bright, suggesting desire without consequence. Whimsy replacing urgency., Billboard pop charts: #1 in 1954-55. Year-end pop: 18 in 1955,

*Country radio followed a parallel path, loosening slightly while remaining grounded:*

Porter Wagoner "Satisfied Mind" A philosophical response to ambition and change, urging calm in a world start to speed up.

Carl Smith "Let Old Mother Nature Have Her Way" Tradition reaffirmed through narrative restraint., Billboard year-end country: 1 in 1951,

Hank Thompson "The Wild Side of Life", was still circulating heavily, Moral tension presented as warning rather than rebellion., Billboard country chart: #1 for 15 weeks in 1952,

Across formats, April radio allowed motion without threat. Rhythm was present, but crowd control remained intact.

The music acknowledged change without surrendering to it.

What Was Playing in Movie Theaters April 1955

Cinema in April started reflecting the same tension radio was handling motion growing under supervision.

Films widely circulating included:

Blackboard Jungle drawing attention following its March release, its opening use of rhythm-heavy music unsettled audiences not because of content, but because of placement. Youth tension introduced where it did not belong.

The Seven Year Itch, heavily promoted for early summer, Desire framed as humor, not disruption. Containment through charm.

Bad Day at Black Rock, still in theaters, Anxiety and moral confrontation presented through stillness and restraint.

Movie houses remained cultural classrooms. Audiences were being trained to notice posture, pacing, and move skills that mattered deeply when encountering a performer like Elvis live.

April cinema acknowledged unease but insisted on control.

*Where Elvis Fit and Pressed Against April Culture*

By April 1955, Elvis Presley was not new to Southern audiences, but he was still new to radio.

Where February radio taught listeners to remain still, and March introduced tension, April flirted with motion without fully accepting it.

Elvis began to live inside that gap.

His performances did not feel accidental. Reaction had become predictable enough to create expectation. Teenagers arrived ready. Adults arrived guarded.

Elvis did not disrupt Aprils culture outright, but he did test its elasticity.

*What Elvis Sounded Like Against April Radio*

April radio allowed rhythm, but only when it arrived safely packaged instrumental, humorous, or abstract.

Elvis's rhythm was none of those things.

*Controlled novelty*

*Emotional distance*

*Rhythmic suggestion*

Elvis offered:

*Direct physicality*

*Sustained tension*

*Immediate response*

In towns where audiences spent the day hearing Perez Prado or the Chordettes, Elvis's sound arrived as something unfinished. Something that did not resolve itself neatly.

This difference did not confuse audiences. It activated them.

*Why April 1955 Matters Culturally*

April arrives with the road warm under the tires. Elvis isn't waiting to be discovered now he's logging miles like a man who knows the next town is listening. The shows are tighter, the travel faster, and the distance between a local name and a national problem starts to shrink. And he feels it in the most ordinary way: behind the wheel. This isn't a kid borrowing crowd pressure, it's a young star learning what speed costs. In early April, that lesson becomes literal, when the pace of the road finally meets the pace of the law. The ticket isn't the headline. It's the symptom. By April, Elvis is moving with the kind of confidence that makes adults frown and teenagers grin because he feels reckless. He is constantly in third gear and refuses to idle.

Radio cautiously introduces rhythm. Cinema cautiously introduces unrest. Audiences cautiously lean forward.

Elvis does not wait for permission. He reveals that it exists.

The culture starts granting small permissions more rhythm on the dial, more talk in the papers, but the institutions still rely on containment. April is where the old rules start to bend without admitting they have moved.

April 1955 captures a country learning how to feel the motion and rhythm of Rock 'N' Roll without naming it.

Elvis gives that motion a figurehead.

**FULL KNOWN APRIL 1955
PERFORMANCE RECORD**

April 1 Ector County Auditorium, Odessa, TX

April 2 City Auditorium, Houston, TX, Louisiana Hayride,

April 30: Louisiana Hayride, Gladewater High School, Gladewater, Texas.

April 29: The Cotton Club, Lubbock, Texas.

April 27: American Legion Hall, Hobbs, New Mexico.

April 26: City Auditorium, Big Spring, Texas.

April 25: M-B Corral, Wichita Falls, Texas. Texas High School, Seymour, Texas.

April 24: Magnolia Gardens, Houston, Texas (afternoon). Not verified but possible.

April 24: Cook's Hoedown Club, Houston, Texas, evening,. Not verified but possible.

April 23: Louisiana Hayride, Heart O' Texas Arena, Waco, Texas.

April 20: American Legion Hut, Grenada, Mississippi.

April 16: The Big "D" Jamboree, Sportatorium, Dallas, Texas.

April 15: High School, Stamford, Texas.

April 14: Owl Park, Gainesville, Texas.

April 13: High School, Breckenridge, Texas.

April 9: Louisiana Hayride, Municipal Auditorium, Shreveport, Louisiana.

April 8: B&B Club, Gobler, Missouri.

April 7: Court House, Corinth, Mississippi, 2:30 and 8:00 p.m.,.

April 2: Louisiana Hayride, City Auditorium, Houston, Texas.

April 1: Ector County Auditorium, Odessa, Texas.

# Chapter 5, May 1955

In May, the Cadillac remained on the road, carrying Presley from engagement to engagement as his reputation moved faster than the highways themselves. The speeding citation had not slowed the schedule, and the court date passed without altering the forward motion. Even though Elvis did not attend the court hearing, it was handled later by paying a fine. It was not unusual for an entertainer who did not live in the area of the citation to miss court. The car continued to do what it had done all year, absorb distance, urgency, and consequence as the year's acceleration showed no sign of easing.

The route this month isn't a tight Delta loop, it's a long swing: New Orleans, and Baton Rouge. Then Mobile, down through Florida's auditoriums and armories, then up the coast into the Carolinas and Virginia, before Presley drops back toward Shreveport and the Texas runs that close the month. Exhausting if you pick up a map and imagine yourself driving it. Then if you imagine the performances and the radio station visits, it looks impossible.

In the earliest days of May, Presley is carried inside a bigger machine than his usual circuit: Hank Snow's All-Star Jamboree. On paper, it's a package show built on known names and reliable set of songs. In the performnce hall, it turns into a nightly test of whether a local big deal can light up a crowd that didn't buy a ticket *for* him.

These were not weak acts. They were the standard polished, practiced, and built for the kind of crowd that wants its entertainment predictable.

On the Hank Snow All-Star Jamboree bills, that "package" can include road-tested names like Mother Maybelle and the Carter Sisters, the Davis Sisters, and seasoned crowd-handlers who know how to keep a room steady. This is exactly why Elvis' effect is so visible.

Presley's presence among them changes how the standard begins to function. They react first, and the venue has to reorganize around it. That lesson repeats across the month's route: bigger halls, tighter schedules, many shows, and the same result attention bends toward him.


May 1, 1955, New Orleans, Louisiana, Municipal Auditorium (Hank Snow All Star Jamboree, 3 shows 2:00, 5:00, 8:00)
New Orleans makes the point immediately. Three dates in one day forces stamina, focus, and discipline. He doesn't have time to "warm up" a room slowly he has to hit it, reset, and hit it again, and each set spreads the rumor faster than the last. New Orleans is not a neutral stop for any act, because the city already lives inside music. Jazz history sits in the same neighborhoods as working clubs and radio habits, and the Tremé area around the room carries its own deep memory of sound and gathering. A civic hall like this one was built to hold big public nights, and it had already hosted every kind of spectacle a city like New Orleans can

generate. That is why the shock lands cleanly. A country package tour arrives with order on the poster, but the room reacts as if something new has slipped in secretly under the official billing.

The All Star Jamboree roster was: Hank Snow, Faron Young, the Wilburn Brothers, Mother Maybelle, and the Carter Sisters, the Davis Sisters, Jimmie Rodgers Snow, and Onie Wheeler. Elvis Presley is billed as the special added attraction, backed by Scotty Moore, and Bill Black, a three piece unit that can sound larger than it looks when the crowd starts leaning forward.

May 2, 1955, Baton Rouge, Louisiana, High School Auditorium (Hank Snow All Star Jamboree, 2 shows 7:00, and 9:00)

Baton Rouge sits on the Mississippi River with the posture of a capital city, shaped by government, university life, and the steady traffic of people moving through for work and school. It is a place used to formal events in formal rooms, even when those rooms are high school auditoriums. In a town like this, the line between a big night, and a civic occasion can blur, and a touring booking becomes part of how a community measures itself against other cities of its stature.. Two appearances in one night means the first crowd teaches the second fans what to expect, and the second turnout arrives ready to react accordingly. For one night the Jamboree splits into two units, and Elvis runs with the unit headlined by Faron Young while Hank Snow plays elsewhere. The same traveling names still define the package, but the weight is shifting toward the act labeled "added," because the seats response keeps deciding the pecking order faster than the program can adjust to Elvis growing fame.

May 3–5, 1955, Mobile, Alabama, with May 4–5 at Ladd Stadium (Hank Snow All Star Jamboree) The road stretches: Mobile, Daytona Beach, Tampa, Fort Myers names that look like dots on a map until you're living them at highway speed. The crowds shift, the accents shift, the local radio favorites shift, but the surge of attraction to Elvis keeps arriving with the same electricity.

Mobile didn't start on a stage. It started with a radio studio: early hours, fluorescent light, a microphone pushed too close, and Elvis answering questions like he's trying not to sound amazed that people care. Between the interviews and the handshakes, Parker keeps the machinery moving: photos, names, phone numbers, and the simple, practical insistence that the record has to be in the DJ's hands today, not next week. It's the unglamorous side of a tour, but it's how a regional act becomes a national one.

Mobile has its own long, public tradition of crowds. It is a port city connected to Mobile Bay, built on movement and commerce, and it carries one of the oldest Carnival histories in the country, the kind of place that already understands parade energy and the way a city can turn loose for a season. That matters, because a stadium crowd in Mobile already knows how to move as one body. Then Ladd Stadium turns the rumor of Elvis Presley's growing legend into a story that will travel on in lore. A football field shouldn't feel like a theater, but the noise climbs the stands the same way it climbs a balcony: fast, contagious, impossible to ignore. After one of the sets, a pack of girls breaks loose, and chases Elvis across the turf, and for a moment the whole scene looks less like entertainment than like weather: a sudden surge you can't reason with, only survive. The adults in the aisle see danger. The kids in the seats see proof. The bill is still the All Star Jamboree machine, Hank Snow and Faron Young, and the Wilburn Brothers, Mother Maybelle and the Carter Sisters, the Davis Sisters, Jimmie Rodgers Snow, and Onie Wheeler, with Elvis Presley, Scotty Moore, and Bill Black as the special added attraction. The shock isn't that Mobile hosted a touring show. The shock is that a young singer could bend a stadium's mood so hard that the kids stops behaving like ticket holders and starts behaving like a tide ready to crash into the shore with no warning.

May 6–7, 1955, with May 7 at the Peabody Auditorium, Daytona Beach, Florida (Hank Snow All Star Jamboree)

By Friday the package plays on without him, and that absence becomes its own headline. Scotty and Bill are there, the show is there, the routing is there, yet Elvis is back in Memphis for a single night, trying to behave like a normal twenty year old again. He dresses up for Dixie Locke's junior prom and slips into a double date, a borrowed slice of normal with Gene Smith and Dixie's friend Bessie Wolverton. It gives the month a human heartbeat. Florida changes the temperature of the story. Not just the weather, but the house texture. These are audiences used to big traveling performances rolling through town. They arrive ready to be entertained, and that expectation forces Presley to land his impact quickly, without the slow build he could sometimes afford in smaller rooms.

Florida, though, is not neutral ground. It's Parker's old map, home territory where he knows which rooms sell tickets and which radio men can tilt a town with a single mention. This is where Parker begins to "show" Elvis his value. In places like Daytona and Tampa, the push is deliberate and due to Parkers connections: publicity, introductions, and the kind of local leverage that makes a "special added attraction" feel like the main event. Even the behind the scenes work bookings, Mae Boren Axton, writer of a future Elvis hit " Heartbreak Hotel" is brought in on publicity for part of the run, another reminder that the Colonel isn't just booking dates; he's building an empire.

Daytona Beach is a beach town that already knows spectacle. Long before a permanent speedway becomes the symbol later in the decade, the city is already selling speed, sun, and crowds. The building, dedicated only a few years earlier, is the kind of performing arts hall a growing Florida city points to with pride, built to bring national acts into a room with good acoustics and civic shine. That shine is exactly why the night hits. The Jamboree arrives with proven stars and a clean program, and then Elvis makes the people feel like it is witnessing something too new and alive to stay polite.

Daytona Beach and Tampa put him in front of people who may know him only as a name on a poster, not a whispered rumor from the next county over. That difference matters. It means the first thirty seconds have to do the convincing. Elvis does not disappoint.

Across these first seven days, the change was

cumulative. Presley was not being discovered town by town anymore. He was being anticipated. Word of mouth traveled faster than the route. DJs referenced his performances before and after witnessing them. Promoters adjusted billing language. Audiences arrived prepared to be part of the next big thing.

Colonel Tom Parker's attention aligned with what the week revealed. Presley's appeal was portable. It survived variation in town size, hall quality, and billing bill placement. That portability mattered more than raw enthusiasm. It meant the phenomenon he was witnessing could scale.

By the end of the first week of May, Presley had not yet crossed into national fame. What he had crossed into was the inevitability of that future.

May 8, 1955, Tampa, Florida (Fort Homer Hesterly Armory, 2 shows)

Tampa is a working city with a port pulse and a cigar town's memory still hanging in the streets, a place built on ships, labor, and loud Saturday nights. The Armory is the kind of room that can hold a crowd without feeling intimate yet still feel personal once the noise starts bouncing off the rafters. Hank Snow's All-Star Jamboree is the official reason everyone bought a ticket, a seasoned package built for families and fairground order, but Elvis is the spark that keeps slipping the leash. The bill carries Hank Snow, Faron Young, the Wilburn Brothers, Mother Maybelle, and the Carter Sisters, the Davis Sisters, Jimmie Rodgers Snow, and Onie Wheeler, with Elvis Presley, Scotty Moore, and Bill Black listed as the special added attraction. The Florida run is already being worked like a campaign, and Mae Boren Axton's publicity efforts are part of why the rooms are filling before the first chord is struck.

May 9, 1955, Fort Myers, Florida (City Auditorium)

Fort Myers has the calm, sunlit confidence of a Gulf town that already knows how to host winter people and visiting money, the kind of place where history is often packaged as leisure sees it. A touring show in a city room isn't unusual, but the reaction to Elvis keeps turning these ordinary nights into something that feels like a change in the weather. The same Jamboree bill rolls in, the same names on the program, the same promise of order, and entertainment. Then Elvis steps into that order and bends it to his will, with a charge in the rhythm that makes teenagers behave like the room is theirs and not their parents.

May 10, 1955, Ocala, Florida (Southeastern Pavilion)

Ocala sits in horse country, a place where the proud local story is built on breeding, training, and the quiet seriousness of work that happens before dawn. The Pavilion crowd arrives with the habits of a town used to fairs and gatherings, used to watching animals move for sport and tradition. The Jamboree bill is steady, professional, and rehearsed. Elvis changes the temperature anyway, because his performance is not simply music, it is a new physical language.

May 11, 1955, Orlando, Florida (Auditorium, 2 shows)

Orlando is still a citrus and resort town in this period, a place with visitors passing through and locals used to entertainment being reliable and predictable. The night doesn't stay contained. It is far from predictable. After the first performance, the crowd refuses to let it end the normal way and calls for Elvis until he comes back out, and then it happens again, a second round of demand as if the audience is learning, in real time, that applause can be a lever. To pull it back and get more for its money.

May 12, 1955, Jacksonville, Florida (Baseball Park)
Jacksonville is a river city with a port identity and a military presence, big enough to feel like a crossroads and restless enough to always be looking for the next thing. A baseball park show changes the geometry, more people, more distance, more open air, and more room for a crowd to become a wave instead of a cluster. The Jamboree package is designed for exactly this kind of stop. Elvis turns it into something else, because the screaming is nothing like the adults have heard before.  It behaves like a signal being broadcast from teen to teen.

May 13, 1955, Jacksonville, Florida (Baseball Park, second night)
May carried the first real backlash in the same breath as the first true mania. Newspaper columns, church talk, and kitchen table conversations began to fix on one question: what exactly was happening to the girls in these crowds? Parents complained, warned one another, and tightened their grip, worried not only about the hips, and the hair, but about the way the music seemed to unhook the manners of their children. To them, it looked like

the devil dressed up as entertainment, a fever that could spread through a venue before any usher could calm it.

At Jacksonville, Florida, on May 13, the fear found a terrifying headline. With more than 14,000 packed into the arena, Elvis teased the front rows and promised the girls he would see them in the backstage hallway. The words hit like a match. Fans surged, security buckled, and the moment turned from concert to chaos. For Parker, the story was not a problem so much as proof he could take to New York: if one sentence from the stage could start a riot, then the popularity of this kid was real. The ceiling was higher than anyone in Sun's small office had dared to say out loud, or for that matter could handle.

That promise, "Girls, I'll see you backstage", changed everything. Parents who had been uneasy about the hips and the hair suddenly had a single sentence to point at: proof, in their telling, that the music came with an invitation to disorder. In the surge that followed, screaming became motion. Fans broke toward the exits and dugouts, hands grabbing at sleeves, shoes, anything that could be kept as evidence. The danger was not abstract. A stampede isn't a metaphor, and Jacksonville made that plain.

What frightened adults also clarified the economics. Promoter Oscar Davis later framed the scene as the moment the situation turned irreversible: the crowd did not just applaud and scream for Elvis. It pursued him. For Parker, it was the kind of raw measurement managers trust more than reviews, an arena full of teenagers willing to risk trouble for proximity to their idol. He didn't have to imagine broader demand. He'd seen a field just prove what was possible. Something Eddy Arnold who was a massive star could not do. After Jacksonville, the complaints kept rising, but so did the proof that Elvis fame was real.

May 14, 1955, New Bern, North Carolina (Shrine Auditorium, 2 shows)
New Bern carries an older America in its bones, a colonial town at the meeting of rivers, the sort of place where history is visible in street names and architecture and civic pride. That makes the contrast sharper when a modern noise arrives. The Jamboree bill reads like established country entertainment, dependable, and proven. Elvis makes the room feel young, and the shock isn't that a singer came through town, but that the town's teenagers suddenly act like the world is larger than the riverbanks they grew up on.

May 15, 1955, Norfolk, Virginia (Municipal Auditorium, 2 shows)
Norfolk is a Navy city, a port with discipline in its posture and movement, a place built around ships, schedules, and uniformed routine. A touring set here is part of the social calendar, but the mood shifts when Elvis comes on, because his act doesn't match the town's normal straight lines. The bill is still Hank Snow's machine, still full of strong performers, but Elvis carries a kind of disorder that

feels thrilling and rather criminal. Two dates in one day do not dilute the reactions, they multiply it.

May 16, 1955, Richmond, Virginia (Mosque Theater)

Richmond is an old capital city with the weight of history and politics in its streets, a place that knows ceremony, and knows reputations. The Mosque Theater gives the night a sense of occasion, and the audience gives it charge. In Richmond's Mosque Theater, the reaction began reaching the people who watched markets for a living. RCA's field representative Brad McCuen and promotion man Chick Crumpacker came to check out the show. Crumpacker would remember not a single trick or gesture but the current that ran through the room, "His energy, and the galvanic effect it had on the ticket holders." Elvis, busy surviving the schedule, could not know who had taken a seat that night. The industry was there, and it was taking notes.

May 17, 1955, Asheville, North Carolina (City Auditorium, 2 shows)

Asheville is a mountain hub, long a resort city, and a cultural center for western North Carolina, a place where tourists come for air and views and locals come for the same reasons plus work. The room is another stop on the same rolling circuit, but the turnout makes it feel like a new test. Elvis passes it the way he keeps passing them, by turning a formal date into something that looks like a release valve of pressure being pulled on the mountain.

May 18, 1955, Roanoke, Virginia (American Legion Hall, 2 shows)

Roanoke is a railroad city, built on junctions, and movement, on people coming through and people leaving again. A Legion Hall appearance has a tighter, closer energy than a ballpark, and it puts the ticket holders near enough to believe they can reach what they are hearing. The bill is still loaded with known names, still meant to be orderly. Elvis makes the hall feel like it is leaning forward into the future of Rock, instead of the stability of country.

May 19, 1955, Raleigh, North Carolina (Memorial Auditorium)
Raleigh is the state capital, a city shaped by government, and universities, where public events tend to arrive with a certain formality. This is the last date on the tour, and the exhaustion is real, but the performance doesn't show fatigue. The booking becomes a marker, one more proof that the package can travel and sell, and that Elvis can turn a civic building into a place that feels briefly out of control. Elvis bursts onto stage as a ball of lightning. When the night ends, it does not feel like a finale of a tour. It feels like the beginning of something the world may not be ready for, but they were still going to get.

May 21, 1955, Shreveport, Louisiana (Municipal Auditorium, Louisiana Hayride)
Shreveport is a river city with broadcast power in its identity, and the Hayride is not just a stage, it is a pipeline. Coming back to the theater means coming back to the place that helped turn his regional noise a few months ago into something that could travel. The Hayride bill shifts week to week, but Elvis returning to that same room to larger and larger

153

crowds begins to make it impossible for anyone to go on stage *AFTER* Elvis.

May 22, 1955, Houston, Texas (Magnolia Gardens, plus Cook's Hoedown listed in some schedules)

Houston is a port city and a growth city, built on trade, shipping, and the kind of expansion that makes everything feel temporary because the skyline keeps changing. Magnolia Gardens is a different kind of room, less civic, and more nightlife, a place where music is not just listened to, it is lived in. The billing in this stretch often includes Onie Wheeler alongside Elvis, with Scotty, and Bill still forming the engine underneath him. The shock here isn't that Houston has entertainment. Houston has everything. The shock is that this one young singer can still make the crowd behave like it has never seen a show before.

May 23, 1955, Tyler, Texas (Mayfair Building)

Tyler sits in the Piney Woods, with a reputation tied to roses and civic pride and the careful cultivation of beauty that can be sold and celebrated. A show here isn't supposed to feel like national news. It is supposed to feel like a good wholesome night out. Elvis keeps refusing to be small-town entertainment, even when the room is small-town sized. The undercard varies by stop, but the constant is the way teenagers react as if something important just passed through and left a mark on their hearts and hormones.

May 25, 1955, Meridian, Mississippi (American Legion Hall, Jimmie Rodgers Memorial Celebration)

Late May in Meridian added a different kind of

legitimacy. The Jimmie Rodgers Memorial Celebration was a civic-scale event, barbecue laid out for thousands, a parade that drew tens of thousands into the streets, and a bill thick with established names. Elvis arrived as the new sensation threaded into tradition, still learning how to carry his own storm inside a setting built to honor a founder. It had mostly forgotten or never realized that he traveled there in 2 years before in 1953, by way of hitch-hiking, the same week as his graduation. It was a reminder that the story was not only teenage frenzy; it was also the older country world deciding whether the boy from Memphis could stand inside its ceremonies and still sound like himself.

Meridian didn't handle him like a new act. It treated him like part of the program. The Jimmie Rodgers Memorial Celebration drew crowds by the thousands, with a barbecue that fed a town's worth of people before the night scattered into smaller stages and halls. One notice in the Meridian Star put it plainly, "Music will be provided by Elvis Pressley. His orchestra", and the phrasing matters, because it's the first time you can feel the institutions trying to fit him into their own language. Country Song Roundup later described the American Legion set as encore-heavy, a room calling him back again, and again. With titles like "Baby Let's Play House," "I'm Left, You're Right, She's Gone," "Milkcow Blues Boogie," and "You're a Heartbreaker" ringing out like proof.

The next day the celebration moved into daylight with a parade estimated at sixty thousand people: politicians, radio men, and country stars all folded into the same rolling pageant. What looks like town ceremony on the surface is also business under the hood: Chick Crumpacker. RCA's Brad McCuen watching Hill & Range's Grelun Landon carrying a Presley song folio. A publicity bio built around sheet-music covers, and Parker measuring the scene the way he measures everything, not just applause, but ownership. In the weeks that follow, even his tone with Bob Neal shifts. There's a sense in his letters that they need to sit down and settle the terms, because the rooms are getting bigger and the stakes are no longer theoretical. The collision course has been set.

May 26, 1955, Meridian, Mississippi (Junior College Stadium, Jimmie Rodgers Memorial Celebration)
The stadium setting makes it feel larger and more public, like the town is staging its identity for itself. The celebration remains anchored in the legacy of Rodgers and the established stars on the program, but Elvis is the detail people leave talking about, because he does not behave like an undercard. The sound coming off that stage is still country by billing, but it is already pressing into a different future.

May 27, 1955, Texarkana, Arkansas (Municipal Auditorium, listed in some logs as a probable date)
Texarkana is a border city by nature, split identity, a place accustomed to travelers and routes and the feeling that everything is passing through on the way somewhere else. That makes it a fitting stop for

a tour that is increasingly defined by movement. The paper trail for this date is not as strong as the others, but it sits in the month's flow like it belongs there, another night where the same small core of musicians is asked to make a room feel like a national event for those who attend.

May 28, 1955, Dallas, Texas (Sportatorium, The Big D Jamboree)

Dallas carries big-city ambition, radio power, and the kind of entertainment appetite that makes a place feel modern even when it is still wearing older clothes. The Sportatorium is a rougher kind of venue, known for drawing crowds that want action, not delicacy. The Big D Jamboree bill includes other names like Onie Wheeler, Arlie Duff, and Texas Bill Strength alongside Elvis, and the room responds like it is built to respond, loud, physical, impatient. This is the kind of stop that teaches a performer how to hold a crowd that isn't automatically friendly. Elvis holds it anyway.

May 29, 1955, Fort Worth, Texas (North Side Coliseum, afternoon), then Dallas, Texas (Sportatorium, evening)

Fort Worth has stockyards history in its posture, a cattle town that learned early how to gather people for spectacle and commerce at the same time. A coliseum crowd in the afternoon has a different feel than a nighttime club house, more families, more daylight energy, and more sense of community watching together. Then the tour swings back to Dallas for a second show, and the day becomes a double-proof that this act can sell twice in two cities and still ignite both rooms. On this stretch, the package often includes names like Ferlin Huskey,

Martha Carson, the Carlisles, J. E. And Maxine Brown, and Onie Wheeler with Elvis, Scotty, and Bill, a traveling stack of talent designed to keep the audience buying tickets even if they came for someone else.

May 30, 1955, Abilene, Texas (tour opening planned, promotion uneven in surviving records) Abilene is West Texas, straight-backed, and practical, a place shaped by distance and the habit of earning everything the hard way. This is the point in the month where the record hints at a problem that isn't musical but logistical. Ther is poor local promotion, thin notices and  a tour that exists on paper more clearly than it exists in the newspapers. Even that is part of the story. The rise is not given for Elvis. It succeeds sometimes even with imperfect routing, inconsistent advertising, and a performer whose impact keeps outrunning the infrastructure around him.

May 31, 1955, Midland, Texas (High School Auditorium, 7:30 pm), then Odessa, Texas (High School Field, 9:30 pm)
Midland, and Odessa sit in the Permian Basin world, oil country cities where money and hardship have a way of arriving in the same decade and changing everything. A high school theater show in Midland carries that familiar small-town intimacy, then the night jumps to Odessa for a later outdoor field performance, and the schedule itself tells the truth about 1955. This is not a world of glamour yet for Elvis. It is mileage and hustle, late hours, quick load-ins, and the constant requirement to win the room again from scratch. By the end of May, the shockwave is no longer only felt locally. It is

cumulative. Town after town has now learned what it feels like when Elvis Presley comes through.

As May ended, the road felt different. Early on, every new town was a chance, and the excitement was still a surprise. Now it was expected. People were already waiting, already screaming, already treating Elvis like the main event before he stepped onstage.

That meant the job changed. He was not just chasing opportunities anymore. He was carrying a pressure. A weight. The crowds were getting bigger, the reactions were getting wilder, and the shows now needed rules. They needed timing, and protection to keep the whole thing from tipping over. The tour was no longer shaping him. He was starting to shape the tour.

The calendar kept filling up. May did what January through April could not do. It squeezed the story tighter, setting June up to turn all that hunger into real consequences.

## CO-BILLED ARTISTS MAY 1955

### Background, Reputation, and Contemporary Hits

During May 1955, Elvis Presley most often appeared on multi-act package bills featuring performers who were familiar to Southern audiences. These artists were not unknowns. Many had radio exposure, local hits, or long-standing touring reputations. Their presence framed how Presley was perceived and amplified the impact of his performances.

### Johnny Horton

Johnny Horton was among the most well-known country performers circulating Southern circuits in 1955. Known for his commanding stage presence and clear vocal delivery, Horton had established himself as a reliable draw. Though his later national hits like "The Battle of New Orleans" were still a few years away, Horton's reputation in 1955 rested on steady radio play and disciplined performance.

Horton's style represented traditional country professionalism. When billed alongside Presley, the contrast was immediate. Horton given precision and polish. Presley given volatility and movement. Audiences accustomed to Horton's crowd-controlled approach often reacted strongly to Presley's looseness, heightening the sense that something new was occurring.

### Slim Whitman

Slim Whitman was one of the most recognizable names on Southern touring bills in the mid-1950s.

His falsetto singing style and smooth romantic ballads had earned him widespread radio exposure. By 1955, Whitman was associated with a soft-sell kind of stardom that played well to mixed-age crowds, the kind that came as families, and left humming.

Whitman's presence lent legitimacy to package shows. His audiences were multigenerational. This meant Presley was often performing before listeners who had not come specifically to see him. The surge and scream of younger attendees during Presley's sets often stood in stark contrast to the calmer reception Whitman received, making Presley's impact more visible.

### Ferlin Husky

Ferlin Husky was another established country artist appearing on Southern bills during this period. Known for something new material and strong crowd engagement, Husky had a seasoned, professional rhythm onstage. He knew how to win a room without letting it run away from him.

Husky's role on these bills mattered because he understood how to work a crowd. When Presley followed or preceded him, audiences could immediately compare two different approaches to performance. Presley's effect was not small by comparison. It felt like the room's center of gravity shifting.

### Louisiana Hayride Alumni

Many of Presley's co-billed performers in May 1955 were Louisiana Hayride veterans, even when Presley himself was not appearing on the radio broadcast. These acts benefited from weekly exposure and local loyalty. Hayride audiences trusted these performers. This made their endorsement of shared bills big.

When Presley appeared alongside Hayride regulars, his presence signaled that he belonged within that professional world. Yet his reception often exceeded that of performers with longer tenure, creating a quiet but noticeable shift in hierarchy.

### Regional Country and Hillbilly Acts

Beyond nationally noticed names, Presley shared bills with many local country singers, hillbilly comedians, and gospel performers. These artists often had strong local followings built through years of touring the same towns repeatedly. Their reputations were deeply rooted in familiarity.

Presley's performances disrupted this familiarity. Audiences who had seen the same performers cycle through town for years responded differently to Presley, whose style felt unpredictable. That reaction became part of the story in towns where the entertainment calendar usually stayed obedient.

### Rhythm-and-Blues Influenced Acts

In Mississippi, Arkansas, and parts of Alabama, Presley occasionally appeared on bills that included performers with rhythm-and-blues influence. Or at minimum artists whose phrasing and set of songs leaned closer to blues and boogie than polite radio country. In those rooms, the groove already lived in the floorboards.

Presley's association with this edge of the circuit was culturally big. His music drew from similar sources, and audiences noticed the connection intuitively. In towns with strong blues traditions, Presley's performances could feel familiar and startling at the same time, like someone saying out loud what had always been implied.

---

## The Hank Snow All Star Jamboree Core Cast

May 1955 adds a new kind of framing device around Presley: a branded traveling package with an established headliner and a recognizable supporting cast. Instead of walking into a town as the whole event, Presley becomes the pressure point inside an event that already has its own reputation and its own order.

### Hank Snow

Hank Snow was not a local draw. He was a national-level professional, a touring machine with a catalogue that already carried weight. Snow's stagecraft was controlled and seasoned. He could hold a crowd without raising his voice, because the turnout already believed in him before the first chord.

That matters for Presley. When a room comes in trusting the headliner, it becomes easier to measure the shock of the newcomer. Snow represented the settled idea of country stardom. Presley represented the unsettled future of it. On the same bill, the contrast did not need explanation. It played itself out right then.

### Faron Young

Faron Young brought honky-tonk bite and youth, but with a different posture than Presley. Young's edge was in the voice and the lyric. In the way a song could sound reckless without the singer ever losing control. In 1955, he was moving fast, building momentum, the kind of act that felt current even to people who did not read trade papers.

On these bills, Young often served as a bridge. He made the package feel modern. Then Presley stepped out and made "modern" feel too small a word. That is how a show can change shape without changing its lineup.

### The Wilburn Brothers

The Wilburn Brothers carried the feel of a tight, road-tested duo. Their harmonies and timing gave audiences something familiar: family-leaning country presentation, efficient, and dependable, built for radio and stage both. That familiarity isn't a footnote. It is the baseline the room stands on.

When Presley hit the stage in the middle of that baseline, the reaction reads louder. He was not just good. He was different. A bill with disciplined harmony acts around him made his looseness register as a force, not a quirk.

### Mother Maybelle and the Carter Sisters

Mother Maybelle and the Carter Sisters brought lineage. Their presence told every promoter and every parent in the seats that this show had roots, not just noise. This was the First Family energy of country music, and it carried a kind of moral credibility in small towns.

That credibility shaped the room Presley walked into. It lowered guardrails for older listeners and raised the stakes for younger ones. When Presley shook a room that had been "approved" by Carter-family respectability, the shock felt bigger, because the room itself had been pre-blessed as safe.

### The Davis Sisters

The Davis Sisters brought something the circuit needed more of female star power that was not something new and not background. Their harmony work had already proven it could dominate a chart and dominate a room. In a package setting, that meant the show did not rely on one kind of excitement.

When Presley followed a female duet that could actually hold attention, the reaction to him becomes more revealing. It suggests the noise around Presley was not just teenage restlessness. It was the sense of a room discovering a new center.

### Jimmie Rodgers Snow

Jimmie Rodgers Snow, billed as Hank Snow's son, carried a built-in storyline: tradition reproducing itself. A young performer with a famous last name gave the package a next generation feel without asking the kids to gamble on an unknown.

That is why his presence matters beside Presley. Jimmie Rodgers Snow represented the expected future of country music, the son stepping into the part. Presley represented an unexpected future, the one that doesn't stay in its part. On the same bill, the house could feel the difference without needing to define it.

### Onie Wheeler

Onie Wheeler is the kind of name that shows up on the edges of several scenes at once. Country, gospel, early rockabilly energy, a performer who could move between styles because the circuit itself did. He carried that borderland feel that Southern audiences understood, even if they did not have a word for it.

That borderland quality pairs naturally with Presley in 1955. Presley was not trying to be a category. He was all categories built into one, forcing a new name of his style. Wheeler's presence on the package is a reminder that the bill was not only country in the strict sense. It was a moving crossroads, and Presley was at the center of it.

### WHY CO-BILLING MATTERED IN MAY 1955

May 1955 was not simply about how Presley performed. It was about how he compared.

Each night, audiences witnessed Presley alongside performers who represented the existing Southern entertainment pecking order. That pecking order was competent, professional, and well known. Presley's effect was to destabilize it without explicitly challenging it.

Promoters noticed. Performers noticed. Managers noticed.

By the end of May, Presley's placement on bills increasingly showed audience behavior in preference to tradition. Co-billed artists mattered, but their function shifted. They became context the frame that made Presley's difference unmistakable.

By the end of May 1955, American radio did not yet sound different on the surface. A listener turning the dial during daylight hours encountered familiarity. The dominant mood remained composed, polite, and emotionally legible. Music continued to serve as reassurance more often than provocation. Yet beneath that surface, routine was doing its work.

In May, radio still plays like it's handling reputations: what's "acceptable," what's "too rough," what belongs on which side of town. But the kids, the jukeboxes, and the after-hours stations don't respect those fences. And the 45s that stick are the ones that swing and talk back: "What'cha Gonna Do", The Drifters, "Ain't That a Shame", Fats Domino, "The Wallflower, Dance with Me, Henry,", Etta James & The Peaches, "Bo Diddley", Bo Diddley, and "Hearts of Stone", The Charms. Elvis is becoming the crossover headline, but the blueprint, the rhythm, the phrasing, the nerve, has been on the dial all year.

In cities and towns across the South and Midwest, radio schedules followed patterns shaped by habit as an alternative to experimentation. Morning and afternoon programming leaned toward calm continuity. Perry Como's "Ko Ko Mo, I Love You So," remained a reliable presence, its relaxed tempo, and conversational vocal style reinforcing the idea that romance was gentle and manageable. Eddie Fisher's "Heart" continued to circulate, its emotional intensity held back within clean phrasing and orchestral restraint. Patti Page's "Croce di Oro" offered exotic suggestion without emotional risk, while Doris Day's "Ready, Willing, and Able" embodied optimism without friction., Billboard DJ chart peak: #2 in 1955,

Vocal harmony groups dominated substantial portions of the pop landscape. The Four Aces' "Love Is a Many-Splendored Thing" played often, its lush arrangement, and blended voices reinforcing emotional certainty. These records did not ask listeners to move. They asked them to feel settled. They fit seamlessly into domestic spaces, reinforcing after World War II stability through sound., Billboard year-end pop: #7 in 1955,

Country radio reinforced similar values. Webb Pierce's "In the Jailhouse Now" remained well-known, its narrative clarity, and traditional setup grounding listeners in familiar storytelling. Hank Snow's "I'm Movin' On" conveyed restlessness, but within moral hierarchy. The song allowed motion without chaos. It suggested independence while maintaining restraint. These 45s reassured listeners that change could occur without disruption., Billboard country charts: #1 for 21 weeks in 1955,

Even when faster or louder records appeared, they were handled with caution. Bill Haley and His Comets' "Rock Around the Clock" spread unevenly in early 1955. It had energy, but many people still treated it like a something new, not a blueprint. Some stations played it hard. Others pushed it late into the night. People heard it, but it still wasn't treated as the main sound on adult radio.

Rhythm-and-blues stations offered more urgency, but familiarity governed rotation. Ruth Brown's records emphasized groove and emotional directness without abandoning setup. The Drifters' vocal arrangements balanced intimacy and crowd control. These records moved bodies, but they did so within patterns listeners understood.

This was the soundscape into which Elvis Presley's records entered in May 1955. They did not dominate charts. They did not displace established favorites. Instead, they spread persistently, appearing again, and again on local playlists. Their influence emerged not through saturation alone, but through contrast.

Presley's recordings sounded unsettled beside the prevailing hierarchy. His voice did not resolve where listeners expected resolution. His phrasing delayed satisfaction. Rhythm pushed forward while melody lingered. The effect was small enough to bypass resistance, but clear enough to register as difference. Listeners did not always know what they were hearing. They only knew it felt alive in a way other records did not.

Radio DJs navigated this difference carefully. Many framed Presley's 45s as responses to listener requests rather than personal endorsements. This rhetorical distance mattered. It allowed DJs to introduce the sound without committing to it fully. Yet once the record played, the hall wherever that room happened to be changed slightly.

Requests followed. At first, they were imprecise. Callers asked for "that song from earlier" or "the one that didn't sound like the others." Over time, the name attached itself to the sound. Elvis Presley became less a something new and more a reference point. DJs adjusted language accordingly, sometimes reluctantly, sometimes with curiosity, always incrementally.

Nighttime programming accelerated this process. After dark, playlists loosened. DJs experimented. Presley's records benefited from that freedom. Played late, they reached listeners in private moments in preference to communal ones. Teenagers heard them alone in bedrooms. Young adults heard them while driving. Parents heard them indirectly, absorbing difference without context.

These moments mattered. Culture rarely shifts in public first. It shifts privately, through routine that feels personal before it becomes collective. Presley's records entered that private space, without announcement, embedding themselves into routine.

Movie theaters reinforced the prevailing emotional hierarchy. In May 1955, film music functioned primarily as reinforcement as an alternative to disruption. Romantic dramas relied on orchestral themes that clarified emotion. Musical numbers emphasized discipline and spectacle. Soundtracks supported narrative instead of competing with it.

Films such as Love Is a Many-Splendored Thing carried songs that crossed easily between screen and radio, reinforcing the idea that music belonged within structured emotional arcs. Even lighter films maintained clear boundaries between sound and movement. Performers sang. They did not release themselves physically. Bodies remained crowd controlled. Move was held back.

This distinction shaped expectation. Music was something heard, not enacted. It accompanied life rather than interrupting it. Presley's live performances contradicted that assumption. His 45s hinted at motion, but his stage presence made it unavoidable. Radio prepared listeners for that confrontation before television ever given it.

As May progressed, juxtaposition became unavoidable. Listeners heard Perry Como followed by Presley. They heard Doris Day followed by a voice that bent rhythm forward and pulled melody back. Sequence altered perception. Presley's music did not exist in isolation. It existed in contrast.

That contrast sharpened awareness. Familiar songs felt calmer. Calm felt more pronounced. Presley's records felt restless even when played. The difference did not announce rebellion. It announced displacement. Something had shifted position, even if nothing had yet been overturned.

Touring and radio fed one another. Performances generated local excitement. Radio carried that excitement outward. Towns not yet visited heard what neighboring towns had experienced. By the time Presley arrived, rooms were primed. Reaction came faster. Expectation preceded exposure.

This feedback loop accelerated saturation without requiring national promotion. Presley's presence became familiar before it became accepted. Acceptance followed familiarity, not the other way around.

Parents encountered this shift indirectly. They heard the music through walls, from passing cars, from radios left on in kitchens. Teenagers encountered it directly, often alone, forming attachments that felt personal in lieu of instructed. DJs acted as intermediaries, translating demand into cautious exposure.

By the end of May, radio playlists had still not been overtaken. Crooners dominated. Ballads reassured. Movie soundtracks reinforced emotional hierarchy. Yet beneath that surface, something had loosened. Presley's 45s lingered longer in memory. They invited replay. They carried physical implication even through speakers incapable of reproducing full bass.

The cultural shift underway did not feel like revolution. It felt like conditioning. Listeners were learning, gradually, to tolerate then expect a different emotional posture in popular music. That learning occurred through routine rather than proclamation.

May 1955 did not crown a new hierarchy. It destabilized an old one gently but persistently. The airwaves carried both reassurance and strain, stability, and unrest. Presley's presence did not overwhelm the system. It bent it, slightly but continuously, until the bend became visible.

What followed would require response. For now, the change existed as sensation in preference to statement. The radio carried it daily, embedding it into routines that did not feel quite as settled as they once had.

## FULL KNOWN MAY 1955
## PERFORMANCE RECORD

May 1955 is among the most heavily traveled months of Elvis Presley's pre-national period. For the first half of the month, he is carried on Hank Snow's All-Star Jamboree big halls, multiple shows, and a bill full of established names before he drops back into the Louisiana Hayride and Bob Neal's routing through Texas. The record below follows the dates as they appear across standard biographies and day-by-day itineraries; where a hall is listed, I use it.

May 1 (Sunday): Municipal Auditorium, New Orleans, Louisiana (2:00, 5:00, and 8:00 p.m.).

May 2 (Monday): High School, Baton Rouge, Louisiana (7:00 and 9:00 p.m.).

May 4 (Wednesday): Ladd Stadium, Mobile, Alabama.

May 5 (Thursday): Ladd Stadium, Mobile, Alabama.

May 7 (Saturday): Peabody Auditorium, Daytona Beach, Florida.

May 8 (Sunday): Fort Homer Hesterly Armory, Tampa, Florida (2:30 and 8:15 p.m.).

May 9 (Monday): City Auditorium, Fort Myers, Florida.

May 10 (Tuesday): Southeastern Pavilion, Ocala, Florida.

May 11 (Wednesday): Auditorium, Orlando, Florida (7:30 and 9:30 p.m.).

May 12 (Thursday): The new baseball park (eventually named the Gator Bowl), Jacksonville, Florida.

May 13 (Friday): The new baseball park, Jacksonville, Florida.

May 14 (Saturday): Shrine Auditorium, New Bern, North Carolina (7:00 and 9:00 p.m.).

May 15 (Sunday): Auditorium, Norfolk, Virginia (3:00 and 8:00 p.m.).

May 16 (Monday): Mosque Theater, Richmond, Virginia.

May 17 (Tuesday): City Auditorium, Asheville, North Carolina (7:00 and 9:00 p.m.).

May 18 (Wednesday): American Legion Auditorium, Roanoke, Virginia (7:00 and 9:00 p.m.).

May 19 (Thursday): Memorial Auditorium, Raleigh, North Carolina.

May 21 (Saturday): Louisiana Hayride, Municipal Auditorium, Shreveport, Louisiana.

May 22 (Sunday): Magnolia Gardens, Houston, Texas.

May 25 (Wednesday): American Legion Hall, Meridian, Mississippi.

May 26 (Thursday): Junior College Stadium, Meridian, Mississippi.

May 28 (Saturday): The Big "D" Jamboree, Sportatorium, Dallas, Texas.

May 29 (Sunday): North Side Coliseum, Fort Worth, Texas (4:00 p.m.); Sportatorium, Dallas, Texas (8:00 p.m.).

May 31 (Tuesday): High School Auditorium, Midland, Texas (7:30 p.m.); High School Field House, Odessa, Texas (8:30 p.m.).

# Chapter 6, June 1955

June 1st, 1955, places Elvis Presley back on the road under the operational structure that had carried him all through the spring: Bob Neal's West Texas touring circuit. The date finds him at a high school auditorium in Guymon, Oklahoma, a town small enough that a touring act does not disappear into anonymity, but large enough that word travels quickly once something unusual arrives.

The run starts with simple town rooms, Guymon on June 1st, then Amarillo's City Auditorium on June 2nd, Places that look ordinary on paper, until you see what they do to a crowd once Elvis steps into the light. Neal is still building a map by hand, town by town, and the audiences keep responding as if the map has always been there.

Somewhere in late May or early June, the Presley's also make a move at home. They move out of the cramped Lauderdale Courts place off Alabama Avenue and into a rented brick house at 2414 Lamar in Memphis. It isn't luxury, but it is a marker: a family trying to give their story a front door. Gladys worries in the same breath she unpacks. Vernon watches the bills. Elvis keeps driving across the country and performing, as if motion itself can hold the year together. Elvis can't stop now. The money he is making is moving his family up. Slowly but surely.

By this point in the year, Elvis isn't an unknown attraction. Radio has done part of the work. Posters and local advertising do the rest. Teenagers arrive early. Adults tell each other about the dangers of this kid. The hall fills with expectation before the first note is played.

The building itself, a school auditorium, sets limits immediately. Stages are shallow. sound are blunt. Crowd fans control relies less on infrastructure and more on local the building's stature figures who have not yet learned what Elvis performances require. This tension between space and response defines much of early June.

Elvis travels with Scotty Moore and Bill Black, the same tight unit that has been refining the act night after night. There is no excess personnel. No buffer between performance and coordination. Bob Neal manages bookings, money, and disputes, often simultaneously. The operation remains lean because it has to be.

Transportation remains the pink-and-white 1954 Cadillac Elvis picked up after the Lincoln was wrecked - a workable tour car, but still one hard mile away from trouble.

### LUBBOCK, TEXAS JUNE 3

Two nights later, on June 3rd, the tour reaches Lubbock, Texas, where the schedule tightens more. Elvis performs twice in the same evening, first at Johnson-Connelley Pontiac, then later at Fair Park Coliseum.

One of the boys in that Lubbock showroom crowd is Mac Davis, just fourteen, watching close enough to remember it for decades. He would later talk about seeing Elvis up close in that car-dealer setting, the kind of afternoon performance that should have felt small but didn't. It felt like the future pressed into a single room. It is an odd, perfect chain: a teenager taking mental notes at a Pontiac showroom who will later write songs Elvis himself would record. Some Elvis greatest hits in the 60's and 70's would be penned by Mac. "In the Ghetto" "Memories" "Don't Cry Daddy". I would attend Mac Davis Hall of fame induction in Nashville, with my Manager Merle Kilgore in 2000. I asked him what his favorite song he wrote that was recorded and he told me "Memories"  It was a fleeting meeting, as everyone was clamoring for pictures, but I was content to hang out with Garth Brooks most of the evening, being given the job of shadowing him by Bart Herbison, the executive director of NSAI.

The trade world is taking notice too. In Billboard, record-shop owner Cecil Holifield reports that Elvis's singles are moving so fast in his stores that they beat any individual artist he's seen across eight years in the business, four Sun sides behaving like a single rolling wave of vinyl. That matters because it's not fan language. It's inventory language. It is the sound of demand becoming measurable. Money being spent.

He continues to not just do one show a day, but often multiple. Many performances in a single night require discipline. Energy has to be rationed. Vocal strain can't be indulged. The band adjusts accordingly. Sets are paced deliberately. The goal is consistency, not spectacle. He has been on the road for nearly 150 days in 1955 alone, not to count 1954.

Lubbock reinforces a pattern that has become familiar by mid-1955: once Elvis is announced, the crowd behaves as if the event belongs to them. Not to the town. Not to the artists. Not to their parents, but to them and them alone. As usual the anticipation builds before arrival. The sustained screaming doesn't need prompting.

These are not polite audiences. They are not disorderly, but they move so quickly, and the room's stature figures are often a step behind. Show planners start to notice that Elvis shows require different planning than standard country bookings.

That observation will matter later.

### SHREVEPORT JUNE 4

On Saturday, June 4, Elvis returns to Shreveport, Louisiana, for his regular appearance on the Louisiana Hayride, radio broadcast from the Municipal Auditorium.

Elvis is, by this point, a reliable presence on the program. The audience expects him. Radio listeners across the region expect him too. The attendees expectation builds instead of easing.

The performance follows the now-established pattern: a crowd-controlled opening, measured escalation, sustained intensity. Screaming arrives early. Movement spreads quickly. The listeners behaves as though they know the sequence.

For Colonel Tom Parker, these appearances carry increasing importance. Regular radio broadcast exposure under scrutiny demonstrates repeatability. Elvis isn't simply generating reaction he is sustaining it. That distinction matters for power.

For Bob Neal, the Hayride anchors the week. It justifies the grind that surrounds it. It makes the smaller weekday bookings defensible.

For Elvis, the Hayride isn't a destination. It is a checkpoint that Elvis keeps returning to again and again. A home base.

### THE ROAD BETWEEN

The distance between Shreveport and the next run of dates is covered quickly, with little rest. Long hours behind the wheel pass the time. Meals are quick. Sleep is fragmented at best.

Fatigue registers subtly. His voice may take longer to warm. Recovery between nights shortens.

Family contact continues at a distance. Gladys Presley worries, though that worry travels through phone calls instead of proximity. Vernon Presley remains involved where he can, but the scale of movement increasingly limits any practical oversight he may have been able to contribute.

Faith remains personal and compressed. Elvis still carries gospel music with him, but the pace leaves little room for formal observance. Belief becomes something internal, folded into quiet moments rather than scheduled rituals.

### HOPE, ARKANSAS JUNE 5

On June 5th, Elvis performs at Fair Park Coliseum in Hope, Arkansas, and returns to an indoor town hall with clear limits. Hope is close enough to the site of the car fire that the incident remains fresh in memory, especially for the band. The road between Texarkana and Hope isn't abstract geography. It now holds a heavy memory.

The Coliseum fills quickly. Teenagers press forward early. Adults position themselves along the edges. The crowd's bodily reaction is familiar now, but familiarity has not dulled intensity. If anything, it has made it more efficient.

Elvis adjusts accordingly. He spaces songs deliberately. He allows reaction to crest and settle before moving on. The band keeps transitions tight. These are learned skills, developed night after crowd pressure in lieu of in rehearsal rooms.

Bob Neal spends much of the evening handling expectations offstage calming show planners, coordinating schedules, and making sure the next run of dates remains intact. Reliability is becoming currency. One missed show would ripple through the circuit. That night the tour is nearly permanently derailed.

After the show Elvis slips away toward Texarkana with a local girl, chasing a few hours of normal in the middle of the noise. Scotty and Bill ride with friends. A little while into the drive the brake linings on Elvis Presley's pink-and-white 1954 Cadillac ignite. The smell comes first, then smoke, then heat rises through the floor and wheel wells. They pull over, get clear, and the car is lost.

No one is injured. That fact matters. But it isn't immediately comforting.

For a small touring unit, the car isn't just transportation. It carries instruments, amplifiers, clothing, money, and the means to reach the next job. Had the fire spread faster had it reached the fuel, had it ignited while driving at speed the consequences could have been far more serious. The margin between hassle and catastrophe is thin on a road like this.

The band understands that instantly. So does Elvis.

The loss of the Cadillac is sudden and complete. There is no spare vehicle waiting. There is no insurance plan that resolves things cleanly. What exists is the next booking advertised, and the knowledge that failure to arrive changes how show planners talk.

For Gladys Presley, the news lands differently. Distance magnifies fear. A car fire isn't a colorful anecdote when your son lives on the road and drives himself through the night. It confirms what she has felt; that the work is dangerous in more ways than one. First the girls storming the stage and now this.

Among the band, the incident lingers. Gear could have been lost. Lives could have been lost. The road has made its first serious claim, and it doesn't feel symbolic in the moment. It feels ominous.

Later, the story will soften in their memories. It will be told with bravado, sometimes even as a way to draw sympathy. But standing on the shoulder of the road watching the car burn, there isn't anything amusing about it.

The tour does not pause.

In the aftermath, they keep moving any way they can. Scotty doubles back toward Memphis to retrieve the pink-and-white Ford Crown Victoria Elvis had bought for his parents, while Elvis and Bill fly ahead to keep the Texas bookings on track. The true replacement comes later: in early July, Elvis buys a pink 1955 Cadillac Fleetwood Sixty with a black top to replace the car that burned.

The tour continues but now everyone involved understands something new.

The road doesn't forgive.

### SWEETWATER, TEXAS JUNE 8

The middle of the week exposes how little margin exists in the schedule.

Behind the scenes, the record business is circling. MGM Records even telegrams Sam Phillips to ask about Elvis's contract status, a blunt inquiry that tells you how loudly the live reports are traveling. Sun is small, but Elvis isn't. By June, Phillips is fielding multiple offers.

Sweetwater's June 8ths booking appears to have gone on at City Auditorium. A telegram from MGM that day even notes strong attendance - one more sign that the draw is widening beyond the usual circuits.

After Sweetwater, the documentation blurs for a beat. Some sources place an Andrews, Texas appearance around this slot, often listed as either June 7th or June 9th, but the next firmly dated stop is in Breckenridge on June 10th.

## BRECKENRIDGE, TEXAS JUNE 10

On June 10th, Elvis plays the American Legion Hall in Breckenridge, Texas, a room built for meetings, and dances, not the kind of crowd now following him. The hall fills fast. The seats press close. Adults try to keep order, but they're making it up as they go because the building isn't built for what's happening.

The performance succeeds, but it underscores a growing mismatch between what Elvis's shows now demand and what most local venues can safely provide. This mismatch has not yet produced crisis, but it is visible to anyone paying attention.

## THE PEOPLE AROUND HIM

Throughout this stretch, the small circle around Elvis carries more responsibility. Every night gets bigger, and there's less room for mistakes.

Bob Neal smooths frictions created by cancellations and rescheduling while keeping the broader circuit intact. His role remains operational, not visionary, but it is very essential.

Colonel Parker remains close enough to observe patterns without being embedded in every decision. He watches how crowds behave when expectations are delayed, how quickly reaction regenerates, and how disruption affects that value. These observations will matter in later negotiations.

Family contact remains strained by distance. Gladys Presley's concern deepens as the pace accelerates. News of the car fire has not faded yet, and the reality of steady travel offers little reassurance. Vernon Presley continues to handle what he can, though the speed of the operation leaves him increasingly reactive rather than proactive.

Religion remains present but compressed. Elvis still carries gospel music with him, often replayed privately rather than performed publicly. Faith isn't structured by routine. It survives in moments.

Romantic relationships remain peripheral. Time and exhaustion limit intimacy. Nothing in this stretch stabilizes that part of his life. It becomes a sacrifice.

By June, audiences don't need to be instructed on how to respond to Elvis. They arrive knowing what they want and how to express it. They have hearing his voice on the radio and playing the records put out by Sun.

June 11th, 1955, Elvis Presley returns to Shreveport, Louisiana, for his regular appearance on the Louisiana Hayride, radio broadcast from the Municipal Auditorium. That night he performed "That's Alright Mama" and teenage girls screamed loud enough to disrupt the broadcast.

Around this period Hayride producer Horace Logan began to instruct Elvis to stand still to try to manage the chaos that was occurring.

**MISSISSIPPI JUNE 14-15**

Following the Hayride, the tour moves into Mississippi, where Elvis plays high school gymnasiums first in Bruce and then in Belden. These venues are familiar and unforgiving. Gyms are built for assemblies and basketball games, not tightly packed crowds pressing toward a shallow stage.

By this point in June, the audience arrives with a working idea of what an Elvis show feels like. Teenagers gather early and push close to the stage. Adults arrive alert, not just curious. The authority figures, principals, teachers, local organizers, stand ready, but they don't have a playbook for the reaction Elvis now brings.

Local DJ Bobby Ritter would later remember the practical chaos of Belden: the crush at the doors was so tight that to get inside, people had to squeeze through like they were slipping between ribcages. In his telling, Elvis's stage clothes were even held together with a safety pin during the performance, a small, human detail that undercuts the legend and makes it more real. This is still a working act, stitched together on the fly, even while the crowd is treating it like a miracle.

Bruce and Belden carry the old school-gym logic, but with a sharper edge. These aren't just concerts. They're senior-class fundraisers, with the profit meant to push the Class of 1956 toward a Washington, D.C. Trip. Elvis shares the bill with local names, and the night turns a town event with teenage electricity inside it. The money is for a class goal. The memory is for a lifetime.

The performances are successful, and it is evident for all who attended that the crowds instinct was to rush the stage the first chance they could get. But Elvis manages it with pacing rather than escalation, allowing reaction to rise, and fall in lieu of build unchecked. These decisions are not stylistic flourishes. They are practical necessities learned through routine. They don't need another crush of a crowd like what happened in Florida.

### AUTHORITY AND RESPONSE

The Mississippi shows underline a growing reality: the crowd is changing faster than the adults running the room can adjust. The old rules still exist, but they're starting to lag behind what the audience is ready to do.

Local officials are not hostile to Elvis. They are just unprepared for what his shows bring, and it puts them all on edge. The rules they rely on; clear aisles, seated audiences, orderly applause doesn't seem to apply to a show that Elvis is in. Elvis himself does not incite chaos, but he draws a collective response that existing setups can't fully contain.

This isn't yet a crisis. But it is a visible issue. Venue managers and show organizers start speaking about it. Crowd size matters less than the audience behavior. Control becomes a consideration alongside ticket sales.

Bob Neal absorbs much of this tension behind the scenes, negotiating with hall operators and calming concerns. His role remains stable, at least to his awareness.

Parker observes. He does not intervene directly, but he notes where friction appears and how it resolves. These observations feed his larger calculations.

### TRAVEL AND FATIGUE

Travel between Mississippi dates remains relentless. The new 1955 Cadillac Fleetwood continues to log heavy mileage immediately after being purchased. There is no lull after the car fire. The replacement vehicle is functioning as a workhorse already by mid-month.

Fatigue accumulates. Elvis's voice requires more careful warm-up as he is in his 6th straight month of touring.

Family contact remains limited. Elvis calls his mother every chance he gets. Gladys Presley's concern deepens with distance and news that never fully reassures her.

Religion remains a part of Elvis' character. Faith functions as grounding Elvis to his roots rather than being ritual.

Romantic relationships remain secondary.

The Mississippi gym shows highlight the contrast between that broader culture and the live environments Elvis now occupies. The fans don't seek closure. They seek release. Release from restrictions. Release from societal boundaries. That difference becomes sharper as the month progresses.

### STAMFORD, TEXAS JUNE 16

On June 16, the tour reaches Stamford, Texas, where Elvis performs at a high school auditorium a space structurally similar to earlier venues, but now facing a different level of demand. The hall fills quickly. Teenagers position themselves close to the stage. Adults cluster along the edges, alert, and watchful.

The surge of noise starts early. It doesn't need to be encouraged. Elvis recognizes this and teases the crowd, while keeping them under control rather than provoking them. The objective is to keep the show intact from start to finish.

This isn't caution born of fear. It is professionalism added through experience. Elvis has learned that sustaining reaction is more useful than igniting it recklessly. He is learning how to pull them in and then let them go. Just enough excitement and then a release.

For Parker, these mid-sized Texas shows offer something clearer than raw excitement: audience consistency. Elvis produces the same response across different rooms, different nights, and different audiences. He is constantly being given proof that Elvis is different then any other artist that came before.

### DALLAS SPORTATORIUM JUNE 17-18

The shift turns unmistakable on June 17 and 18, when Elvis appears at the Dallas Sportatorium as part of the Big D Jamboree. This isn't a local event or a local booking. The Sportatorium is a known hall, accustomed to wrestling crowds, and large-scale events. It is built to handle volume and movement.

The crowd reflects that. Attendance is heavier. The audience is mixed teenagers, young adults, and curious older listeners drawn by reputation rather than something new. Reaction arrives quickly, but it spreads differently in a larger room. Noise becomes sustained as an alternative to explosive. Movement ripples in lieu of surges.

Elvis adjusts without hesitation. He fills the building without overdriving it. The band plays with confidence shaped by weeks of routine. The act scales upward without losing cohesion.

For Colonel Tom Parker, the Sportatorium appearances confirm something he has been tracking. Elvis can command a large room without losing crowd control of it. This isn't simply popularity. It is adaptability.

Around this same time, Parker puts his impatience into letters. Writing to Tom Diskin, he complains that Neal still can't handle Elvis the way the moment requires. He insists that building in unfamiliar territory takes patience and skill, not luck. His conclusion is cold and instructive: go slow, watch Neal, and watch what Neal does with Elvis.

He writes Neal as well, in the language of a man measuring loyalty like money. When the summer pushes Elvis into bigger rooms, Parker suggests Neal will have to prove his worth. The sentence sounds like business, but it carries something personal inside it: Parker isn't just trying to book

Elvis. He is trying to control the acceleration, so he can control the destination.

Bob Neal, meanwhile, focuses on execution making sure shows get booked, payments are cleared, and the next sequence of dates remains viable.

### THE COST IS RISING

It is around this time that Neal also makes the trip to Parker's headquarters in Madison, Tennessee, the talk he has been circling for months. It doesn't remove Neal from Elvis's daily life. It reshapes the chain above him. Neal remains the manager in practice, the man handling schedules, payments and damage control, but Parker starts positioning himself as the architect of the next leap, the one aimed straight at getting Elvis off Sun and into a major-label world. June is where the handshake turns into a setup.

June 19th, 1955, at Magnolia Gardens in Houston, Texas, pushes Elvis Presley into a stretch where endurance matters as much as talent.

The tour moves back into Houston, Texas, a city big enough to take repeated exposure without burning out its curiosity. Houston isn't a one-night market. It is a place where radio, word of mouth, and live appearances feed one another over days instead of hours. That changes how a performer is received, and it changes how mistakes echo back. Houston had a population of over 600,000 so there were plenty of new fans to be won over.

The crowd is heavy and mixed, and it comes in less tentative now. Teenagers still drive the noise, but adults stay longer, watching instead of drifting toward the exits. Elvis adjusts by tightening transitions and keeping the set lean. The goal is to leave the audience hungry, not to push them until the night turns ugly.

By this point, the act doesn't warm up onstage. Warm-up happens off to the side, fast, and intentional. They get on stage, set it on fire, and then get off.

### BEAUMONT, TEXAS -MULTIPLE SHOW NIGHTS

From Houston, the tour moves into Beaumont, Texas, where the breakneck schedule continues. Two and sometimes three performances in a single night become normal.

Multiple shows per night is a challenge for anyone, Elvis included. Reaction must be kept under control, or it would ruin the next shows. Energy must reset quickly. There is no emotional recovery between audiences, only minutes.

Elvis handles this by narrowing focus. He does not attempt to escalate each set beyond the last. He delivers consistency. The band follows, maintaining tempo, even as fatigue accumulates between all three of them. It is summer. In Texas. That will exhaust you.

These nights are physically demanding. Sweat accumulates. Clothing is changed quickly. Food is taken where it can be found. Sleep is deferred.

Yet the shows succeed. The crowd responds each time as if the performance belongs only to them. That illusion of singular experience repeated endlessly is part of what starts to separate Elvis from other touring acts.

Beaumont isn't casual success. The city auditorium seats roughly 2,400, and the run fills again, and again, five shows in the stretch, each one packed. That routine is the point. Anybody can spike a single night. Beaumont proves Elvis can hold demand across many performances without the demand cooling.

From Beaumont, Neal wires Parker with the kind of update that reads like a siren: the rooms are full. The money is real, and the question isn't whether Elvis is rising, but how fast. Neal even invites RCA's Steve Sholes to make a bid for Elvis, to handle the singer not as a local curiosity, but as an acquisition. June doesn't announce a deal to the world, but it announces that the conversation has become unavoidable.

Bob Neal manages logistics relentlessly. Payments are handled between sets. Schedules are adjusted on the fly. Arguments are smoothed quickly. There is no room for prolonged dispute when the next audience is waiting outside.

## THE PEOPLE AROUND HIM

By mid-week, the small circle around Elvis functions less like companions and more like a crew.

Scotty Moore and Bill Black conserve energy deliberately. Playing turns economical instead of expressive. Precision replaces flourish. This isn't artistic retreat. It is survival.

Colonel Parker remains close but not intrusive. He watches how Elvis performs under pressure and routine, how audiences behave when given multiple shows to respond, and how show planners react to sustained demand rather than small spikes.

Some trade listings even place Elvis in Vernon, Texas, on June 22, though supporting documentation is thin. That uncertainty is part of how 1955 survives on paper: the schedule moves faster than record-keeping at the time did.

### LAWTON, OKLAHOMA JUNE 23

On June 23, Elvis performs in Lawton, Oklahoma, marking the end of one of the most demanding stretches of the month. The hall is smaller than Houston or Beaumont, but the surge of the crowd doesn't diminish with size. If anything, the crowd arrives sharper, primed by his reputation in in spite of a lack of big city advertising.

By now, Elvis does not need to announce himself. His name travels ahead of his arrival. Audiences show up prepared to respond. The performance becomes less about introduction to Elvis and more about the fulfillment of their fantasies.

## PROFESSIONALISM UNDER PRESSURE

What distinguishes this stretch isn't spectacle. It is reliability.

Elvis appears on time. He delivers consistently. He absorbs exhaustion without visible fall apart.

That reliability changes how industry figures talk. Not in grand declarations, but in tone. Elvis isn't discussed as a promising act. He is discussed as a working one capable of sustaining demand without unraveling. We are nearing 6 straight months of doing music and Elvis is growing stronger.

This matters.

By June 23, the grind has settled into a pattern.

June 24, 1955, Elvis Presley heads back into Oklahoma, starting in Altus. It is a town that has seen touring acts before, but it isn't ready for the kind of reaction that follows him now. The room is small. The house isn't. Teenagers show up hours early and press close to the front. Adults hang back along the walls curious and watching with that careful look people get when they realize this isn't going to behave like a normal set.

The performance stays under control because Elvis keeps it that way. He doesn't push the room harder than it can handle. He lets the excitement rise, then lets it settle, then moves on. By late June, that choice isn't something he has to think about. It is instinct. It comes from repeating the same kind of night so many times that the body learns what works before the mind explains it. This doesn't meant eh crowds don't explode or scream and tear their hair out, they do. But Elvis learns to settle them down before it becomes a riot.

The 1955 Cadillac Fleetwood keeps swallowing miles like it is built for it. The "new car" feeling is long gone, even after one month. All the dust builds up from the thousands of miles of Texas and Oklahoma roads. It is just a car now, another tool. Travel is still overnight. Meals happen whenever they can. Sleep gets squeezed into whatever hours are left between one town and the next.

### Return to Shreveport

By June 25, Elvis is back in Shreveport for another Louisiana Hayride appearance. The radio broadcast is the steady point in a month that keeps sliding forward. For listeners across the region, it is a regular appointment. For Elvis, it is routine he can count on, a show he looks forward to. A reunion of sorts.

The performance meets expectations without trying to top them. The reaction is strong, but familiar. Screaming starts early. Movement follows. The room behaves the way it has learned to behave, only it reacts stronger each time.

Colonel Parker watches more than he steps in. What he is paying attention to now isn't only popularity. It is whether this pace can last. Elvis is deep into a cycle that keeps repeating, and it has not broken him yet.

Bob Neal stays focused on the practical work. The schedule is holding. Payments are getting made. Show planners want him back. Those facts matter more than excitement, because they are what keep the whole machine moving. Bob Neal is realistic about this.

### THE GULF COAST LATE JUNE

The final days of the month move Elvis toward the Gulf Coast, with performances in Biloxi, Mississippi, and Mobile, Alabama. These towns introduce different audiences military personnel, tourists, and locals accustomed to transient entertainment. Reaction remains strong, but it manifests differently. Crowds are broader, less concentrated, but no less responsive.

Biloxi is a different kind of test because the room itself is trying to be modern. The Slavonian Lodge, newly air-conditioned, opens its doors to a sellout, and Elvis, Scotty, and Bill are booked as the draw that makes the upgrade feel worth it. Comfort does not tame the reaction. If anything, it keeps people inside longer.

The next nights move onto the Airman's Club at Keesler Air Force Base, and this is where a name enters the Elvis story that will echo later: June Juanico. She attends with a friend who has already seen the act, and later memories say Elvis notices her in the crowd, calls her out, and spends the rest of the evening with her. The take for the Biloxi stretch is reported at $600 for three nights, a clean number that hides how hard those nights are on a voice. Some accounts even place Gladys at Keesler for at least one show. The kind of mother-presence that's less celebration than reassurance.

The month closes in Mobile with two more nights at Curtis Gordon's Radio Ranch, playing alongside Gordon's Radio Ranch Boys. It is the same grind in a different climate: humid air, close rooms, and an audience that has learned the pattern: arrive early, push forward, and demand the moment in person.

The venues vary. Some are better prepared than others. None are fully designed for the kind of reaction Elvis now generates. Adults do what they can. Control is improvised, not planned.

Elvis continues to handle the pacing of the show carefully. By this point, he has learned that sustaining reaction across a set is more effective than igniting it repeatedly.

As June closes, the circle around Elvis has narrowed functionally even as it has widened socially.

Bob Neal remains indispensable, handling planning and smoothing friction. His role has grown heavier, though it remains largely invisible to audiences.

Colonel Parker's presence carries more weight. He hasn't reshaped the operation yet, but his influence shows up in conversations and plans.

Future opportunities aren't hypothetical. They're getting close.

July waits without offering relief.

## June 1955 Radio, Film, and Cultural Environment

June's soundtrack is a tug-of-war: the clean, smiling songs up front, and the harder, funnier, hungrier ones that actually move bodies in the back of the room. Black artists are shaping the feel of 1955 right then, rhythms that don't ask permission. Lyrics that don't apologize: "Bo Diddley", Bo Diddley, "Don't Be Angry", Nappy Brown, "Every Day I Have the Blues", Count Basie Orchestra with Joe Williams, "Sincerely", The Moonglows, and "Feel So Good", Shirley & Lee. As Elvis keeps showing up on package bills, that energy gets carried into bigger whiter rooms, same beat, different faces in the seats.

By June 1955, American popular culture sits in a tense middle space. The old systems still crowd control distribution radio playlists, studio contracts, film exhibition but the listeners has started to behave independently of those systems. Teenagers are not waiting for permission. They are responding where they stand.

Radio in June doesn't sound revolutionary. It still sounds crowd controlled. Ballads dominate daytime rotation. Rhythm 45s circulate after dark or on select local programs. What changes this month isn't what stations play, it is how listeners react when Elvis steps onto a stage carrying a sound that radio has not yet fully absorbed.

Stations across the South and Southwest continue to rely on late-1954 and early-1955 hits still heavy in rotation, rather than brand-new chart climbers. These are the songs audiences are arriving with in their ears:

"Sixteen Tons", Tennessee Ernie Ford Still a dominant presence on AM radio. Its restraint and fatalism stand in sharp contrast to the very strong reaction Elvis generates live.

"Hearts of Stone", The Fontane Sisters Often heard on daytime programming, especially on stations favoring clean vocal harmony.

"Earth Angel", The Penguins Heavy local airplay continues into June, especially at night. Its emotional directness resonates with the same teenage audience now attending Elvis shows.

"Sincerely", The McGuire Sisters Still widely played, reinforcing the polish-and-crowd control model that governs mainstream radio.

"Speedoo", The Cadillacs Common on R&B-friendly stations and jukeboxes, reflecting a parallel youth culture not yet integrated into national programming.

These songs are not weak 45s. They represent the standard of mid-1955 radio: emotionally held back, vocally centered, and structurally predictable.

Elvis's live performances run into with that standard rather than extending it.

*Disc Jockeys and Regional Influence*

By June, local DJs matter more than national charts in shaping audience behavior. Stations in Shreveport, Dallas, Houston, and along the Gulf Coast increasingly handle Elvis as a known quantity instead of a something new.

Louisiana Hayride broadcasters continue to give Elvis sustained exposure, reinforcing familiarity across state lines.

Independent DJs in Texas and Mississippi introduce Elvis records in rotation without framing them as novelties, allowing audience reaction to build organically.

Nighttime programming remains crucial. Elvis's strongest resonance aligns with the same hours that R&B records circulate most freely.

The result is an unusual feedback loop: radio familiarity fuels live reaction, and live reaction feeds demand for more radio exposure without formal industry coordination yet catching up.

### Film Culture June 1955

American movie theaters in June 1955 remain spaces of crowd control, polish, and narrative containment. The films audiences are actually seeing reinforce emotional distance and orderly resolution values increasingly at odds with the live, bodily response Elvis Presley is already provoking onstage.

Among the films in U. S. Theatrical release during June 1955:

The Seven Year Itch Released June 3, 1955. A major Marilyn Monroe vehicle that frames sexuality as fantasy and flirtation held back, comedic, and safely resolved. Desire is suggested, not acted upon, and always kept within social boundaries.

Love Me or Leave Me Released June 1955. A musical biopic centered on discipline, ambition, and consequences. Performance is shown as work governed by the hall's stature, contracts, and setup.

Bad Day at Black Rock Released May 1955 and still widely playing through June. A tense, crowd-controlled drama emphasizing moral reckoning and restraint. Conflict is internalized and resolved through confrontation in lieu of release.

Strategic Air Command Released April 1955, still in broad circulation. A prestige picture emphasizing duty, pecking order, and hierarchy values strongly aligned with adult the hall's legitimacy and institutional crowd control.

East of Eden Released April 1955 and continuing strong box office play into June. James Dean's performance introduces youthful tension and emotional volatility but still frames it within narrative consequence and cinematic distance.

Teenage Culture Mid-Year Shift

By June, teenage culture has moved decisively ahead of adult permission.

High school gyms and auditoriums now function as testing grounds, not scene centers.

Movement starts before music fully settles.

Screaming is not spontaneous. It is anticipated.

Authority isn't challenged head-on. It gets stepped around. The kids don't argue with the rules. They act like the rules aren't there.

Elvis does not instruct it, but he does triggers it.

**FULL KNOWN JUNE 1955 PERFORMANCE RECORD**

June 1, Wednesday,: High School Auditorium, Guymon, Oklahoma.

June 2 (Thursday): City Auditorium, Amarillo, Texas.

June 3, Friday,: Johnson-Connelley Pontiac Showroom, Lubbock, Texas. Fair Park Coliseum, Lubbock, Texas, 8:00 p.m.,.

June 4, Saturday,: Louisiana Hayride, Municipal Auditorium, Shreveport, Louisiana.

June 5, Sunday,: Hope Fair Park, Hope, Arkansas.

June 8 (Wednesday): Auditorium, Sweetwater, Texas.

June 10, Friday,: American Legion Hall, Breckenridge, Texas.

June 11, Saturday,: Louisiana Hayride, Municipal Auditorium, Shreveport, Louisiana.

June 14, Tuesday,: Bruce High School Gym, Bruce, Mississippi.

June 15, Wednesday,: Belden High School Gym, Belden, Mississippi.

June 17, Friday,: Roundup Hall, High School Gym, Stamford, Texas.

June 18, Saturday,: The Big "D" Jamboree, Sportatorium, Dallas, Texas.

June 19 (Sunday): Magnolia Gardens, Houston, Texas.

June 20, Monday,: City Auditorium, Beaumont, Texas, 7:00 and 9:00 p.m.,.

June 21, Tuesday,: City Auditorium, Beaumont, Texas, 2:30, 7:00, and 9:00 p.m.,.

June 23, Thursday,: McMahon Memorial Auditorium, Lawton, Oklahoma, 8:00 p.m.,. Southern Club, Lawton, Oklahoma, 11:00 p.m.,.

June 24 (Friday): Altus, Oklahoma.

June 25, Saturday,: Louisiana Hayride, Municipal Auditorium, Shreveport, Louisiana.

June 26 (Sunday): Slavonian Lodge, Biloxi, Mississippi.

June 27, Monday,: Airman's Club, Keesler Air Force Base, outside Biloxi, Mississippi.

June 28, Tuesday,: Airman's Club, Keesler Air Force Base, outside Biloxi, Mississippi.

June 29, Wednesday,: Curtis Gordon's Radio Ranch, Mobile, Alabama.

June 30, Thursday,: Curtis Gordon's Radio Ranch, Mobile, Alabama.

# Chapter 7, July 1955

By July 1955, the American South settles into a summer pattern that has nothing to do with romance or tidy storylines. The heat is not background scenery. It is the condition under which everything happens in the world Elvis is living in. It shapes how crowds gather, how long they remain, and how quickly patience thins. In dance halls and armories, it clings to uniforms, cotton dresses, and worn guitar straps. It gives new buildings an old scent. It frays tempers. And when applause finally lifts into the air, it is earned rather than automatic.

And it makes music matter differently.

On July 11, Sun Records captured one of the year's defining pairings. "Mystery Train," drawn from Junior Parker's blues recording, and "I Forgot to Remember to Forget," written by Stan Kesler and Charlie Feathers. The session joined something rooted and something forward-looking. The band struck the rhythm steady and insistent, and Elvis sang with restraint that made the heartbreak sound older than his years. Sam Phillips later said of "Mystery Train" that it had "a strange, almost haunting quality," and that Elvis understood how to carry that mood without overselling it.

If March was the month when his value became clear, when Elvis shifted from being noticed to being debated, then July is when that debate spreads outward into places that do not follow the same customs. The shows are no longer limited to towns shaped by Saturday night country or weekly radio jamborees. July carries him into a wider mix of small-town halls, open fields, and Florida auditoriums. Onto package bills where a crowd may arrive for another headliner and leave speaking about the young man who closed the program.

This is not a month with one tidy narrative. It is a month of shifting conditions. Spiritual, physical, and cultural currents crossing the same calendar.

Baton Rouge: Proximity and the heat of the first night

On July 1, Elvis opens the month at the Plaquemine Casino Club in Baton Rouge, Louisiana.

A casino club in 1955 is not Las Vegas. There is no spectacle. It is an adult night spot built for close quarters. Tables nearly touch. Aisles are narrow. Conversations overlap. It is a space where people notice one another. No one fades into the background. You are visible.

Baton Rouge carries its own sense of rank. As Louisiana's capital, it lives within layers of civic awareness. Not everyone is political, but the city is accustomed to structure and order. Even leisure carries a sense of measure. A performer who unsettles a Baton Rouge audience risks more than a complaint. He risks a story that travels through the local social network by morning.

Elvis enters that building with a divided reputation.

Teenagers respond to him as ignition. Adults respond with reserve. In a club like Plaquemine, those audiences sit within sight of one another. They observe each other's reactions. They measure themselves against what they are seeing.

So the atmosphere of the night carries weight.

Elvis does not attempt to overwhelm the space. He works within it. The set unfolds rather than bursts. He follows the approach he has learned in conservative venues. Gain acceptance first. Then increase intensity. Not through apology. Not through dilution. Through control and awareness of sequence.

A crowd that begins in evaluation ends in involvement. That is the method he continues refining in 1955. He does not require unanimous approval. He requires enough interest that reluctance loses its authority.

By the close of July 1, the club has changed. Applause arrives in uneven waves. The front tables respond openly. Toward the rear, quieter faces remain attentive, aware that what unsettles them also holds attention.

Shreveport: The Hayride as checkpoint

On July 2, Elvis returns to Municipal Auditorium in Shreveport for the Louisiana Hayride.

The Hayride is more than a broadcast. By 1955, it functions as an ecosystem. A weekly gathering that trains audiences to recognize emerging performers and grants touring acts legitimacy beyond a single booking. The Library of Congress maintains an archive of Louisiana Hayride materials, including photographs and documentation of Elvis's appearances on that stage.

By July, Elvis's connection to the Hayride is no longer a simple story of opportunity. Each appearance serves as confirmation. Reaction is measured against previous weeks. Management can point and state clearly that this response repeats.

Shreveport in mid-summer carries familiarity. The audience has already seen him. They arrive anticipating a response. They do not only watch Elvis. They watch one another watching him. That circular awareness multiplies the effect. Teenagers react to him and to each other's reaction at the same time.

The Hayride audience remains mixed. Families and older listeners maintain loyalty to established country tradition. Younger listeners approach the evening differently. For a few hours, Municipal Auditorium becomes a civic vessel holding two versions of America. One that prefers order. One that welcomes release.

Elvis does not attempt to reconcile those impulses. He operates within them.

That same weekend, Cash Box reports that country disc jockeys have voted Elvis Presley the number one "Up-and-Coming Male Vocalist." The language is formal. The implication is direct. The response is not confined to one region.

Corpus Christi: The Gulf and movement

On July 3, Elvis performs at the Hoedown Club in Corpus Christi, Texas.

Corpus Christi is shaped by flow. Sailors, refinery crews, oil workers, and tourists pass through. The audience is less supervised than inland towns. Fewer parents. Less formality. The dance culture is direct. In a place like the Hoedown Club, music answers one question. Does it move the floor?

Elvis fits that standard. Even before the label "rock and roll" settles into common speech, his performance leans forward. It invites physical response.

In a Gulf city in July, restlessness already hangs in the air. Elvis does not manufacture that mood. He directs it.

July 4: Stephenville, De Leon, Brownwood

July 4, 1955 is not a single engagement. It is a chain of appearances. Daytime Gospel All Day Picnic programs in Stephenville and De Leon, followed by an evening show in Brownwood at 8:00 p.m.

The schedule reveals range. Elvis is not confined to one identity. His gospel foundation remains active and visible.

Stephenville, 10:00 a.m.

The morning begins at Stephenville Recreation Hall. The format resembles a rotating bill rather than a headlining concert.

Stephenville sits in ranch and farm country. The Recreation Hall functions as a community meeting place. Attendees gather to sit, eat, and sing hymns they already know. This is fellowship, not spectacle.

Within that context, Elvis is familiar rather than controversial. A young man formed by the same Southern church harmonies as the rest of the program.

De Leon, Hodges Park

The afternoon continues at Hodges Park in De Leon. Accounts describe performers rotating between towns to keep the program active across multiple stops.

Gospel promoter W. D. Nowlin anchors the day. Two of Elvis's preferred quartets, The Statesmen Quartet and The Blackwood Brothers, help define the atmosphere. Some recollections suggest Elvis performs only gospel in De Leon. Reaction is described as respectful, perhaps reserved.

If accurate, that choice speaks clearly. Even as his broader profile expands, gospel remains central. In mid 1955, sacred and secular versions of Elvis exist without division.

Brownwood, 8:00 p.m.

The day concludes at Memorial Hall in Brownwood. The setting shifts from open park to indoor evening audience.

He shares the bill with Slim Willet, widely known for writing "Don't Let the Stars Get in Your Eyes," and the Farren Twins. The structure of the program follows established order. Elvis does not erase that order. He alters the response within it.

After hours of gospel under daylight, the evening gathers a different atmosphere. Yet the same voice carries through both settings.

Memphis, his home, July 5 to 15

On July 5, Elvis returns to Memphis, his home, for roughly two weeks that appear quiet on paper.

They are not idle.

Jackson Baker later recalled hearing Elvis rehearse "Mystery Train" repeatedly during this period. Adjusting phrasing. Reworking emphasis. Playing the acetate again and again after sessions.

The image is telling. The performer drawing growing crowds sits in Memphis studying his own record closely.

On July 7, Scotty Moore trades his Gibson ES-295 for a Gibson L-5 at O. K. Houck Piano Company. The instrument better suits his Ray Butts Echosonic amplifier. Elvis appears with a new Martin D-28 fitted with a tooled leather back to protect it from belt wear. After losing his previous Cadillac to fire, Elvis purchases a pink 1955 Cadillac Fleetwood Sixty with a black top and removable roof rack.

Then July 11 brings the Sun session.

"I Forgot to Remember to Forget," "Mystery Train," and "Trying to Get to You." Memphis drummer Johnny Bernero participates on all but "Mystery Train." The first two become the next single.

Shreveport, July 16

On July 16, Elvis returns again to the Louisiana Hayride.

That same week, "Baby Let's Play House" appears at number 15 on the Country and Western chart in

Cash Box. For the first time, his name sits visibly on a national chart.

Cape Girardeau, July 20

On July 20, Elvis performs at the Arena Building in Cape Girardeau, Missouri.

A Mississippi River town shaped by commerce and travel. The Arena Building serves as a civic structure for sports and large gatherings. Appearing there signals movement beyond youth-oriented venues.

Wanda Jackson later recalled that Elvis encouraged her to lean into rockabilly rhythm during this period, saying he told her she could "do it as good as any of the boys."

Behind the scenes, Colonel Parker advises Tom Diskin to distribute Presley press materials regionally rather than nationwide to focus booking demand. Parker understands it is not time yet to introduce Elvis to the national audience. It will take a larger label to do this.

Newport, July 21

On July 21, Elvis performs at the Silver Moon Club in Newport, Arkansas.

Clubs require direct command. Reaction is immediate. Stories from a single evening travel quickly.

Minden, July 22

On July 22, Elvis appears at the Joy Drive-In in Minden, Louisiana.

Outdoor performances demand constant attention control. Attendees can remain in cars. Focus must be drawn back repeatedly.

Earlier that day, Colonel Parker, Bob Neal, Hank Snow, and Tom Diskin discuss contract terms by phone. Parker and Snow offer $10,000 to secure Elvis's release from Sun in exchange for 2 percent of royalties. RCA proposes either $12,000 flat or $5,000 plus $20,000 recoupable and a television guarantee within sixty days.

Dallas, July 23

On July 23, Elvis appears at the Big D Jamboree at the Sportatorium in Dallas.

The Sportatorium is built for volume and large turnout. The trio is unchanged. The venue is larger. The exposure is widening.

By July 24, Elvis is formally represented by Colonel Parker and Hank Snow Attractions, with Bob Neal continuing as manager.

Florida Week, July 25 to 31

Elvis joins the Andy Griffith tour package across Florida.

Mae Boren Axton works press coverage. Griffith later remarked in interviews that Elvis's reception "almost stole the show" on certain nights.

Fort Myers, July 25

New City Auditorium hosts the opening Florida date.

The bill includes Ferlin Husky, Marty Robbins, Tommy Collins, Glenn Reeves, and others.

Orlando, July 26 to 27

At Municipal Auditorium, mixed audiences respond strongly. Later accounts recall Griffith acknowledging the strength of the teenage reaction.

Jacksonville, July 28 to 29

Baseball park appearances bring larger attendance.

Daytona Beach, July 30

Two shows at Peabody Auditorium at 7:30 and 9:30.

Tampa, July 31

At Fort Homer Hesterly Armory, two shows at 2:15 and 8:15.

Photographer William S. Randolph captures images later used for Elvis's first album cover.

July 1955: Radio and film

Radio balances polished pop and rhythm-driven recordings.

"Rock Around the Clock" reaches number one. "Learnin' the Blues" remains high. "Cherry Pink and Apple Blossom White," "A Blossom Fell," "Unchained Melody," and Pat Boone's "Ain't That a Shame" circulate widely.

The airwaves present contrast. Elvis is moving through it in person.

The variety is significant. Up tempo rhythm records share space with orchestral pop and crooner ballads. Radio programming reflects coexistence rather than replacement.

Elvis performs within that landscape. Audiences may hear Sinatra or Perez Prado during the day and encounter Elvis live at night. The contrast lies in format. Radio delivers sound at a distance. Live performance presents it in person.

---

## What is playing in theaters

Earlier in 1955, the film Blackboard Jungle introduced Rock Around the Clock in its opening sequence, bringing a rhythm driven record into a mainstream cinematic context.

By July, that association remains familiar. Film culture continues to frame youth themes within structured narratives. Music in theaters is presented within storylines that guide interpretation.

Live performance operates differently. In auditoriums, armories, and ballparks, interpretation happens in real time among audiences. The broader culture in July 1955 reflects multiple formats carrying evolving sounds at once.

## FULL KNOWN JULY 1955
## PERFORMANCE RECORD

July 1, Friday,: Plaquemine Casino Club, Baton Rouge, Louisiana.

July 2, Saturday,: Louisiana Hayride, Municipal Auditorium, Shreveport, Louisiana.

July 3, Sunday,: Hoedown Club, Corpus Christi, Texas, 4:00 to 8:00 p.m.,.

July 4, Monday,: Hodges Park, De Leon, Texas. Recreation Hall, Stephenville, Texas. Memorial Hall, Brownwood, Texas, 8:00 p.m.,.

July 16, Saturday; Louisiana Hayride, Municipal Auditorium, Shreveport, Louisiana.

July 20, Wednesday,: Cape Arena Building, Cape Girardeau, Missouri.

July 21, Thursday,: Silver Moon Club, Newport, Arkansas.

July 23, Saturday,: The Big "D" Jamboree, Sportatorium, Dallas, Texas.

July 25, Monday,: New City Auditorium, Fort Myers, Florida.

July 26 (Tuesday): Municipal Auditorium, Orlando, Florida.

July 27 (Wednesday): Municipal Auditorium, Orlando, Florida.

July 28, Thursday,: The new baseball stadium, Jacksonville, Florida.

July 29, Friday,: The new baseball stadium, Jacksonville, Florida.

July 30, Saturday,: Peabody Auditorium, Daytona Beach, Florida, 7:30 and 9:30 p.m.,.

July 31, Sunday,: Fort Homer Hesterly Armory, Tampa, Florida, 2:15 and 8:15 p.m.,.

# Chapter 8, August 1955

## August 1st, 1955, Tupelo Fairgrounds, Tupelo, MS, The All Star Jamboree

Tupelo is not neutral ground. It is where Elvis was born and where he grew up under the hard weight of poverty and prejudice. In 1955 it is still a small Mississippi city shaped by commerce and church life, a place where family names travel fast and reputations travel faster. A fairgrounds appearance here is not like a big city auditorium. It is a public gathering where you are seen before you are heard. Dust hangs in the air. Fried food drifts through the lanes. The humidity makes people feel closer than they are. This is a homecoming that does not behave like a homecoming, because the hometown already holds a version of Elvis in its mind. They arrive to measure the distance between that boy and the man who steps onto the stage.

Bob Neal's new four day All Star Jamboree package is built around headliner Webb Pierce, with Wanda Jackson, Bud Deckelman, the Miller Sisters, and a young Charlie Feathers, a twenty three year old rockabilly talent recording for Sun's Flip imprint. For Elvis, the symbolism is blunt. This is his first performance in Tupelo since he sang at these same fairgrounds as a ten year old. He is doing it in front of roughly 3,000 people who still feel a personal claim on him.

The All Star Jamboree format is designed to spread attention across the bill, but the crowd's focus shifts early. Teenagers arrive already excited. Adults arrive already cautious. In a hometown, applause can feel like pride, but it can also feel like resistance. A hometown does not always enjoy being surprised by its own success. Elvis is not here to introduce himself. He is here to carry the weight of recognition.

Although he will have immense success with RCA in 1956, it is still Sun in early August 1955 that has released the record carrying him beyond the South. "I Forgot to Remember to Forget," backed with "Mystery Train," moves like mail that cannot be intercepted. It will reach the top of Billboard's country chart in February 1956, making him, for the first time, a nationally known country star and proving that the Sun sound can compete in the wider marketplace. But that time is not here yet, for now Elvis is happy and excited to be on the charts anywhere.

Nationally, the world is also shifting into a new era of observation. August 1st is tied to the first flight of the Lockheed U 2 prototype, a Cold War step toward seeing farther than anyone could before. That same hunger to see, to know, and to get ahead of the story is present in the fairgrounds crowd too.

By August 1955, the idea of Elvis Presley having a long career is still a fragile idea. At this point anything could happen. What exists instead is a path that can be seen, recorded, and increasingly hard to manage. The meaning of August begins not with a contract or a headline, but with geography. When Elvis steps onto a stage in Tupelo that summer, he is not yet returning as a conquering hero or a fully formed star. He is returning as someone in motion, whose reputation is traveling faster than his body, and whose hometown is meeting him again through the lens of growing national curiosity.

Tupelo in August 1955 does not yet understand what it is witnessing. The fairgrounds appearance is not framed as history being made. It is framed as a jamboree date, another stop on a traveling bill. Yet the younger listeners respond with a new urgency. This is not pride alone. It is pride mixed with displacement, the sense that something born locally is already slipping into a wider world.

That matters. Elvis's first truly professional hometown appearance is not about validation. It is about separation. The boy who once stood in these spaces as a spectator now commands them, and the crowd feels both ownership and loss at the same time. That emotional contradiction becomes one of the defining forces of his early rise.

August also marks a shift in how Elvis is seen, not only where he performs. By this point, cameras have started capturing his stage presence with intention. These early filmed moments are rough and limited, far from the polish of later television appearances, but they preserve something crucial. Radio cannot explain the way he moves, or how audiences respond before they fully understand why they are responding. This is not yet cinematic ambition. It is evidence gathering.

It shows a performer whose appeal is not confined to sound. Elvis's impact is multisensory, and it unsettles the neat categories of singer and entertainer. That is why August feels like a threshold month. The culture is beginning to see that Elvis cannot be held to a single channel, not radio alone, not stage alone, and eventually not film alone.

Behind the scenes, August also brings the tightening of forces that have been circling Elvis for months. The growing involvement of Colonel Parker does not arrive as a sudden takeover, but as a response to a demand that now requires stronger management. Parker's early contractual arrangements reflect not just ambition, but urgency. Elvis's schedule is intensifying. Public reactions are escalating. The risk of missteps, financial, legal, or reputational, is rising alongside popularity.

What Parker recognizes, and what August makes unavoidable, is that Elvis has moved beyond the stage where talent alone can guide the path. Structures are being built around him because demand now exceeds improvisation. This does not yet mean the later version of domination. It means an attempt to shape disorder before it overwhelms the operation entirely.

Media attention in August 1955 reflects this same shift. Coverage remains local and cautious, but it is more frequent, more curious, and increasingly alert to controversy. The focus is not yet superstardom. It is behavior. Audience response. Teenage enthusiasm. Adult concern. Elvis is becoming news not just for what he sings, but for what happens when he sings.

That distinction is crucial. It marks the moment when success stops being measured only by applause and starts being measured by impact. How crowds change. How venues change. How expectations change.

By the end of August 1955, nothing is settled, not contracts, not media narratives, not long term plans. But the direction is unmistakable. Elvis has crossed from something new into something sure. His hometown has seen it. Cameras have caught it. Management has moved to formalize it. Audiences have begun arriving prepared to feel something they cannot yet name.

This is the start of Elvis Presley's legend in the way history later simplifies it. It is the start of consequence. And August is the month where that consequence becomes visible.

---

## August 2nd, 1955, Community Center, Sheffield, AL, All Star Jamboree, two shows at 7:00 and 9:30

Sheffield sits along the Tennessee River in northwest Alabama, close enough to the Muscle Shoals region to feel music in the air even before Muscle Shoals becomes a national name famous for Aretha Franklin, The Rolling Stones, Lynyrd Skynyrd and Cher. A community center show in 1955 carries the town's sense of order. Bright lights, folding chairs, and an implied expectation of proper behavior. Two shows in one night turn that order into a live comparison. The first audience teaches the second what they are allowed to feel.

At 7:00, the crowd arrives guarded. People watch themselves as much as they watch the stage, gauging whether clapping too hard looks foolish, whether letting teenagers drift forward looks careless. Elvis works inside that restraint. He does not have to push the crowd. He stays steady until the crowd loosens on its own. At intermission, the parking lot becomes a fast moving conversation. The 9:30 crowd does not arrive curious. It arrives informed. The response begins earlier and with more confidence because someone has already said, you will not believe what he does.

On paper, Webb Pierce is still the headliner, but the center of attention shifts quickly. Elvis pulls the focus way from him, and Sun newcomer Johnny Cash has also been added to the bill. Behind the scenes, the pressure is building in letters and wires. Tom Diskin writes Colonel Parker that Bob Neal is still trying to get Elvis committed to a move to a major label, hoping to have him pinned down soon.

Outside the tour, Cold War headlines are building a culture trained to think in rival futures, in speed, and in escalation. That mindset, faster, bigger, next, is the same logic you can feel in the late show crowd.

---

## August 3rd, 1955, Robinson Auditorium, Little Rock, AR, All Star Jamboree

Little Rock is a capital city with a public spine, government buildings, newspaper offices, and a strong sense of how people are supposed to behave in public. This is not a honky tonk. It is a formal venue designed to keep response polite. In places like this, the first hurdle is not volume. It is permission.

Elvis steps into a venue that wants to watch without fully participating, the way adults sometimes watch youth culture like it is weather. The set works the crowd gradually. Applause does not burst all at once. It spreads. A few teenagers start it. Parents hesitate. Then the larger crowd follows, not as surrender, but as acknowledgment that something is happening whether they approve or not. Elvis does not have to tear down the formality. He performs until the formality begins to feel old in real time. That is the July to August shift. The crowd is no longer deciding whether Elvis is good. It is deciding how it is supposed to or allowed to act while watching him.

On the wider calendar, early August headlines lean toward Cold War technology, surveillance, and rockets, the feeling that the next decade is arriving early. Popular music is doing something similar, teenagers hearing themselves in public.

---

### August 4th, 1955, Municipal Auditorium, Camden, AR, All Star Jamboree, two shows at 7:00 and 9:30

Camden is smaller, more intimate, and more exposed. A municipal auditorium here can feel like the town's shared living space. People know someone in the crowd, and people know who is watching. Two shows create an immediate before and after in the same building. The 7:00 crowd arrives half curious and half defensive. The first show introduces Elvis to some and confirms him to others. By the time the doors open for the late show, the building is carrying the earlier crowd's energy like heat stored in wood.

At 9:30, the response begins sooner. The aisles feel narrower. The distance from seats to stage feels shorter. The crowd behaves as if it already knows what the night is supposed to become, the one you will talk about tomorrow. Elvis thrives in that preloaded atmosphere because he does not need to build belief from scratch. He only needs to guide what is already there so it does not scatter.

Nationally, August 4th carries a Cold War governance marker. President Eisenhower signs a bill authorizing funding for construction of a CIA headquarters, commonly cited as $46 million. It is another institutional future moment, America building the system that will watch, collect, and handle information. In a smaller mirror, these auditoriums are also trying to handle information, who Elvis is, what he does, and what public response is acceptable.

Back in the office, Parker learns what was discussed in Meridian, the Hill and Range song folio idea. It infuriates him. In his mind it is another example of Bob Neal's lack of foresight, another moment where a decision should have been made cleanly and was not. The Colonel does like surprises. He looks at that moment as bad management.

---

## August 5th, 1955, Overton Park Shell, Memphis, TN, The Bob Neal Jamboree

Overton Park Shell is Memphis in public mode, open air, a place meant to present wholesome culture to itself. And Memphis is Elvis's home base, his ground, his center of gravity, Sun, radio, and the familiar streets where his rise has been taking shape. He is here not as a kid slipping into a studio world, but as a featured act on a jamboree bill that signals legitimacy. The stage is outdoors, which means the city can hear itself react.

It is Bob Neal's eighth annual Country Music Jamboree, stacked with names like Webb Pierce, Sonny James, and Johnny Cash, and it draws over 4,000 people into the open air shell where Elvis began his professional run. That is what makes this date feel like a test. Memphis is not a random stop. It is his home base checking its own reflection.

Teenagers arrive with a sense of ownership. Adults arrive with an evaluative stare, wondering what this is becoming. The Shell makes that divide visible, two audiences sharing the same seats, one there for the music, the other there for the social argument happening in the crowd.

Nationally, August 5th is marked by the death of Carmen Miranda, a reminder that show business is an industry with turnover, not just sparkle. In the same week, Elvis is not yet the King, but he is forcing the business to rethink who becomes a star, and how fast.

---

### August 6th, 1955, River Stadium, Batesville, AR, White River Carnival

Batesville is a river town, and the White River Water Carnival is the kind of event that belongs to the whole community, parades, festivities, and civic pride. This is not a concert crowd only. It is families, elders, teenagers, and people who came for the carnival before they came for the singer. That mix matters, because Elvis's reception in 1955 often divides along age lines.

The staging is part of the story. Arkansas sources note the friction of the evening, younger girls thrilled, older townspeople disapproving of the movement they viewed as improper. The night persists in memory because it captures 1955 clearly. Elvis is not just entertainment. He is a public argument. The crowd watches him, and it also watches itself responding.

This date has an unusually solid archival footprint. Arkansas sources preserve the fact of the event and its controversy, and even artifacts like posters tied to the Water Carnival appearance. That matters because it means this stop is not just another night on the road. It is a recorded dividing line.

But the real aftermath of Batesville is correspondence. Promoter Ed Lyon writes an angry letter to the Colonel, accusing Elvis of unprofessional behavior, off color jokes, then leaving after only four songs and demanding an adjustment for a show he felt was ruined. Parker responds the way he often does when the brand is threatened, fast, with a refund of fifty dollars, then with a lecture to Neal about standards. Elvis is still young and inexperienced, Parker insists, and it takes more than a couple of hot records in one territory to become a real big name artist. The adults around him are trying to set rules before the crowd sets them.

---

## August 7th, 1955, Magnolia Gardens, Houston, TX, afternoon

Houston in 1955 is big enough to hold many cultures at once, oil money, working neighborhoods, church life, and nightlife, with no single crowd speaking for the whole city. An afternoon appearance at Magnolia Gardens catches Houston in daylight mode. Families, casual listeners, people who wander in with curiosity rather than urgency. Afternoon crowds do not surge as quickly because the day still belongs to errands, obligations, and heat.

So Elvis's work here is subtler. He plants the effect. Teenagers drift forward a little at a time. Adults listen longer than they planned. The afternoon show becomes information that can travel ahead of the night.

Nationally, early August headlines remain thick with Cold War forward motion, satellites, surveillance, and institutional decisions. It is a culture training itself to live in what is next. The afternoon crowd at Magnolia Gardens feels like watching to learn what will matter later.

---

### August 7th, 1955, Cooks Hoedown, Houston, TX, evening

Night changes Houston. Cooks Hoedown is built for participation, music as motion, not background. By evening, the afternoon story has done its work. People arrive ready. They do not need proof. They want the experience.

By this point Elvis is not introducing himself anymore. He is arriving with expectation already in the air. The crowd behaves less like a polite audience and more like a gathered force. Once the response begins, it does not reset neatly between songs. It keeps moving forward, carried by momentum and repetition.

This is also where tour context sharpens. Sources that track this period note that around this time Elvis begins a weeklong Tom Perryman presented East Texas swing. This is also associated with the band's evolving live rhythm, with D J Fontana joining regularly often placed in this general window. Whether this Houston night is the logistical start line or simply feels like one, it marks the July to August difference in one place. July showed portability. August shows certainty.

---

## August 8th, 1955, Mayfair Building, Tyler, TX, Tom Perryman Tour

Tyler is East Texas with a public face, courthouse town energy, commerce, and that mix of pride and gossip that makes crowds feel like extended family even among strangers. The Mayfair Building is not a field. It is enclosed and concentrated. That makes Elvis's effect arrive faster and feel denser.

Tom Perryman's role matters because it reframes this stop. It is not random routing. It is local promotion driven by a radio power who knows how to gather people. The teenagers come not as accidental foot traffic, but as assembled listeners who have been told what they are about to see. That changes the first minute. It removes the slow climb.

This East Texas package pairs Elvis with Jim Ed and Maxine Brown, and around this run D J Fontana stops being an occasional Hayride drummer and becomes part of the regular traveling sound, salaried rather than on a percentage. It is another quiet sign that Parker is turning the band into payroll and the show into a repeatable machine.

Local reporting and later retrospectives in East Texas treat these early shows as formative. It is not just that he played Tyler. It is that people remembered the night as a before and after in what a concert could mean in the region.

---

## August 9th, 1955, Rodeo Arena, Henderson, TX, Tom Perryman Tour

Henderson's rodeo arena is built for spectacle and movement. Rodeo crowds understand volume and physicality. They do not require permission to respond. Elvis steps into an environment where motion is already culturally acceptable, so the crowd's body level response can feel immediate and communal rather than scandalous.

What changes here is the scale of participation. The arena invites standing, shifting, and calling out. A seated, polite posture does not dominate. Elvis does not have to break etiquette because etiquette is looser. The show becomes less about whether response is allowed and more about how large it gets.

Within the Perryman presented East Texas run, this stop functions like an amplifier. Once the tour enters open venues, rodeos, parks, and baseball fields, word of mouth travels faster because more people can witness it at once. Henderson is not just a night. It is an enlargement of the story.

---

## August 10th, 1955, Baseball Park, Gladewater, TX, Tom Perryman Tour

Gladewater is oil country with boomtown roots, radio driven community life, and a sense that entertainment is a public event, not a private luxury. A baseball park is designed for distance. It is supposed to flatten performers into small figures against a large field.

Elvis refuses this concept by changing how his crowd would use the space. He makes people drift closer. Proper viewing angles become less important than proximity. The field stops behaving like a sports ground and starts behaving like a gathering place. You can feel the ticket holders create a new shared space inside the open air, using bodies and attention as boundaries.

This is also Tom Perryman's home zone. His name is tied to the region and its bookings. The logic of the run is visible here. Put Elvis where the most people can see him. Let the people become the advertisement. Then move to the next town before the story cools.

---

## August 11th, 1955, Reo Palm Isle Club, Longview, TX, Tom Perryman Tour

Longview brings the run back into intimacy. Clubs change the chemistry. In a club, you can see Elvis's face clearly. You can measure the crowd's response in real time. The Reo Palm Isle is a night spot where people arrive prepared for entertainment rather than stumbling into it.

Here, the power of the show is sustained attention. The response does not have to be explosive to be memorable. It only has to be steady. People stay.

They linger afterward. They talk. That after show conversation is how the legend travels to towns where Elvis has not arrived yet.

This is why clubs matter in the middle of a run of parks and fields. The story becomes personal again. The crowd does not just say, we saw him. They say, he looked right at us.

---

## August 12th, 1955, Driller Park, Kilgore, TX, Tom Perryman Tour

Kilgore is oil country with muscle work rhythms, paydays, pride, and a crowd that can be generous and unforgiving in the same breath. Driller Park is a town gathering place where people come to be together, not to be refined. Elvis meets that energy without needing to translate himself.

Response here arrives with less hesitation. There is less of the quiet debate that appears in formal auditoriums. Some older listeners may disapprove of style, but the younger listeners respond strongly enough that the evening belongs to them. That generational claim, teenagers taking ownership of a public area, becomes one of the defining images of 1955.

Years later, fellow rockabilly singer Bob Luman remembered one of these East Texas nights as a lightning flash, Elvis walking out in loud colors, then standing behind the microphone for a beat that felt like a dare. That pause, the calm before the crowd fully commits, becomes part of the new formula. The crowd does not need to be convinced anymore. It needs a moment to gather itself.

Offstage, the Colonel is tightening his reach. Around this date he writes directly to Vernon Presley because he cannot get Bob Neal on the phone, saying a very good deal is pending. It is the subtext of the whole month. Parker does not just want to book dates. He wants to control the decisions between them.

## August 13th, 1955, Municipal Auditorium, Shreveport, LA, Louisiana Hayride

Shreveport is not just a town. It is a radio broadcast engine. The Municipal Auditorium is a venue with a reputation, and the Hayride is the machine that turns local excitement into repeated proof. Elvis returning here after the East Texas run feels like bringing field tested response back to the place that records it.

The crowd in Shreveport is not discovering Elvis. It is confirming him. That changes the mood. The response becomes less like surprise and more like ritual. The audience knows where to clap and when to call out. Elvis, in turn, learns how to ride that ritual without letting it grow stale.

August's spine shows clearly. Certainty. Shreveport proves the response survives repetition because it is being repeated in the most formalized setting Elvis has.

## August 15th, 1955, Memphis, TN, business meeting

Memphis is Elvis's home base, the place where his professional life has been built in real time, Sun, radio, and the streets that still hold the day to day version of him. And on August 15th, the business catches up. In Memphis, Parker meets with Bob Neal and Vernon Presley and locks in a new contract that calls him Elvis's special advisor, language that gives him control over nearly every moving part, bookings, publicity, negotiations, and money. It is a moment where the road stops being a scramble and starts becoming a system.

---

## August 17th, 1955, letters and leverage

On August 17th, Parker writes Hill and Range publisher Julian Aberbach to confirm the new reality, a three year representation deal and talks edging toward a major label. He has also learned that Elvis's 1955 record sales are already a little over 100,000 copies. Put that number beside the demand on the road and the month becomes more than performance. It becomes power.

Around the same time, promoter A V Bamford writes Parker with a blunt assessment. Elvis is hot only in certain pockets, and radio outlets like KXLA in Pasadena are not playing him at all. The letter reads like a map of the problem. Parker's preferred solution is simple. Book new territories when you can pair Elvis with an established drawing card so the crowd arrives for the headliner and leaves talking about the young man who pulled the spotlight.

---

## August 20th, 1955, Municipal Auditorium, Shreveport, LA, Louisiana Hayride

A week later, Shreveport arrives even more ready. Familiarity does not settle the crowd. It primes it. People come not to evaluate but to participate. This is the difference between a show and an event the community talks about afterward.

In a Hayride setting, where the program is structured and the venue expects order, the public response becomes more noticeable. Small shifts read big. Small calls from the crowd register as disruption. Elvis is learning something crucial. He does not have to increase his own behavior for the night to feel bigger. The crowd does that.

Somewhere in this stretch, likely around August 21st, there is also a Mount Pleasant, Texas stop at the American Legion Hall. The exact date wobbles in the paperwork. The meaning does not. Small town halls like that are where the summer tour keeps its heartbeat one night at a time, whether anyone writes it down perfectly or not.

This Hayride is also one of the rare nights where live recordings survive, songs like "Baby Let's Play House," "Maybellene," and "That's All Right." Not studio clean, but clear enough to remind you what the place sounded like before later legend polished it.

---

## August 22nd, 1955, Spudder Park, Wichita Falls, TX, Louisiana Hayride

Wichita Falls sits in North Texas with one foot in prairie practicality and one foot in oil and industry. A park show feels communal. People spread out, families and groups staking informal territory. Outdoor parks are supposed to diffuse intensity. This is also the opening night of a weeklong package run with Johnny Horton and Betty Amos on the bill. Another example of Parker's method. Stack the night, borrow a crowd, and let Elvis walk out like the unexpected center of attention.

The offstage story is gentler. Elvis visits local DJ Bill Mack at the hospital to talk about Mack's newborn daughter. A small human moment that survives history because it is Elvis at his core.

Elvis compresses the expanse of the park anyway. Teenagers drift closer as a unit, like a tide. The response becomes communal, less I like this and more we are here together for this. In August, these open air settings prove a new truth. Elvis's effect is not dependent on architecture. The crowd becomes the architecture.

---

## August 23rd, 1955, Rodeo Grounds, Bryan, TX, Louisiana Hayride

Bryan, TX is tied closely to the Texas A&M world, an area shaped by tradition, youth, and public events that can swell quickly. Rodeo grounds invite volume and physicality. Elvis does not need to manufacture energy. He needs to steer it so it does not scatter.

The crowd response in a rodeo setting has a different flavor than a club. It is broader and less intimate, more like a town roar. The sound carries. People who are not close still feel included because the shared response becomes part of the experience.

These mid Texas Hayride tour dates also function as an expanding music marketing network. Every stop feeds the next town. By the time Elvis reaches the next show, people are arriving with a shared expectation of what it is supposed to feel like.

---

## August 24th, 1955, High School Football Field, Conroe, TX, Louisiana Hayride

A high school football field is not just a venue. It is a symbol of the town. It is the town's youth stage, the place where rules and supervision normally dominate. Bringing Elvis into that space is like dropping a match into dry grass.

Conroe's setup is as makeshift as it sounds. The stage is built from two flatbed trucks pushed together. At one point Elvis trips and goes down hard enough to hit his head. He gets up and finishes anyway, as if pain has become part of the job.

Teenagers respond first and claim the front. Adults hover farther back, doing their best to keep order. That physical separation becomes the picture of the night, youth pressing forward while the town's authority watches from a distance. Elvis does not have to deliver a speech about rebellion. The layout says it for him.

---

## August 25th, 1955, The Sportscenter, Austin, TX, Louisiana Hayride

Austin brings a different kind of attention, curiosity mixed with skepticism, a city that thinks of itself as observant. The Sportscenter suggests organized entertainment, ticketing, and structure. Elvis steps into a crowd that wants to decide what it thinks.

He wins them gradually. The response grows in layers. Applause grows more confident. The crowd posture loosens. By the end, people are no longer evaluating whether Elvis deserves a reaction. They are participating as if it was always going to happen.

This is a quiet strength of August. Elvis does not need instant chaos. He needs certainty.

---

## August 26th, 1955, Baseball Field, Gonzales, TX, Louisiana Hayride

Gonzales carries Texas symbolism, historic pride, and a town identity built on memory and story. A baseball field is meant to keep spectators separated from performance. Elvis turns separation into suggestion. The crowd drifts inward, tightening the shape of the gathering until the field feels less like a wide open ground and more like a shared space.

Open air does not weaken the show anymore. It makes it feel like the whole town is present. And in a place like Gonzales, the whole town matters, because stories are currency. A night like this can turn into local legend quickly.

That folklore is what Elvis is riding in August. The idea that if you missed it, you missed something the town will keep talking about.

---

## August 27th, 1955, Municipal Auditorium, Shreveport, LA, Louisiana Hayride

The month closes where the record remains strongest. Shreveport does not just host Elvis. It continues to documents him. Returning again at the end of August turns the month into a loop. The road proves the response, and the Hayride confirms it.

By this point, the audience arrives with ritual confidence. Response starts earlier. The evening feels pre-arranged, not by staff, but by the expectations that build with each return. Elvis's challenge becomes keeping a known night from becoming a routine night. The stage is beginning to be not big enough to hold him.

August ends not with something new, but with confirmation. Elvis's eclectic effect now precedes his arrival.

### AUGUST 1955: RADIO, CINEMA, AND A COUNTRY LEARNING TO ANTICIPATE

August feels like the country drawing a long breath before something changes. Radio continues to rotate its dependable favorites, but if you listen past the surface playlist, a different current is moving. "Maybellene" by Chuck Berry, "What'cha Gonna Do" by The Drifters, "Tweedle Dee" by LaVern Baker, "Unchained Melody" by Roy Hamilton, and "The Door Is Still Open to My Heart" by The

Cardinals are circulating in ways that signal movement beneath the official charts. Elvis's name is becoming easier to say on stations that might have avoided it only months earlier. And once that door opens, it does not open for him alone. It opens space for many Black rhythm and blues records to travel further up the dial.

By August 1955, American radio is not a single conversation. It is a split signal.

On one side, the industry still favors polish. Smooth vocals. Orchestral arrangements. Songs that keep their posture. On the other side, often later at night and often on local stations, rhythm, backbeat, and youthful drive are pushing through. The national charts still look cautious but listening habits are shifting faster than official records can capture.

That delay matters.

Because the crowds gathering for Elvis in August are responding to something radio has not fully named yet. They are reacting to what feels like it is coming next, even while labels and networks debate how to classify it.

**What America is hearing on the radio**

In August 1955, many dominant radio 45s emphasize reassurance and control.

"Rock Around the Clock" by Bill Haley and His Comets is still riding the aftershock of *Blackboard Jungle*. The song is loud, fast, and aimed at youth, but it presents rebellion in a manageable frame. Haley's image offers reassurance even as the beat excites. It is rock and roll dressed for approval. It is paving the way for Elvis.

"A Blossom Fell" by Nat King Cole delivers elegance and restraint. Heartbreak is expressed carefully, with distance and composure. Adult radio reminds listeners that emotion can be handled without disruption.

"The Yellow Rose of Texas" by Mitch Miller leans into nostalgia. Whistling replaces backbeat. The past is presented as comfort.

"Dance With Me Henry" by Georgia Gibbs smooths and softens a rhythm and blues hit for broader consumption. Its success over Etta James's original shows how the industry redirects youthful drive into safer channels.

"Love and Marriage" by Frank Sinatra speaks in confident tones about stability and order. It tells the country what security sounds like.

These are not weak records. They are popular because they connect. But together they reveal a radio landscape attempting to steady emotion at a moment when many younger listeners are seeking something more immediate.

That is the atmosphere Elvis is breathing in August.

Teenagers are not rejecting these songs outright. They are adding to them. They tune in to local broadcasts. They follow late night DJs. They listen for voices that reflect how they feel rather than how they are told to feel. Elvis is one of those voices, even when his records are not yet dominating the national charts.

## Regional radio and repetition

By August, Elvis's presence on Southern radio, especially through the Louisiana Hayride broadcasts, has taught listeners something important. Reaction can be repeated.

That lesson is stronger than any single chart position.

When listeners hear crowd response week after week, they absorb it. They learn how to answer before they ever see Elvis in person. By the time he arrives in town, the emotional rhythm has already been practiced over the airwaves.

This is why August crowds come prepared.

They do not need persuasion. They want participation.

## What America is seeing in movie theaters

Cinema in August 1955 reflects the same split that radio reveals.

On screen, the country is watching stories that maintain order and resolution. Films that explain the world rather than unsettle it.

*Mister Roberts* plays widely. Authority is questioned, but gently. Conflict is framed with humor and structure. Dissent is allowed, yet it lands safely.

*The Man with the Golden Arm*, starring Frank Sinatra, circulates in discussion and theaters. It acknowledges darker subjects such as addiction, suggesting adult cinema is beginning to admit unease. Yet it presents that unease within clear moral boundaries.

Musicals and romantic dramas continue to fill neighborhood theaters. Feelings are expressed, but they are concluded neatly.

Teenagers attend these films, but they are not yet centered in them. Youth is present as an audience, not as a driving force within the story.

That space between what youth feels and what mainstream cinema shows is where Elvis is operating.

## Why August matters

In July, Elvis proves that response can travel from town to town.

In August, radio and cinema reveal something else. The culture is slower than its own momentum.

While national radio continues to emphasize reassurance and polish, and while films present youth energy as something to guide rather than unleash, Elvis's live audiences behave as if permission has already been granted.

They call out sooner. They move closer. They arrive knowing what they want to experience.

That expectation does not come from charts alone. It grows from repetition, from local amplification, and from the speed of word of mouth, the same patterns that August tour routing uses so effectively.

By the end of August 1955, much of American media is describing yesterday.

Elvis's audiences are already practicing tomorrow.

## FULL KNOWN AUGUST 1955 PERFORMANCE RECORD

August 1st, Monday: Fairgrounds, Tupelo, Mississippi.

August 2nd, Tuesday: Community Center, Sheffield, Alabama, 7:00 p.m. and 9:30 p.m.

August 3rd, Wednesday: Robinson Auditorium, Little Rock, Arkansas.

August 4th, Thursday: Municipal Auditorium, Camden, Arkansas, 7:00 p.m. and 9:30 p.m.

August 5th, Friday: Overton Park Shell, Memphis, Tennessee.

August 6th, Saturday: River Stadium, Batesville, Arkansas.

August 7th, Sunday: Magnolia Gardens, Houston, Texas, afternoon. Cook's Hoedown, Houston, Texas, evening.

August 8th, Monday: Mayfair Building, Tyler, Texas.

August 9th, Tuesday: Rodeo Arena, Henderson, Texas.

August 10th, Wednesday: Baseball Park, Gladewater, Texas.

August 11th, Thursday: Reo Palm Isle, Longview, Texas.

August 12th, Friday: Driller Park, Kilgore, Texas.

August 13th, Saturday: Louisiana Hayride, Municipal Auditorium, Shreveport, Louisiana.

August 20th, Saturday: Louisiana Hayride, Municipal Auditorium, Shreveport, Louisiana.

August 22nd, Monday: Spudder Park, Wichita Falls, Texas.

August 23rd, Tuesday: Bryan, Texas.

August 24th, Wednesday: Davy Crockett High School Football Stadium, Conroe, Texas.

August 25th, Thursday: The Sportcenter, Austin, Texas.

August 26th, Friday: Baseball Park, Gonzales, Texas.

August 27th, Saturday: Louisiana Hayride, Municipal Auditorium, Shreveport, Louisiana.

# Chapter 9, September 1955

September 1, 1955. Pontchartrain Beach, New Orleans, Louisiana

Music at the beach is supposed to drift. It is meant to fill space while people keep walking, keep buying tickets, keep moving from one attraction to another. The midway rarely falls silent. Rides flash. Gears rattle. Loudspeakers compete with one another. The crowd arrives without a fixed destination, pulled by heat, lights, and whatever seems entertaining from a short distance away.

The evening is advertised locally as a Hillbilly Jamboree connected to WBOK personality Red Smith. The program includes a country music lineup and a Miss Hillbilly Dumplin contest meant to distribute attention across the grounds. Elvis Presley is presented as part of the bill, not the centerpiece. He is one name among several, positioned as something you might stop and watch before heading elsewhere.

That arrangement lasts only briefly.

When Elvis steps forward, the direction of movement changes. Teenagers pause. Then they remain where they are. Conversations trail off unfinished. Applause comes earlier than expected, cutting through the steady clatter of the amusement grounds. It does not arrive in a single unified swell. It moves in sections, spreading from one group to another until attention begins to concentrate.

Attendance is described in the thousands. In a place designed to keep people dispersed, that turnout alters behavior. It is not a sudden rush toward the

247

stage. It is a change in priorities. Families postpone rides. Groups that planned to wander continue standing in place. The Ferris wheel keeps turning, but fewer people watch it.

From the platform, Elvis can see the shift happening in real time. He has played dance halls and auditoriums where attention was already fixed on the stage. This is different. Here, he feels attention being pulled toward him from every direction. He understands that if he holds steady, the crowd will come the rest of the way. He does not force the moment. He lets it gather.

Event staff do not intervene immediately because nothing appears disorderly at first. Instead, they reposition themselves for better visibility, monitoring where clusters form and where walkways begin to narrow. Elvis does not hurry or exaggerate the moment. He stands in the center of it, aware that this is a larger test than it appears. The atmosphere grows heavier minute by minute. The beach remains active, but the center of gravity has shifted. Elvis becomes the focus.

When the set concludes, the crowd does not instantly return to its earlier pattern. The midway resumes gradually, as though routine must be reintroduced. Walking offstage, Elvis carries a new awareness. If he can command an amusement park designed to scatter attention, he can command almost any setting. September opens with proof that the reach of his presence is expanding.

---

September 2, 1955. Arkansas Municipal Auditorium, Texarkana, Arkansas

Texarkana brings the first interruption of the month.

The Municipal Auditorium is formal, structured for schedules and hierarchy. Advertisements promise two evening performances, a practical solution to demand without altering the order of the program. The audience arrives early, seated, composed, confident it understands what it has heard described in other towns.

Then the evening falters before it fully begins.

Earlier that day, roughly fifteen miles south of Texarkana, the touring party's pink and black Cadillac Fleetwood is involved in a collision. Scotty Moore is driving when an oncoming car, attempting to pass a pickup truck, cuts into their path. The impact leaves the car damaged enough that Scotty later estimates nearly a thousand dollars in repairs. The immediate cost, however, is delay. Elvis arrives late.

The audience waits. The air grows heavier. Local performers extend their minutes. Teenagers stand, sit, and stand again. Anticipation sharpens into impatience.

Elvis steps into the auditorium aware of the delay and the frustration it has caused. He knows he is walking into a room that has been building energy without release. There is no time for easing in. He must meet the crowd at its current temperature.

When he finally appears, the applause does not gently begin. It breaks free.

The sound is louder than the auditorium anticipated, edged by the long wait. Teenagers lean forward instinctively. Adults glance toward ushers for cues that never arrive. By the second number, applause interrupts transitions. Quiet does not land where it is intended.

Onstage, Elvis feels the edge created by the delay. He understands that the crowd's reaction is not only about music. It is about relief. He keeps his footing, leaning into rhythm and familiarity, trusting the material that has carried him through other volatile nights.

Ushers stop trying to enforce neat rows and begin tracking movement instead. The auditorium does not collapse, but it no longer directs behavior. Its authority shifts from instruction to reaction.

The later performance does not restore calm. It adds to what has already formed. By then, the crowd is no longer responding out of surprise. It is responding out of certainty. On paper, the schedule remains intact. In practice, the room has learned that calm becomes optional once Elvis steps forward.

Backstage, Elvis recognizes something else. Even a delayed entrance does not weaken the pull. If anything, it intensifies it.

---

September 3, 1955. Dallas, Texas. Afternoon. Sportatorium, Big D Jamboree

Elvis returns to Dallas.

The Sportatorium is built for participation. It expects volume and involvement. Posters and radio promotion frame the event as part of an ongoing city tradition, a machine that runs on audience engagement.

Elvis enters that system and redirects it.

Applause erupts the moment he moves forward, not as a brief surge but as sustained force. Sound strikes the high ceiling and returns amplified. Teenagers respond together, shouting without delay. Movement spreads across sections rather than concentrating near the front.

Standing under the lights, Elvis feels the difference between a receptive crowd and a charged one. Dallas does not need convincing. It arrives ready. He senses that the stories about him have traveled faster than he has. He does not try to overpower the reaction. He rides it, shaping songs around the crowd's volume instead of fighting it.

His set, constructed around rhythm driven numbers familiar to much of the audience, deepens physical response. Stagehands shorten resets instinctively. Announcements lose their authority. Silence feels unnatural and unwanted.

This marks a clear signal for September. A larger venue does not soften reaction. It enlarges it. And Elvis begins to understand that bigger halls are not obstacles. They are amplifiers.

---

September 3, 1955. Dallas, Texas. Late Night.
Round Up Club

The day does not conclude with the Sportatorium.

After the major performance, Elvis and the band are associated with a late night appearance at the Round Up Club, a far more intimate setting that draws what the afternoon scattered. People arrive carrying the earlier charge with them. There is no pause between events, no period of cooling.

Faces are close. Reaction is immediate. Shouts replace structured applause. Chairs become obstacles rather than seats. Sound has nowhere to disperse.

In the small club, Elvis feels the crowd almost physically against him. There is no buffer of distance. Every movement is seen at arm's length. Every lyric returns instantly in the form of a shout or a call. He recognizes the intensity but also the responsibility. He must keep control of himself so the room does not lose control entirely.

Staff abandon traditional enforcement and concentrate on maintaining space where they can. Elvis performs within inches of the audience, and the crowd presses inward, dense and constant. It is not a different response from the afternoon. It is the same response held inside smaller walls.

Dallas, taken together, reveals the pattern clearly. Elvis unsettles both large halls and intimate clubs without altering his core approach. The night runs late. His voice carries the strain of back to back performances, yet the demand does not lessen. He leaves Dallas aware that endurance is becoming part of the job.

September 5, 1955. Smith Stadium, Forrest City, Arkansas

Forrest City introduces the fair circuit.

This appearance is tied to the St. Francis County Fair Jamboree. The setting draws a varied crowd. Families already attending the fair. Teenagers arriving specifically for Elvis. Local residents curious about the attention gathering around a performer barely into his twenties.

Smith Stadium is open air, built on the belief that space will moderate response.

It does not.

As Elvis performs, people stand, then more people stand. The geometry of the field changes as attention pulls inward. Sound travels through the stands and returns louder with each rebound.

From the stage, Elvis sees clusters forming across the field. He understands that open space does not dilute energy. It spreads it before drawing it back. He adjusts instinctively, giving the crowd moments to respond, letting them hear themselves.

Accounts describe a temporary stage consistent with fairground shows of the period, placing Elvis closer to the audience than a formal theater might allow. The proximity alters behavior immediately. Groups shift positions. Families abandon earlier seating choices.

Open air does not soften reaction. It exposes how quickly a crowd can form its own boundaries once attention locks into place.

By September 5, the pattern of the month is evident.

Elvis does not arrive to test whether a venue will respond. He arrives knowing it will, and the venue adjusts accordingly. Amusement parks redirect movement. Municipal auditoriums lose their timing. Large arenas absorb response. Small clubs draw it tight. Stadiums pull it inward.

The travel schedule grows more demanding. Time between appearances shrinks. The window for vocal rest narrows. Elvis feels that pressure physically. Yet each crowd's response reinforces his belief that the effort is building something larger than any single night.

September is not about proving intense response exists. It is about discovering how much a crowd will sustain before something else must yield.

---

September 6, 1955. High School Gym, Bono, Arkansas

Bono's high school gym announces oversight before Elvis appears. The building is compact and familiar. Bleachers frame the space. The floor reflects sound sharply. Administrators and local officials are present to maintain order.

The assumption is simple. Closeness plus supervision will keep behavior contained.

Elvis overturns that belief in minutes.

The crowd is young, filled with teenagers who have heard reports from Dallas and Texarkana. Applause begins before he finishes his first line. Teenagers stand instinctively. The sound rebounds off the gym walls, merging music and response into one sustained roar.

Elvis feels the echo wrap around him. He recognizes that in a gym like this, every sound doubles back. There is no hiding inside the music. He must anchor the room through steadiness. He keeps his posture controlled, trusting rhythm rather than reacting to every shout.

Adults hesitate. No one intervenes because nothing openly defiant has occurred. Yet the room moves faster than supervision can process. Ushers abandon strict seating enforcement and begin watching for sudden shifts instead.

What falters is not authority itself but its timing. By the moment anyone considers stepping forward, the reaction has already taken control.

Elvis remains composed. The surge comes entirely from the hall. And as he leaves Bono that night, he understands something clearly: the crowds are no longer tentative. They arrive prepared. And he must arrive prepared as well.

September 7, 1955. National Guard Armory, Sikeston, Missouri

The armory carries its own posture before the music even begins. It is a building associated with order, with discipline, with the idea that public behavior can be directed. Adults arrive believing that if reaction crosses a line, it can be corrected.

Elvis walks into that assumption and feels it immediately. The room is waiting to see whether it will have to assert itself.

Applause breaks early, sharp and uneven. Movement starts in clusters rather than rows. Sound strikes the armory's hard surfaces and returns stronger, doubling back on itself. Ushers stop pointing people toward chairs and instead take positions along the walls, watching how the flow shifts from one section to another.

The armory does not completely surrender structure, but it does not dictate the tone either. Elvis senses that shift. He knows he is performing inside a room that expects control yet cannot fully apply it. He steadies his breathing, keeps his phrasing measured, and allows the crowd to answer him.

For him, the lesson is quiet but clear. Authority on paper does not equal authority in practice once the music begins.

---

September 8, 1955. City Auditorium, Clarksdale, Mississippi

Clarksdale listens differently than Arkansas or Missouri.

This is not a town encountering unfamiliar sound. The audience brings memory into the hall. Blues is not an imported style here. It is part of the local fabric.

Applause is deliberate rather than explosive. It does not flash and fade. It continues. Respect moves through the audience alongside excitement.

Onstage, Elvis feels the distinction. The response is not built on novelty. It is built on recognition. He understands that this crowd is measuring him against something deeper than radio reputation. That awareness sharpens his focus. He leans into phrasing, into rhythm, into the parts of his sound that connect to the region's musical roots.

Even so, staff watch carefully as the volume grows beyond what they expected. Announcements shorten. Workers shift from trying to shape the mood to simply managing its direction. They cannot reverse it. They can only guide it.

This is not reaction born from curiosity. It is reaction grounded in connection.

---

September 9, 1955. High School Auditorium, McComb, Mississippi

McComb places Elvis back inside a supervised setting.

The presence of school officials suggests structure. That structure dissolves quickly. Teenagers move forward early. Applause cuts across transitions. Noise fills spaces that were meant for quiet.

Elvis sees the adults hesitate. He senses that the authority in the room is unsure how far to press. He keeps his posture steady, aware that any visible challenge might harden positions. He performs as though the room is larger than it is, refusing to mirror the crowd's urgency.

Adults do not rush to intervene. They watch instead. In doing so, they move from prevention to reaction. The room sets its own tempo.

What stands out is the absence of strong resistance. No public reprimands. No removals. There is a collective understanding that heavy handed action would only heighten the reaction.

Elvis leaves McComb aware that the pattern is becoming consistent. Supervision alone does not redirect the audience.

---

September 10, 1955. Municipal Auditorium, Shreveport, Louisiana

By this point, Elvis's connection with the Louisiana Hayride is established. The Municipal Auditorium treats his appearance as part of routine. The broadcast structure is ready. The sequence of performers is known.

Elvis steps into a system that does not appear unsettled by him. He performs. The audience responds in ways that feel expected.

Applause lands where it usually lands. Volume increases and settles in familiar cycles. Nothing in the hall appears startled. The Hayride captures the moment without commentary or embellishment.

For Elvis, this neutrality carries weight. Shreveport does not react emotionally. It records. The performance feels less like a challenge and more like confirmation. He has moved from curiosity to fixture within the program's structure.

The Hank Snow All-Star Jamboree is built on reliability. Names appear in predictable order. Transitions are practiced. The audience understands when to respond and when to listen. Hank Snow's reputation reinforces that steadiness.

Elvis joins that structure not as its architect but as its most unpredictable element. He senses the balance. He knows he must work inside the framework without overturning it completely.

---

September 11, 1955. Municipal Auditorium, Norfolk, Virginia. Afternoon and Evening

Norfolk changes the tone of conversation.

The Municipal Auditorium is large and civic in character. It represents public order. The Hank Snow All-Star Jamboree arrives with advertising that highlights Snow first, promising dependable country professionalism.

Elvis's name appears lower on the bill.

Yet radio has already shaped anticipation. Local disc jockeys have spoken cautiously about crowd reaction. Teenagers interpret caution as invitation. Parents interpret it as warning.

The afternoon performance begins smoothly. Hank Snow steadies the hall. The audience behaves as expected.

When Elvis steps forward, applause breaks earlier than the program anticipates. It cuts across introductions and disrupts the established rhythm. Teenagers rise without prompting. Adults watch aisles rather than the stage.

Elvis feels the shift immediately. He understands that this is not only about music. It is about attention changing direction inside a civic space. He keeps his movements controlled, careful not to inflame the moment, yet unwilling to retreat from it.

By the evening performance, word has traveled. The second audience arrives louder from the outset. Applause interrupts formalities. Sound fills the building more aggressively than in the afternoon.

Ushers reposition themselves closer to the stage. Announcements shorten. No one halts the program. They adjust around it.

Newspaper coverage the following day uses measured language. Words such as excited and unexpected appear. Elvis is described less as a singer and more as a phenomenon that must be interpreted.

Elvis recognizes the shift. The tour continues to function, but it must now account for him in ways it did not before.

---

September 12, 1955. Municipal Auditorium, Norfolk, Virginia

The second night confirms the first.

The audience arrives informed. Teenagers take their places early. Parents sit farther back. Applause begins before Elvis reaches the microphone. The reaction no longer surprises the staff.

What changes is acknowledgement. Radio commentary now refers to Elvis directly when discussing audience management. The phrasing remains careful, yet the message is clear. This response is consistent. It is not fading.

Hank Snow remains the headliner. His presence frames the show. Yet the emotional center of the evening gathers around Elvis's segment. When his set concludes, the room remains energized beyond the program's arc.

Onstage, Elvis senses that he is operating inside a professional touring system that must bend around him. He understands the responsibility. He also understands the opportunity.

---

September 13, 1955. Shrine Auditorium, New Bern, North Carolina

New Bern offers a smaller hall but sharper contrast.

The Shrine Auditorium carries local pride. The audience includes families, teenagers, and older couples drawn by Hank Snow's name. Advertising emphasizes tradition and order. Elvis is presented as an addition rather than the draw.

The reaction challenges that framing.

When Elvis appears, attention narrows quickly. Applause arrives sooner than anticipated. Teenagers stand and remain standing. Adults glance toward exits, measuring the room.

Elvis feels the narrowing of focus. In a smaller hall, every sound returns immediately. He adjusts his timing, allowing the applause to crest before continuing. He understands that forcing the pace would only create friction.

Local reporting describes the night as lively and unusual, noting the youth enthusiasm without condemning it.

The tour continues, and with it, Elvis's awareness that each town is no longer asking whether something will happen. It is preparing for it.

---

September 14, 1955. Fleming Stadium, Wilson, North Carolina

Wilson brings the tour back into open air under civic supervision.

The stadium suggests that space will keep reaction manageable. At first, the audience spreads out.

When Elvis appears, attention gathers inward again. Movement increases along the aisles. Sound travels outward and returns stronger. The open setting does not disperse response. It makes it visible across distance.

Elvis notices how quickly the field reorganizes itself around him. He remains steady, conserving his voice while allowing the crowd to supply volume. He knows the road is long and the nights are stacking.

Radio mentions the event in neutral language but advises early arrival and preparation for crowds. Elvis is increasingly framed not simply as entertainment but as an event that changes logistics.

---

September 15, 1955. American Legion Auditorium, Roanoke, Virginia

Roanoke reveals fatigue.

The schedule has been tight. Travel has been constant. Elvis performs cleanly, yet he feels the accumulation of nights in his throat and shoulders.

The American Legion Auditorium expects decorum. The audience includes veterans and community leaders. The building carries authority.

Applause begins early anyway. Sound rises unevenly. Staff remain on their feet, observing rather than intervening. The approach has shifted to management rather than prevention.

Elvis senses the difference between enthusiasm and strain. He measures his breathing carefully, spacing phrases, protecting his voice. He understands that stamina is becoming as important as charisma.

Local reporting calls the youth response remarkable, without taking a firm position. The language feels cautious.

September 16, 1955. City Auditorium, Asheville, North Carolina

Asheville's venue carries mountain formality and strong musical awareness. The audience listens closely. Reaction is less explosive and more sustained. Respect is audible.

Elvis recognizes the listening quality of the room. This is not a crowd seeking spectacle alone. It is evaluating tone, phrasing, delivery. He leans into clarity, allowing notes to settle before moving on.

The response is layered. Excitement is present, but so is attention and focus.

Radio commentary now refers to Elvis as one of the most discussed attractions on the tour. The phrasing avoids judgment but acknowledges reality.

By mid September, Elvis feels the change in his own footing. He is no longer wondering whether audiences will respond. He is considering how to sustain himself as they do.

## September 17, 1955. High School Auditorium, Thomasville, North Carolina

Thomasville draws everything close again.

A high school room combines supervision, proximity, and youth density in one tight space. The reaction begins instantly. Teenagers stand. Adults hesitate. Teachers watch rather than step forward.

Authority is not confronted. It is bypassed. What fills the room is collective hunger.

Onstage, Elvis must have felt the closeness in his chest. A high school auditorium leaves no distance between performer and consequence. He was only twenty. He likely recognized that many in the room were his age, some younger. Their response was not polite admiration. It was identification.

He would have understood something else as well. This was no longer curiosity. These students were not waiting to decide what they thought of him. They had already decided before he walked in.

By the end of the night, the internal balance of the tour has shifted again. Hank Snow's structure still frames the program. But Elvis's segment now defines the emotional crest of the evening.

Elvis must have sensed that shift. A mixture of pride and unease. Gratitude and awareness. The applause was growing, but so was responsibility.

By September 17, Elvis Presley is no longer simply traveling with the Hank Snow All-Star Jamboree.

He is altering it from inside.

Advertisements still list names in traditional order. Radio still speaks cautiously. Newspapers still hedge tone. But the pattern is undeniable.

Crowds arrive early. Response begins quickly. Venues prepare instead of pretending nothing unusual will occur.

September has crossed its midpoint. The road is no longer regional.

It is stretching outward.

Elvis must have begun to understand that this was no longer a string of good nights. It was something larger forming around him.

---

## Broadcast Gravity and the Limits of Containment

By the third week of September, Elvis Presley is not moving faster than coverage.

Coverage is moving with him.

What changes now is not the reaction itself. That has proven steady. What changes is the system surrounding it. The road becomes a chain of anticipation, threaded by radio mentions, newspaper notices, and quiet adjustments made before he arrives.

The shows happen at night.

Talk about them happens all day.

Elvis must have felt that invisible weight. He was not just walking into rooms. He was walking into rooms already shaped by rumor.

---

## September 18, 1955. WRVA Theater, Richmond, Virginia. Afternoon and Evening

Richmond introduces broadcast consequence.

The WRVA Theater connects directly to one of the strongest radio signals in the region. The Jamboree arrives under visible conditions. The show is expected to represent itself well. To sound professional. To sound manageable.

Elvis does not directly challenge that expectation.

The audience does.

The afternoon performance begins restrained. The crowd is aware of microphones. Aware that what happens here may travel beyond the hall.

Applause begins measured, then grows freer as his set continues. Teenagers stand despite the formality of the space. Sound rises where clarity is expected.

Elvis must have felt the pressure of that awareness. Microphones change a room. They also change a performer. He likely understood that this was no longer just a hall reacting. It was a broadcast reacting.

He would have known that anything uncontrolled could echo farther than the building.

By the evening performance, restraint has faded. Word has moved through the city. The second crowd arrives louder and more certain. Applause interrupts introductions. The sound pushes against the limits preferred by a broadcast environment.

Staff reposition. Announcers shorten remarks. The program continues.

Elvis must have felt both thrill and caution. The energy was undeniable. But so was the sense that adults were now discussing him in more serious terms.

Local commentary avoids harsh language. Instead it speaks of packed houses and youthful enthusiasm. His name appears more prominently.

He would have recognized that he was no longer a side attraction in print.

---

## September 19, 1955. WRVA Theater, Richmond, Virginia

The second night confirms exposure.

The audience arrives fully aware. Teenagers gather closer to the stage. Parents sit farther back. Applause begins early and sustains itself longer.

Microphones do not soften the response. They heighten it.

Elvis must have felt the difference between being heard and being carried. This was no longer sound contained in walls. It was transmission.

He may have felt pride. A twenty year old recognizing that his name was traveling beyond his physical reach.

But there must also have been uncertainty. Success expanding this quickly leaves little time to adjust.

Radio discussion afterward addresses the difficulty delicately. His impact is described as challenging to contain within traditional programming.

Elvis would have understood what that meant.

He was changing expectations faster than language could comfortably describe.

---

### September 20, 1955. Fairgrounds, Danville, Virginia

Danville returns to open air.

The fairgrounds suggest distance. Families assume space will soften reaction.

It does not.

When Elvis performs, movement pulls inward. Sound spreads across the field and returns louder.

Elvis must have felt the contradiction. Even without walls, the crowd gathers tightly around him. The energy does not need enclosure.

At twenty, that realization would have been intoxicating. The ability to command attention without architectural help.

Local notices describe the turnout as lively and unusually energetic.

No one calls it a problem.

Yet.

## September 21, 1955. Memorial Auditorium, Raleigh, North Carolina

Raleigh restores civic formality.

The Memorial Auditorium is structured to preserve order. Ushers position themselves carefully. Announcements emphasize courtesy.

The audience still leans forward when Elvis appears.

Applause begins early. Teenagers stand. Adults monitor aisles.

Elvis must have sensed the careful watchfulness. He likely understood that each night now carried scrutiny along with applause.

He performs cleanly. Controlled. Focused.

He must have been learning in real time how to balance excitement with survival.

Newspaper coverage remarks on the contrast between orderly hall and responsive crowd.

The tone is cautious.

Elvis would have known that caution is not indifference. It is attention.

---

## September 22, 1955. Civic Auditorium, Kingsport, Tennessee

Kingsport tightens the space again.

The room is smaller and more immediate. Reaction begins quickly. Applause swells. Shouting replaces polite cheering.

Sound rebounds sharply from the walls.

Elvis must have felt the physical force of it. In a smaller room, reaction lands directly in the chest. It is not abstract.

At twenty, he likely felt both invincible and vulnerable in the same breath. The crowd energy lifted him. It also demanded stamina.

Radio commentary begins repeating familiar phrasing. Youthful enthusiasm. Strong response.

Repetition itself signals permanence.

Elvis would have recognized that this pattern was no longer isolated.

---

## September 24, 1955. Municipal Auditorium, Shreveport, Louisiana

The return to Shreveport is almost plain.

The Louisiana Hayride treats his appearance as scheduled routine. He arrives. He performs. The audience responds as expected.

The broadcast captures it without drama.

For Elvis, this must have felt grounding. Shreveport is not surprised by him. It documents him.

He likely felt both pride and pressure. Being routine inside the Hayride meant stability. It also meant he was no longer the unknown.

Radio adjusts tone. Newspapers calibrate language. Venues prepare in advance.

Elvis must have begun to sense that he was no longer chasing opportunity. Opportunity was organizing around him.

---

## September 25–26, 1955. Trinity High School Auditorium, Gilmer, Texas

Louisiana Hayride Jamboree

Gilmer places him again inside a space built for obedience.

A high school auditorium suggests assemblies and authority. The Hayride format relies on order.

The audience arrives already primed.

Applause begins before Elvis reaches the microphone. Chairs become optional. Sound strikes flat surfaces and returns louder.

Elvis must have felt the youth of the room intensely. These were not distant admirers. They were peers. Faces his age. Voices his age.

He may have felt exhilaration. He may also have felt responsibility pressing in.

Teachers observe instead of intervene. They have learned suppression increases reaction.

The second night builds on the first. There is no reset. The crowd knows what it wants.

Elvis must have realized that anticipation was now part of his entrance. The moment he appears, reaction begins.

That is a powerful realization for a twenty year old.

---

### September 27, 1955. High School Auditorium, Watson Chapel, Arkansas

Watson Chapel reduces distance further.

The room is small. Supervision visible. Response immediate.

The audience answers his first movement before he completes a line.

Elvis must have felt the immediacy as almost overwhelming. In a space this tight, applause and shouting leave no margin.

Adults choose observation over confrontation.

The striking detail is familiarity. No one looks shocked.

Elvis would have understood that this was no longer new behavior.

It was expected behavior.

That knowledge must have carried weight.

---

## September 28, 1955. B & B Club, Gobler, Missouri

Louisiana Hayride Jamboree

Gobler removes nearly every buffer.

A club offers no institutional posture. No hierarchy beyond proximity.

Elvis enters and reaction arrives at full strength.

There is no gentle beginning. Sound fills the room instantly. Bodies press inward. Staff focus on preventing physical harm rather than preserving order.

For Elvis, this must have felt electric and dangerous at once. Close faces. No separation. No distance between applause and touch.

At twenty, that kind of intensity can feel like proof of destiny.

It can also feel like something that could tip too far.

When the set ends, the energy remains suspended.

Elvis must have walked out of that club aware that this thing surrounding him was no longer fragile.

It was powerful.

And it was growing.


Radio: Occupying the Days

By late September, radio doesn't introduce Elvis.

It manages him.

Disc jockeys frame him as something listeners should be aware of rather than just entertained by. Mentions emphasize crowd behavior as much as music. Some stations caution parents obliquely. Others lean into the excitement with knowing humor. None ignore him.

Elvis's name now travels independently of his records. His appearances are discussed before they happen and analyzed afterward, not critically, but behaviorally. The language is careful, but routine does the work. Listeners learn that an Elvis appearance changes the shape of a room.

## Music, Cinema, and Popular Culture

By September 1955, American popular culture isn't moving in unison. The systems that once advanced together. Radio, cinema, fashion, and public behavior. Start to separate into different speeds. The result isn't chaos, but tension. September does not feel loud because culture is changing quickly. It feels unsettled because culture is changing unevenly.

September isn't one sound, it's a collision. Pop still wants polish, but the 45s people remember are the ones with teeth. And a lot of that bite is coming from Black performers and Black labels that have been doing this work for years. Across jukeboxes, dance floors, and the bolder radio slots, you hear: "Maybellene", Chuck Berry,. "I Hear You Knocking", Smiley Lewis, "Story Untold", The Nutmegs, "Soldier Boy", The Four Fellows, and "Most of All", The Moonglows,. Elvis is the face on the marquee more often now, but the sound underneath the marquee is getting older, deeper, and already proven.

Radio in September leans toward reassurance.

Playlists favor records that sound composed and emotionally legible. Ballads return to prominence. Vocal phrasing is careful. Rhythms are present but disciplined, often carried by orchestration in preference to percussion. Songs emphasize memory, distance, longing, and emotional clarity instead of urgency.

Records such as Love Is a Many-Splendored Thing, Moments to Remember, and Seventeen dominate the air with gentleness and polish. These are songs that move slowly, resolve cleanly, and leave no excess behind. Even when youth is referenced, it is framed nostalgically instead of urgently.

This matters because Elvis Presley's presence now circulates through radio differently. His 45s may still be played, but his reputation travels faster than the music itself. Disc jockeys start referencing audience behavior rather than sound. Elvis becomes something listeners are told to prepare for rather than simply enjoy. The language is careful, indirect, and repetitive. A sign that radio has not yet found a vocabulary for what his live performances provoke.

Cinema responds by reinforcing hierarchy.

September movie houses continue to offer stories where the room's stature is visible, masculinity is held back, and resolution is guaranteed. Motion on screen is purposeful and framed. Even suspense arrives with boundaries.

Films such as Mister Roberts, The Night of the Hunter, and Guys, and Dolls present crowd-controlled worlds where rebellion is either stylized or punished, and emotion is guided toward closure. These films ask audiences to sit, watch, and trust the setup around them.

What cinema provides in September is certainty.

Elvis's live performances provide none.

The contrast sharpens because cinema resolves feelings while Elvis leaves it suspended. The film ends. The lights rise. The listeners exits calm. An Elvis performance ends, and energy remains active, unresolved, carried outward into streets, and memory. The body reacts differently in each space. September makes that difference impossible to ignore.

Popular culture absorbs this imbalance gradually.

Fashion stays neat. Hair stays trimmed. Authority still looks solid on the surface. But posture loosens. Movement changes. Youth culture starts responding less to instruction and more to rhythm. Elvis's influence isn't fully visible in dress or language yet, but it is visible in behavior, in how quickly crowds form, how long reaction lasts, and how hard it is to restore calm afterward.

Parents, teachers, and town leaders don't yet speak openly about this shift. Instead, they adjust. Curfews are discussed. Seating is watched. Announcements are softened or shortened. Elvis is rarely named directly in these conversations, but he is present in all of them.

September doesn't introduce a new cultural hierarchy. It reveals strain in the existing one.

Radio offers calm routine. Cinema reinforces rules and tidy endings. Live performance, led by Elvis Presley, disrupts both because it refuses an easy resolution.

The difference isn't abstract. It is physical, visible, and increasingly familiar.

## FULL KNOWN SEPTEMBER 1955 PERFORMANCE RECORD

September 1, Thursday,: Pontchartrain Beach Amusement Park, New Orleans, Louisiana.

September 2, Friday,: Arkansas Municipal Auditorium, Texarkana, Arkansas.

September 3, Saturday,: The Big "D" Jamboree, Sportatorium, Dallas, Texas. The Round-Up Club, Dallas, Texas, later in the evening,.

September 5, Monday,: St. Francis County Fair and Livestock Show Jamboree, Smith Stadium, Forrest City, Arkansas.

September 6, Tuesday,: High School Gym, Bono, Arkansas.

September 7, Wednesday,: National Guard Armory, Sikeston, Missouri.

September 8 (Thursday): City Auditorium, Clarksdale, Mississippi.

September 9, Friday,: McComb High School Auditorium, McComb, Mississippi.

September 10, Saturday,: Louisiana Hayride, Municipal Auditorium, Shreveport, Louisiana.

September 11, Sunday,: City Auditorium, Norfolk, Virginia, 3:00 and 8:00 p.m.,.

September 12 (Monday): City Auditorium, Norfolk, Virginia.

September 13, Tuesday,: Shrine Auditorium, New Bern, North Carolina.

September 14, Wednesday,: Fleming Stadium, Wilson, North Carolina.

September 15, Thursday,: American Legion Auditorium, Roanoke, Virginia.

September 16, Friday,: City Auditorium, Asheville, North Carolina.

September 17, Saturday,: High School Auditorium, Thomasville, North Carolina.

September 18, Sunday,: WRVA Theater, Richmond, Virginia, 2:30 and 8:30 p.m.,.

September 19 (Monday): WRVA Theater, Richmond, Virginia.

September 20 (Tuesday): Danville Fairgrounds, Danville, Virginia.

September 21, Wednesday,: Memorial Auditorium, Raleigh, North Carolina.

September 22 (Thursday): Civic Auditorium, Kingsport, Tennessee.

September 24, Saturday,: Louisiana Hayride, Municipal Auditorium, Shreveport, Louisiana.

September 26, Monday,: Junior High School Gym, Gilmer, Texas.

September 28 (Wednesday): B&B Club, Gobler, Missouri.

## October 1, 1955. Municipal Auditorium, Shreveport, Louisiana

Louisiana Hayride

The Municipal Auditorium operates with practiced calm. Staff know the rhythm. Radio equipment is arranged efficiently. Announcers prepare language that stays measured. Elvis arrives as scheduled. He performs as scheduled. The audience reacts as it has learned to react.

What stands out is not surprise. It is familiarity.

Applause begins quickly. Shouting follows. Teenagers stand. Ushers monitor aisles instead of correcting seats. No one in the hall looks startled.

The Hayride does not dramatize the moment. It documents it.

Elvis must have felt something grounding in that. Shreveport is not chasing him. It is recording him. He is no longer a novelty there. He is part of the family.

At twenty, that realization carries weight. Being expected to do something is different from being discovered.

---

## October 3, 1955. G. Rollie White Coliseum, College Station, Texas

Louisiana Hayride

College Station introduces wider space.

The G. Rollie White Coliseum spreads outward.
Seating is broader. The assumption is that distance
will soften reaction.

It does not.

Students gather near the stage before assigned
sections settle. Applause builds before Elvis finishes
his first phrase. Sound travels across the coliseum
and returns layered and stronger. Movement is
visible from far corners.

University staff adjust quickly. Aisles are watched.
Access points monitored. No one attempts to
restore an older order. The goal is endurance.

Elvis must have felt the difference in volume alone.
A university crowd carries its own energy. Youth
concentrated and confident. He likely felt pride
seeing so many his own age reacting without
hesitation.

He may also have felt the beginning of scrutiny.
Administrators observing. Institutional eyes
measuring.

This is not resistance.

It is evaluation.

---

**October 4, 1955. Boys Club Gymnasium,
Paris, Texas**

Louisiana Hayride Jamboree

Paris compresses the room again.

The Boys Club Gymnasium is intimate and filled with teenagers who arrive knowing what to expect. Reaction begins before Elvis reaches the microphone.

There is no gradual build. The response arrives complete and remains steady. Organizers observe instead of intervening. They have learned that confrontation sharpens reaction.

Elvis must have felt the youthfulness of the room intensely. Faces close. Voices sharp. Energy immediate.

At twenty, he likely felt both understood and exposed. These were not distant adults applauding politely. These were peers who saw him as something happening in their own time.

That kind of connection can feel powerful.

It can also feel overwhelming.

---

## October 5, 1955. City Auditorium, Greenville, Texas

Louisiana Hayride Jamboree

Greenville brings civic structure.

The City Auditorium is built on order. Seating firm. Sightlines controlled. Announcements emphasize courtesy.

The structure holds briefly.

When Elvis begins, applause cuts through before transitions are completed. Teenagers stand and remain standing. Adults look toward staff. Staff look toward the youth.

The program continues under adjustment.

Elvis must have sensed the shift in posture. Adults no longer pretending nothing unusual is happening. They are watching.

Local reporting the next day focuses less on music and more on reaction. Words such as excitement and unusual enthusiasm appear carefully.

He must have begun noticing that coverage was changing tone.

That kind of attention brings hope.

It also brings caution.

---

## October 6, 1955. Southwest Texas State University, San Marcos, Texas

Afternoon Show, Louisiana Hayride Jamboree

Daylight changes the atmosphere.

Students move between classes. Faculty presence is visible. The assumption is moderation.

Applause interrupts early. Sound travels beyond the immediate hall. Students who were not planning to attend drift toward the building. Reaction sustains rather than peaks.

Elvis must have felt the intrusion into routine. This was not night entertainment. It was daytime interruption.

At twenty, he may have felt a surge of pride that his presence could disrupt ordinary campus rhythm.

He also may have felt the edge of controversy forming. Daytime attention invites broader conversation.

---

## October 6, 1955. Skyline Club, Austin, Texas

Evening Show, Louisiana Hayride Jamboree

Austin narrows the space again.

The Skyline Club offers proximity without institutional buffer. There is little distance between stage and crowd. Reaction arrives immediately and remains constant.

Staff abandon any attempt at hierarchy and focus on preventing physical harm. Bodies press inward. Sound saturates the room.

Elvis must have felt the intensity physically. No separation. No cushion. The audience nearly within reach.

For a young performer, that closeness can feel electric.

It can also feel fragile. The line between celebration and chaos becomes thin in rooms like this.

---

## October 8, 1955. Louisiana Hayride, Municipal Auditorium, Shreveport, Louisiana

Returning to Shreveport brings steadiness.

Staff anticipate response. Announcements are concise. Ushers position themselves before doors open. The audience arrives informed.

Applause begins early and continues between songs. Movement is managed only because the hall enforces structure physically.

The Hayride does not deny what is happening.

It braces for it.

Elvis must have felt a strange duality. In Shreveport, he is part of a system. On the road, he is the catalyst altering systems.

That contrast likely stayed with him.

---

## October 9, 1955. Cherry Springs Dance Hall, Cherry spring, Texas

Cherry Springs removes ceremony.

The dance hall is informal and crowded. There are no ushers guiding behavior. No formal announcements moderating tone.

Reaction is immediate and sustained. Bodies gather tightly. Sound fills every corner.

Elvis must have felt the rawness of it. No protection. No framing. Just direct exchange between performer and crowd.

At twenty, that kind of response can feel like validation of something personal rather than professional.

It can also hint at how little control remains once momentum begins.

---

## October 10, 1955. Memorial Hall, Brownwood, Texas

The Elvis Presley Show

Brownwood marks a change in billing.

This is not a shared marquee. It is promoted directly as The Elvis Presley Show.

The name alone organizes the night.

Attendance is strong. Applause begins early and lasts longer than the printed program suggests. The energy feels focused rather than scattered.

Elvis must have noticed the difference immediately. His name stands alone. No buffer of other headliners. No shared responsibility.

At twenty years old, that kind of billing must have felt like arrival.

It also must have felt like exposure.

If the crowd surges, it is because of him.

If the night falters, it is because of him.

By mid October, the shift is unmistakable.

Elvis Presley's name now does work before he steps onstage. Not suggestion. Not promise. Organization.

Crowds gather knowing what will happen when he appears.

For a young man who began the year hoping to be heard, that realization must have carried both excitement and fear.

The shows no longer need explanation.

They carry their own gravity.

## October 11, 1955. Fair Park Auditorium, Abilene, Texas

The Elvis Presley Show, Two Performances

Abilene approaches the night carefully.

The Fair Park Auditorium schedules two performances, spaced deliberately, as if division might moderate intensity. It does not. The afternoon between shows becomes part of the event. Teenagers linger outside. Word moves quickly across town. By the time the evening performance begins, the air inside the building feels heavier.

The first show breaks seating discipline quickly. Applause interrupts transitions. Shouting overtakes structured cheering. Staff stop attempting to reseat ticket holders and focus instead on maintaining clear aisles.

The second show opens louder than the first.

What stands out is endurance. Reaction does not spike and dissolve. It holds. The hall never fully settles. Even after Elvis leaves the stage, the sound continues, as though the audience has not yet remembered how to be still.

The structure of the evening bends to the crowd instead of shaping it.

Elvis must have felt the difference between momentum and control. Two shows in one day leave little room for recovery. His voice would have felt the strain. His body would have felt the fatigue. Yet the response in front of him would have offered something powerful in return. At twenty, that trade may have felt worth it. Applause sustained longer than exhaustion.

---

## October 12, 1955. High School Auditorium, Midland, Texas

The Elvis Presley Show

Midland compresses the experience again.

The high school auditorium carries institutional language. Seating is tight. Supervision is visible. The assumption is compliance.

Elvis steps into the hall and compliance fades almost immediately.

Applause begins before his first line finishes. Teenagers stand and remain standing. Teachers watch without intervening. Administrators exchange looks and choose observation instead of enforcement.

The reaction is not violent. It is not traditionally disorderly. It is simply persistent.

This is where the distinction becomes clearer. Elvis does not provoke rebellion. He makes instruction feel secondary.

He must have sensed that shift. In earlier months, authority sometimes attempted correction. Now, authority hesitates. At twenty, he may have felt both pride and uncertainty in that realization. The adults are no longer certain how to respond. That kind of influence can feel empowering. It can also feel larger than intended.

---

## October 13, 1955. Municipal Auditorium, Amarillo, Texas

The Elvis Presley Show

Amarillo brings size again, but under new conditions.

The Municipal Auditorium is broader, with more distance between rows and clearer sightlines. Earlier in the year, space like this might have softened response. In October, it reveals how unified response has become.

Sound carries farther. Applause moves in waves. Movement appears across the hall at once. Staff take positions along the edges early, not to prevent reaction but to manage it.

This is a hall responding as one body.

Elvis must have felt the collective nature of it. Not pockets. Not sections. Entire rooms rising together. That kind of unity would have felt thrilling to a young performer who had started the year playing smaller halls.

He also may have begun recognizing that the reaction now precedes him. The crowd knows what to do before he sings.

---

### October 14, 1955. High School Field House, Odessa, Texas

The Elvis Presley Show

Odessa removes ceremony.

The Field House is built for physical competition, not decorum. Bleachers rise steeply. Sound rebounds sharply. There is no softening surface.

Reaction arrives immediately and remains constant. Shouting replaces measured applause. Teenagers lean forward as one group. Adults observe from the margins.

The building stops behaving according to design and reshapes itself around the audience.

Elvis must have felt the intensity physically. The echo alone would have pressed against him. At twenty, he may have felt both excitement and a flicker of apprehension. There is less distance now between performer and consequence.

When every sound returns amplified, so does every mistake.

---

## October 15, 1955. Fair Park Coliseum, Lubbock, Texas

The Elvis Presley Show

Lubbock introduces confidence.

The Fair Park Coliseum is substantial and prepared. The billing is direct. The audience arrives early and in large numbers.

Reaction begins immediately and holds steady. Noise fills the coliseum and does not thin. Ushers monitor aisles throughout. Announcements remain brief. The performance continues under steady adjustment.

Elvis commands a large building without changing his act. The crowd carries the rest.

He must have felt the growing weight of his own name. When a coliseum fills under your billing alone, the room feels different before you even walk out. At twenty, that kind of realization could bring exhilaration.

It could also bring pressure.

---

## October 15, 1955. Cotton Club, Lubbock, Texas

The Elvis Presley Show

The second show strips the evening back to proximity.

The Cotton Club is intimate and compressed. The audience presses inward immediately. Sound fills the room quickly. Movement is limited by closeness.

The difference between coliseum and club is architectural, not emotional. The reaction remains equally strong. Only the shape changes.

This confirms what October has been revealing.

Elvis's effect does not depend on setting.

He must have felt the contrast in his body. Large rooms require projection. Small rooms require steadiness. At twenty, moving between those extremes in a single day demands focus beyond experience.

The name on the ticket now organizes the crowd.

The reaction no longer fades quickly.

Some venues prepare in advance. Adults often observe rather than intervene.

October is not experimenting.

It is solidifying.

---

## October 16, 1955. Oklahoma Auditorium, Oklahoma City, Oklahoma

Hank Snow All Star Jamboree, Two Shows

Oklahoma City brings back formal structure.

The Hank Snow All Star Jamboree restores position on the bill. The Oklahoma Auditorium is large and accustomed to national touring acts. Two shows divide the evening carefully.

The audience responds in layers.

Hank Snow steadies the room. Other performers move through their portions predictably. When Elvis appears, tone shifts immediately. Applause breaks rhythm. Teenagers rise without hesitation.

The program does not collapse. It adjusts.

Elvis must have felt the contrast sharply. Within the same show, the room moves from calm professionalism to youthful intensity. At twenty, he may have felt both gratitude for the platform and awareness that he is becoming the volatile center within it.

By the second show, the crowd arrives louder. Reaction starts earlier and holds longer. The system accommodates without comment.

This is not disruption.

It is adaptation.

---

## October 17, 1955. Memorial Stadium, El Dorado, Arkansas

El Dorado opens the sky again.

The stadium promises distance and air. It offers neither moderation nor restraint. Sound travels outward and returns layered. Movement pulls inward despite space.

Clusters form and move together. Applause rolls across the stadium in unison.

Elvis must have felt the scale in his chest. Outdoor sound behaves differently, yet the response remains unified. At twenty, he may have begun understanding that geography no longer determines reaction.

His presence does.

---

## October 19, 1955. Circle Theater, Cleveland, Ohio

Two Shows

Cleveland signals transition.

The Circle Theater introduces a different mix. Urban. Slightly older. More familiar with national entertainment. The assumption is polish and composure.

The first show challenges that assumption.

Applause begins early and grows louder than expected. Teenagers stand. Adults remain seated but attentive. Ushers position themselves along aisles early.

By the second show, word has moved quickly through the city. The audience arrives primed. Reaction mirrors what has been seen throughout the South.

This is not regional behavior traveling north.

It is something broader taking form.

Elvis must have felt the shift geographically. New city. Same response. At twenty, that realization likely carried a surge of hope. If Cleveland reacts like Texas, then the map has changed.

---

## October 20, 1955. Brooklyn High School Auditorium, Cleveland, Ohio

Afternoon

The afternoon performance compresses youth and supervision again.

A high school auditorium means proximity and oversight. The seats fill with students. Reaction begins immediately. There is no gradual build.

Teachers and administrators observe instead of intervene. Experience has taught them intervention sharpens reaction.

Elvis must have felt the immediacy of youth response again. At twenty, he was not far removed from these students. That closeness may have felt validating. They are not reacting to nostalgia. They are reacting to the present.

---

## October 20, 1955. St. Michael's Hall, Cleveland, Ohio

Evening

The evening performance returns to enclosure.

St. Michael's Hall is crowded and tight. Sound fills the space quickly. Bodies press inward. Reaction remains strong and sustained.

There is little structural relief in a room like this.

Elvis must have felt the physical closeness deeply. The applause does not disperse. It surrounds. For a young performer, that kind of immersion can feel overwhelming and affirming at the same time.

When the final note fades, the energy does not dissolve immediately.

It lingers.

By late October, Elvis Presley is not simply touring.

He is carrying a response that repeats itself across cities, buildings, and formats.

At twenty years old, that repetition must have felt like proof.

And also like a huge responsibility.

### October 21–22, 1955. Missouri Theater, St. Louis, Missouri

### Two Shows Each Night

St. Louis get to know Elvis.

The Missouri Theater schedules multiple performances across consecutive nights. The arrangement is practical. Divide demand. Control flow. Preserve order.

It does not function that way.

Each performance begins louder than the one before it. Reaction carries across shows instead of resetting. Crowds remain outside between performances. Teenagers do not disperse. Anticipation gathers rather than thinning.

The theater adjusts operationally. Transitions shorten. Announcements are trimmed. Aisles are monitored continuously.

By the second night, ticket holders behave as though attending something established. Reaction arrives immediately and follows a familiar pattern.

This is Elvis's effect repeated across time without decline.

Elvis must have felt the strain of repetition in his body. Four shows across two nights leave little margin for rest. His throat would likely have felt worn by the final encore. His legs heavy. Yet the sound waiting each time he stepped forward would have reminded him why he kept moving.

At twenty, he may have felt pride and disbelief in equal measure. These were not small-town gyms. This was St. Louis. The applause did not shrink with geography.

Gladys, back home, would have heard about the crowds. She would have heard numbers. Perhaps newspaper mentions. She must have worried about exhaustion, about the pace, about whether he was eating enough or sleeping enough. To her, he was still her son first. Four shows in two days would not have sounded triumphant. It would have sounded dangerous.

Colonel Parker saw something different.

He saw repetition under pressure.

Four performances. No drop in turnout. No softening in reaction. The same intensity reproduced in a major city. To a manager, that is measurable demand.

---

**October 23, 1955. Missouri Theater, St. Louis, Missouri**

## Three Shows

The third day confirms saturation.

Three performances compress endurance. Neither audience nor hall fully resets between shows. Reaction remains strong, though fatigue appears faintly at the edges.

What matters is durability.

Elvis's presence continues to organize the building. His name alone fills seats. The pattern repeats with consistency.

This is not a spike. It is steadiness.

Elvis must have felt the toll by the final performance. The roar would still arrive, but the effort required to answer it would feel heavier. At twenty, that contrast between exhaustion and exhilaration can be confusing. The body asks for stillness. The crowd asks for more.

Gladys would have heard it in his voice if he called. A rasp. A tired laugh. She would have asked if he was all right. He would have reassured her quickly. He always did.

Parker would have been studying receipts.

Three shows in one day demonstrate elasticity. If St. Louis sustains that demand, other cities can as well. Parker did not hear fatigue. He heard capacity.

By October 23, the pattern is established.

Elvis does not enter halls to test them. He enters halls that have adjusted to him.

The national corridor is open.

The reaction holds steady across regions and schedules.

The spotlight has widened.

Control of the narrative has not caught up.

---

## October 24, 1955. Silver Moon Club, Newport, Arkansas

Newport removes protection.

The Silver Moon Club is tight and informal. There is no separation between stage and crowd. Reaction arrives instantly and remains constant.

Sound saturates the room. Bodies press inward. Movement becomes difficult. Staff focus on keeping people upright.

What stands out is accumulation beneath intensity. Not decline. Weight.

Elvis must have felt the closeness sharply. In rooms like this, there is nowhere to hide. Every note is exposed. Every shift visible. At twenty, performing inside that proximity night after night requires nerve.

He may have felt both invincible and fragile at once.

Gladys would not have liked the sound of a crowded club with no distance between him and the audience. She would have imagined pushing and falling. A mother calculates danger differently than a promoter.

Parker saw portability. If the response holds in a club and in a theater, then it belongs to the performer, not the architecture. That distinction carries financial consequence.

---

## October 26, 1955. Vigor High School, Prichard, Alabama

### Morning Performance

Daylight brings exposure.

A school performance during morning hours interrupts routine. Students sit under supervision. Faculty presence is visible. Discipline is expected.

Reaction arrives immediately.

Applause breaks early. Shouting follows. Students stand without hesitation. Teachers observe rather than intervene.

Elvis must have felt the strangeness of applause in daylight. There is something surreal about hearing cheers inside a building meant for instruction. At twenty, he may have felt disbelief that his presence could override a school schedule.

Gladys would have imagined classrooms disrupted and worried about what adults might think. She

understood small towns. She understood
reputation.

Parker would have recognized range. A performer
who can draw response during school hours is no
longer confined to night bookings. That widens
opportunity.

---

## October 26, 1955. Greater Gulf States Fair, Prichard, Alabama

### Two Shows

The fair attempts diffusion.

Open space and multiple attractions are expected to
soften response. They do not. Elvis's performances
pull attention inward. Noise gathers. Movement
clusters.

Two shows divide time but not intensity. The
second begins louder than the first.

Elvis must have felt the familiarity of it. Open air
does not alter outcome. He steps forward and the
pattern unfolds. That consistency may have brought
confidence.

It may also have brought pressure. When something
works every time, failure feels less permissible.

Gladys would have worried about the stacking of
appearances. Morning school. Two fair sets. Travel.

Parker saw stamina converted into booking leverage. Density without decline increases negotiating power.

---

## October 27, 1955. National Guard Armory, Jackson, Alabama

The armory restores civic formality.

The building is structured for order. Seating is fixed. Expectations are clear.

Reaction overrides design.

Applause breaks through the formal atmosphere. Teenagers stand. Noise rebounds off hard surfaces and returns amplified. Staff monitor aisles rather than enforce seating.

Elvis must have felt the weight of that civic room. Armories carry authority. When applause overtakes that authority, the moment expands.

At twenty, that shift can feel empowering.

It can also feel larger than intended.

Gladys might have wondered whether institutions would eventually respond more forcefully.

Parker would have noted adaptation. When buildings adjust rather than resist, the market has shifted.

---

## October 28, 1955. Curtis Gordon's Ranch Club, Mobile, Alabama

The Ranch Club removes distance entirely.

It is informal and crowded before Elvis arrives. Reaction ignites instantly. Sound fills every corner. Bodies press forward.

There is no hierarchy here. Only proximity.

Elvis must have felt the intensity in his chest. In small clubs, sound does not dissipate. It surrounds. At twenty, that immersion could feel intoxicating.

It could also feel unstable.

Gladys would have imagined the crowd too close. She always feared the physical risk.

Parker would have recognized loyalty forming. Club audiences return. They multiply through word of mouth. They create repeat markets.

---

## October 29, 1955. Municipal Auditorium, Shreveport, Louisiana

### Louisiana Hayride

October closes where it often does.

Shreveport receives Elvis without ceremony. The Hayride operates efficiently. He performs. The audience responds. The broadcast records it.

The difference is not intensity. It is normalization.

The reaction no longer requires explanation.

Elvis must have felt this stage differently now. Earlier in the year, Shreveport was opportunity. By late October, it is confirmation.

He may have felt pride stepping back into that spotlight knowing what the road has demonstrated.

Gladys would have sensed her son's world widening beyond the boundaries she could picture.

Parker understood something decisive.

The reaction had stabilized.

Stability allows strategy.

---

## October 1955. Management Strategy Takes Form

By October, Colonel Tom Parker is no longer assisting growth. He is structuring it.

Show planners are routed through him rather than Bob Neal. Appearance fees increase steadily. Billing language shifts toward **The Elvis Presley Show.** Posters enlarge his name. The rest of the bill contracts.

Parker studies repetition.

High schools. Theaters. Armories. Clubs. Fairs. Universities.

The response holds across all of them.

That repeatability becomes leverage.

Elvis remains under contract with Sun Records. Parker allows live demand to outpace distribution. The imbalance becomes visible. Drawing power exceeds infrastructure.

From New York's Warwick Hotel, Parker wires Sam Phillips and tests numbers. What would it take to acquire the contract outright.

It is framed as a question.

It is not casual.

Option dates. Deposits. Deadlines. Money discussed plainly.

Elvis must have sensed movement, even if details were not fully shared. At twenty, knowing larger companies are circling can feel thrilling.

It can also feel uncertain.

Gladys would have felt that uncertainty sharply. Contracts mean permanence. Permanence means change.

Parker watched money coming in.

Touring density converts into negotiation power. Crowd behavior converts into corporate interest. Timing becomes critical.

By the end of October, nothing publicly has shifted.

Privately, everything is in motion.

Elvis continues performing as though the road is the only focus.

Gladys watches the calendar expand.

Parker watches the deal coming together.

**FULL KNOWN OCTOBER 1955
PERFORMANCE RECORD**

# Chapter 11, November 1955

November probably began without Elvis noticing.

He does not step into the month restored or reset.
He arrives carrying October with him, the residue of
halls that did not empty quickly and nights that
refused to release their energy when the lights came
up. The road no longer offers contrast. Towns do
not feel new on arrival or distant on departure. They
merge into forward motion, separated only by the
architecture of the next room and the hour of the
next performance.

What remains distinct is the response.

It arrives earlier now, before the first chorus settles,
and it lingers after the final note. This is the month
where routine stops feeling repetitive and starts
revealing durability. Elvis is no longer
demonstrating that something is happening. He is
demonstrating that it continues under strain.

Behind the scenes, Colonel Parker has altered his
stance.

The issue is no longer whether Elvis can gather
crowds or unsettle order. The issue is duration. How
long can Sun Records hold an artist whose reach
exceeds its structure. How quickly might a national
label decide that hesitation equals loss.

None of this is spoken plainly to Elvis.

He does not sit in negotiation rooms. He is not
asked for terms. His responsibility remains simple.
Arrive. Sing. Leave.

November will test whether that responsibility can remain isolated from the machinery building around it.

---

On November 20 at Sun Studio in Memphis, Elvis and the band worked on Billy Emerson's "When It Rains, It Really Pours." The take was not finished to release standards, and for years its existence lived more in documentation than in circulation. Still, its presence matters.

Even as conversations multiplied and contracts shifted direction, Elvis continued doing what he had always done. He stepped to a microphone and tried to bend another man's song into something personal. That discipline did not change.

By late summer, the business side of his life had begun moving faster than the miles under the car.

Parker was no longer hovering near the edge of arrangements. He stood in the center of them, tightening schedules, pressing promoters, treating each appearance not as an evening but as inventory. Where others heard noise, he heard arithmetic.

The same mothers who worried about their daughters also worried about tone, about what the music suggested. To them, something restless had entered public space. To Parker, that restlessness translated into long-term revenue.

---

On November 21, he pulled the largest lever available.

Negotiations with RCA Victor resulted in an agreement to purchase Elvis's Sun recording contract for $35,000, plus $5,000 to settle back royalties, a sum unprecedented for a singer still touring largely across the South. The figure signaled valuation beyond regional expectation.

The deal did not alter the young man stepping onstage that night.

But it altered what waited behind the curtain.

Parker did not speak in emotion. He thought in multipliers. National distribution. Royalty streams. Catalog longevity. He understood that Sam Phillips had created a sound small enough to live inside a Memphis studio and strong enough to travel beyond it.

Elvis may have sensed movement without understanding every detail. At twenty, hearing that larger companies were circling could feel thrilling.

It could also feel destabilizing.

Gladys would have sensed that instability more sharply. Contracts meant distance. Distance meant permanence. Permanence meant change she could not slow.

Parker watched numbers settle into position.

On November 10, in a Nashville hotel room during the Country Music Disc Jockey Convention, songwriter Mae Axton played Elvis a rough demo she had co-written with Tommy Durden. The title was "Heartbreak Hotel."

He listened.

He snapped his fingers.

He asked to hear it again.

He was months away from recording it, yet something in the phrasing held him. He began carrying the song with him, speaking about it as something certain.

The setting mattered.

Not a stage. Not a screaming crowd. A hotel corridor atmosphere where songs were exchanged like rumors. Around him were disc jockeys who could turn a regional record into a national habit. Trade language had begun shifting. He was no longer described merely as curious. He was increasingly described as promising.

That word looked controlled on paper.

It felt anything but controlled on the road.

---

## November 5, 1955. Shreveport, Louisiana

Municipal Auditorium, Louisiana Hayride

The month opens in familiar territory.

By November 5, Shreveport operates less as introduction and more as observation post. The

Hayride is not presenting Elvis to a region. It is tracking him.

Newspaper listings remain plain. Names. Times. No ornament.

He shares the bill with Webb Pierce and Faron Young, artists whose careers rest on radio steadiness. Their performances draw applause that rises and falls predictably.

When Elvis steps forward, the difference is immediate.

Front rows lean in before the first chorus completes. By the second song, engineers are adjusting levels as the roar sustains longer than scheduled. He runs through his late-1955 set. "That's All Right." "Baby Let's Play House." "Blue Moon of Kentucky." Motion controlled. Intensity intact.

Backstage, conversation is minimal.

Scotty Moore watches Elvis's hands, aware of stiffness that does not fully disappear between appearances. Bill Black keeps the mood light without pressing.

Parker is not visible on the floor. His presence is felt in the lack of interruption. The night proceeds without correction.

Another entry in the ledger.

No declarations.

Only continuation.

Elvis may have felt familiarity differently now. Earlier in the year, this stage represented opportunity. By November, it represents confirmation. That recognition could feel grounding.

It could also feel heavy.

Gladys would have heard about it and wondered how long such intensity could be sustained.

---

## November 6–8, 1955. Biloxi, Mississippi

Biloxi interrupts rhythm by compressing contrast into a weekend.

On November 6, the Scene House hosts two performances. The split exposes how quickly anticipation multiplies. The afternoon audience includes families and churchgoers alongside teenagers. The room is modest, intended for meetings more than sustained volume.

Reaction builds unevenly, then overtakes itself by the second song. Chairs scrape. Aisles narrow. Adults stand along walls, uncertain whether to participate or monitor.

Between sets, Elvis eats quickly and rests without fully sleeping. Fatigue does not announce itself dramatically. It accumulates.

By evening, tone shifts entirely.

Teenagers arrive early and clustered. He opens with "I Got a Woman." The sound ignites instantly.

On November 7 and 8, the venue shifts to the Airman's Club. Servicemen crowd the floor. The ceiling sits low. Sound rebounds sharply. Reaction becomes physical rather than polite.

Lyrics are shouted back in fragments.

These nights run late.

Elvis stands between sets, wiping sweat from his face. His voice holds, though strain would likely have begun settling into the edges. At twenty, that strain might have felt both exhausting and energizing.

Gladys would not have liked the idea of late club nights filled with servicemen and noise. She worried about proximity. About unpredictability.

Parker saw confirmation of transferability. Family audience. Military audience. Same response.

That consistency mattered more than atmosphere.

---

During the Biloxi stop, Elvis meets June Juanico.

The encounter is brief. Ordinary in structure. They speak only for a short time. There is no immediate sense of permanence.

What distinguishes it is continuation.

Unlike most road interactions, this one does not disappear entirely when he leaves town. Contact resumes intermittently over the following months, shaped by distance and schedule.

Even so, the emotional center of Elvis's life remains unchanged. Gladys remains the person he calls most often. The voice he waits for late at night.

June enters the story without displacing anything already in place.

---

## November 12, 1955. Carthage, Texas / Shreveport, Louisiana

November 12 compresses strain into a single day.

The afternoon finds Elvis in Carthage, Texas, appearing at a Carthage Milling Company event framed as community program rather than concert. Notices are spare. The setting is functional and open.

Workers pause. Families drift closer. Teenagers gather near the front. Sound travels across open ground and reorganizes attention.

He performs the same songs heard in Shreveport and Biloxi. Here, the effect feels intrusive rather than contained. Daily rhythm bends around it.

That evening, he is back in Shreveport for the Louisiana Hayride broadcast.

The contrast is sharp.

The hall absorbs him efficiently. Reaction arrives early, almost impatient. Engineers adjust without delay. Announcers shorten introductions.

Backstage, he sits longer than usual before leaving. Shoulders tight. Conserving energy for the drive ahead.

Elvis may have felt the doubling of the day in his body. Afternoon field. Evening broadcast. The same intensity delivered twice under different skies.

Gladys would have heard about such days and worried about accumulation.

For Parker, days like this were instructive.

They demonstrated that Elvis required no elaborate framing to command attention. Context did not determine reaction. Presence did.

That realization was not discussed in dressing rooms.

It traveled forward into negotiation rooms instead.

## November 13, 1955. Memphis, Tennessee

### Ellis Auditorium

Ellis Auditorium in Memphis becomes the first legitimacy test of the month.

On November 13, Elvis appears as part of a Western-Swing Jamboree, sharing the bill with established figures such as Hank Thompson and Carl Smith. Advertisements emphasize hierarchy and variety, positioning Elvis beneath names secured by years of radio presence and steady touring. On paper, placement still carries authority.

Hank Thompson brings the polish of "The Wild Side of Life." Carl Smith carries the confidence of "Loose Talk." Their songs are shaped for controlled reception. Applause rises and settles as intended.

The afternoon performance confirms that institutional order still matters to organizers. Reaction to Elvis is strong but initially concentrated near the front rows. Applause gathers in sections rather than across the full hall.

The evening performance redraws that arrangement audibly.

Teenagers arrive early. Aisles fill before the first set concludes. By the time Elvis reaches "I Got a Woman," the response overrides the printed billing. This is not rebellion. It is volume directing attention where it chooses. The loudest reaction determines the focal point of the room.

Backstage, Elvis speaks quietly with Scotty Moore about the road, about stiff hands, about how tightly the calendar has been drawn. At twenty, standing in Memphis and hearing that same sustained roar must have felt different than earlier months. Memphis is home. Yet the response no longer belongs to home. It belongs to the road.

That realization could bring pride. It could also bring awareness that there is no smaller room to return to.

Gladys would have understood Memphis differently. This was her city. Hearing reports of that response inside a hall she knew must have felt both thrilling and unsettling. Pride never erased her concern.

Colonel Parker is not present on the floor, yet his influence is evident. Nights like this alter conversations. Sun Records cannot overlook them. RCA's interest does not feel distant anymore.

Elvis leaves Memphis carrying both fatigue and forward motion into a month that offers little space for either to fade.

---

## November 14, 1955. Forrest City, Arkansas

Forrest City receives Elvis inside a high school building meant for assemblies and graduations, not sustained noise.

Local notices are cautious. Two showtimes are emphasized as if division alone might restore order. Teenagers line sidewalks before doors open. Teachers and parents hover near entrances, hoping their presence will steady the evening.

It does not.

Elvis appears mid-bill as part of the Western-Swing Jamboree, but placement loses relevance once he begins to sing. By the second song, aisles narrow and the shape of the front rows dissolves. Applause spills into introductions of subsequent acts. Organizers shorten transitions.

Between shows, Elvis sits with elbows on knees. His fingers stiffen enough that Scotty Moore massages them briefly before retuning. Bill Black jokes about coffee no one has time to find.

A minor disagreement surfaces backstage regarding how long Elvis can remain onstage. It ends not through resolution, but through reluctance to test the room further.

At twenty, performing twice in one evening inside a building built for restraint must have carried a mixture of adrenaline and strain. The response no longer surprises him, yet it still demands something physical each time it arrives.

Gladys would have heard about the packed gym and imagined narrow aisles and crowded exits. Her worry would not lessen with repetition.

The second performance comes louder and less patient than the first.

When Elvis leaves that night, the town remains active longer than usual. Sound carries outward into parked cars and quiet streets.

---

## November 15, 1955. Sheffield, Alabama

The Western-Swing Jamboree moves into a scene center proud of modernity and order.

Advertisements highlight reserved seating and precise timing. The language suggests structure. The crowd suggests otherwise.

Families and teenagers share space uneasily at first. When Elvis approaches the stage, the younger audience presses forward instinctively. Reserved sections dissolve within minutes.

He performs efficiently, conserving energy without appearing withdrawn. "That's All Right." "Mystery Train." Delivered with restraint that sharpens response rather than inflames it.

Between appearances, he drinks water and rests without sleeping. Eyes closed. Jaw set. At twenty, the line between concentration and fatigue must have felt thin. Earlier months allowed space for casual interaction. November narrows that space.

Girls gather during breaks hoping for a glance or word. Interaction remains brief and polite. The flirtation of earlier stops has tightened into focus.

Colonel Parker is not present, yet the tightened schedule reflects his direction. Downtime has nearly disappeared.

The second appearance mirrors the first but arrives faster and louder.

Sheffield hums long after the lights rise.

---

## November 16–17, 1955. Camden and Texarkana, Arkansas

Camden and Texarkana compress strain into consecutive nights that blur together.

Camden's city auditorium has hosted civic meetings where sound rises briefly and then settles. On November 16, it does not settle.

Police presence is advertised openly. Elvis's voice sounds rougher between sets. Scotty adjusts keys to ease strain. These accommodations remain invisible to the audience but necessary for endurance.

At twenty, singing through that roughness must have required calculation. Push too hard and tomorrow suffers. Hold back and the room senses it.

The following night in Texarkana, advance tickets sell out. The municipal venue fills impatiently. Reaction arrives before the first line finishes.

Border-town energy dominates. Crowds draw from both sides of the state line, more invested in participation than in decorum.

After the second show, a promoter complains backstage about traffic congestion and delayed exits, invoking Parker's name even though he is not present.

Elvis listens. He does not respond.

He leaves both towns late, shoulders tight, carrying accumulation rather than release.

---

## November 18–19, 1955. Longview and Gladewater, Texas

The Reo Palm Isle Club in Longview magnifies everything the month has built.

The ceiling is low. Air is dense. There is no seating plan to dissolve. The audience presses forward immediately. Sound rebounds until it feels physical.

"Good Rockin' Tonight" becomes endurance rather than celebration. Elvis delivers it without embellishment, focused on completion.

A minor disagreement surfaces regarding backstage access. It fades quickly but leaves irritation behind.

At twenty, nights like this must have felt powerful and precarious at once. No distance between performer and crowd. No margin for misstep.

On November 19 in Gladewater, the setting shifts to a high school gym sponsored by the Louisiana Hayride. Youth dominates the floor early. Teachers line the walls with expressions closer to resignation than intervention.

Reaction breaks loose before the first chorus concludes.

Elvis sings through it with precision, conserving movement, aware that the noise does not require encouragement.

After the show, he calls home.

Gladys worries about his health and the pace of travel. He reassures her carefully. The reassurance sounds measured rather than effortless.

---

## November 25–26, 1955. Port Arthur and Shreveport

Thanksgiving brings no pause.

On November 25 in Port Arthur at Woodrow Wilson High School, post-holiday restlessness saturates the night. Families remain in town. Teenagers are uncontained. The hall fills beyond capacity.

Noise spills into corridors and parking areas. Police redirect traffic.

This is repetition under strain.

The following night returns Elvis to Shreveport for another Louisiana Hayride broadcast. The evening proceeds efficiently. Reaction recorded without commentary.

Behind the scenes, negotiations intensify.

Sun Records feels its limits. RCA presses forward.

Elvis continues the only task assigned to him. Arrive. Sing. Leave.

By the end of November 26, fatigue has settled into his body as a constant companion. At twenty, enduring that rhythm must have felt like strength. It also may have felt unsustainable.

Gladys senses the pace. Parker senses opportunity.

---

## November 29, 1955. Richmond, Virginia

### Mosque Theater

The month closes in Richmond at the Mosque Theater, a formal urban hall built for seated listening.

Notices emphasize exclusivity and restraint. Reserved seating. One night only.

The audience arrives dressed for decorum.

That decorum does not survive long.

Elvis steps forward carrying accumulated weariness. Movement controlled. Delivery focused. The reaction rises anyway, traveling from floor to balcony before ushers can reposition.

By "That's All Right," people stand instinctively.

The architecture holds. The volume presses against its intention.

At twenty, stepping into such a hall and hearing the same sustained response found in smaller towns must have altered perspective. Geography no longer changes outcome.

He finishes without flourish. Nods once. Leaves the stage.

Outside, cars idle longer than anticipated.

Richmond absorbs what dozens of towns have already experienced.

Distance does not soften it.

---

## The Buildup of Fatigue

By the end of November, exhaustion is not episodic. It has become steady.

His voice remains strong, yet recovery takes longer. Fingers stiffen before shows. Sleep fragments under travel and early arrivals. Scotty Moore and Bill Black adjust without comment. D. J. Fontana reads posture rather than waiting for instruction.

Elvis speaks less between performances. Energy conserved. Attention narrowed.

Calls home become more frequent. Gladys worries openly. He reassures her carefully.

In quieter moments, memory drifts briefly back to Biloxi and June Juanico. Not as escape. As reminder of human proportion. The interaction required nothing beyond conversation. It did not compete with the central gravity of his mother's presence.

November leaves little room for romance. Only acknowledgment.

---

## Colonel Parker's Position Hardens

While Elvis carries fatigue forward, Colonel Parker carries advantage.

November supplies repetition under pressure. Each completed night strengthens bargaining position.

Sun Records still holds the contract. The limits of that arrangement are increasingly visible. Regional success is no longer the question. National transfer is.

Parker spends more time on telephones than in auditoriums. He allows the road itself to accumulate evidence.

RCA does not require excitement. It requires endurance.

Western-Swing Jamboree dates demonstrate dominance within multi-act bills. Hayride broadcasts confirm that reaction sustains across regions. Schools, clubs, theaters, and fairs produce the same result.

Parker does not rush public announcement.

He tightens schedules. Eliminates downtime. Let's the results speak for themselves.

Elvis remains mostly separate from negotiation.

He is not shielded from fatigue.

He is shielded from strategy.

His role remains unchanged.

Arrive. Sing. Leave.

## Sun Records Under Strain

Sun Records feels November tightening around it.

The label provided the room where the sound first formed. It provided the microphone, the acetate, the early radio relationships. It created the frame in which Elvis Presley first appeared. What it no longer controls is the magnitude of response that now surrounds him nightly.

Memphis makes that visible. Texarkana confirms it. Richmond seals it.

The infrastructure that once felt sufficient now feels narrow. Regional distribution. Limited pressing capacity. A promotional network built for steady growth, not sustained uproar across state lines. Elvis's performances now produce reaction that extends beyond the channels Sun built to carry it.

Executives at Sun would have watched November with rising awareness. Not panic. Not yet. But urgency.

Delay now carries consequence.

And still, no formal break occurs.

Ownership remains intact. Contracts remain signed. The paperwork has not shifted. The imbalance remains suspended between control and inevitability.

Elvis himself does not publicly articulate this strain. He keeps stepping into the same songs. "That's All Right." "Mystery Train." "I Got a Woman." He delivers the set as he always has. He bows. He exits. He boards the car.

At twenty, he must have sensed movement around him without being given the language for it. Hotel room whispers. Phone calls that quiet when he enters. Conversations that do not include him.

Gladys would have felt tension in a different register. Contracts meant permanence. Permanence meant change. She would have understood that business decisions travel faster than comfort.

Meanwhile, Parker watches alignment.

He does not need theatrics. He needs repetition. Each night that closes without collapse strengthens his hand. Each hall that fills without advertising overhaul strengthens his position.

The business decisions move around Elvis without touching him directly. They tighten gradually, not through spectacle, but through accumulation.

November does not explode.

It constricts.

---

## November Locked In and Focused

November does not bring a dramatic turning point. It brings endurance.

There is no single incident that defines it. No collapse. No confrontation that announces transformation. Instead, the month establishes something steadier and more consequential.

Elvis Presley sustains the pace.

He carries exhaustion forward without visible loss of control. He enters halls built for structure and leaves them altered. He repeats songs already familiar and receives reaction that does not diminish.

At twenty, that durability must have felt like validation. It may also have felt like confinement.

When every room answers the same way, there is no smaller version of yourself to retreat into.

Superstardom does not stand ahead of him as a distant milestone.

It surrounds him as pressure.

The road moves into December without pause. Parker advances methodically. Sun studies the imbalance. RCA inches closer.

Elvis continues the only role assigned to him.

Arrive. Sing. Leave.

November does not celebrate the collision forming between independent label, national corporation, and rising performer.

It records it.

And that record begins to determine what December will demand.

---

## NOVEMBER 1955

Radio, Cinema, and American Culture

By November, the old categories begin to strain.

Elvis is no longer easy to place within a single regional bracket. Once a station makes room for him, it becomes harder to ignore the rhythm and blues records that shaped the year.

The dial carries a layered mix of romance, grit, and harmony.

"At My Front Door" by The El Dorados.

"What'cha Gonna Do" by The Drifters.

"The Door Is Still Open to My Heart" by The Cardinals.

"Tweedle Dee" by LaVern Baker.

"Every Day I Have the Blues" by Count Basie Orchestra with Joe Williams.

Change does not arrive with declaration. It arrives through rotation.

Ballads remain strong. Patti Page's "Allegheny Moon" moves through living rooms with polished restraint. Tennessee Ernie Ford's "Sixteen Tons" continues steady airplay, its labor-worn gravity resonating with working listeners. Bill Haley and His Comets maintain presence with "Rock Around the Clock," still unsettling established programming patterns even when framed cautiously.

Country radio remains steady. Webb Pierce's "Love, Love, Love." Carl Smith's "Let Old Mother Nature Have Her Way." Their phrasing favors melodic clarity and emotional control. Programmers understand these structures.

Yet requests begin to blur lines.

Disc jockeys introduce unfamiliar 45s carefully. They soften edges with commentary. They contextualize rhythm before playing it.

Elvis's Sun recordings circulate inside this atmosphere as objects that do not sit comfortably within the existing grid. Not yet nationally dominant. Not easily dismissed.

Particularly in the South and border regions, where listener appetite shifts faster than institutional approval.

Cinema mirrors the tension.

Rebel Without a Cause continues drawing young audiences with its portrayal of isolation and unspoken anger. Love Me or Leave Me explores ambition through the structure of performance and consequence. The Man from Laramie leans on discipline, justice, and moral authority.

On screen, structure still prevails.

In theaters, narrative closes cleanly.

Television preserves composure even more carefully. Variety programs, family dramas, and carefully staged musical appearances project calm and order. Performers smile. Choreography remains controlled. Applause fades predictably.

Nothing broadcast nationally resembles the sustained bodily reaction Elvis generates live.

Television stabilizes.

Live performance destabilizes.

In daily life, November retains visible order. Postwar optimism remains present, though worn by routine. Factories operate. Schools enforce rules. Churches prepare for Thanksgiving services.

Teenagers, however, occupy more space than before. Their taste is louder. Their posture more forward.

Adults sense change without naming it.

Institutions respond with caution rather than confrontation.

Against this cultural landscape, Elvis Presley's nightly appearances do not feel isolated. They align with broader tension moving through American sound and image.

Radio favors polish. Cinema favors resolution.

Live performance becomes the site where restraint falters.

November 1955 sits at that intersection.

The country has not agreed on what it is becoming.

Yet the signals move steadily.

Through radios.
Through jukeboxes.
Through movie houses.
Through crowded halls at night.

And at twenty years old, Elvis stands inside that current, carrying fatigue, momentum, and the unspoken awareness that the road is no longer regional.

It is becoming national.


## FULL KNOWN NOVEMBER 1955 PERFORMANCE RECORD

November 5, Saturday,: Louisiana Hayride, Municipal Auditorium, Shreveport, Louisiana.

November 6, Sunday,: Biloxi Community House, Biloxi, Mississippi, 2:00 and 8:00 p.m.,.

November 7, Monday,: Keesler Air Force Base, outside Biloxi, Mississippi.

November 8, Tuesday,: Keesler Air Force Base, outside Biloxi, Mississippi.

November 12, Saturday,: Carthage Milling Company, Carthage, Texas, 2:00 p.m.,. Louisiana Hayride, Municipal Auditorium, Shreveport, Louisiana.

November 13, Sunday,: Ellis Auditorium, Memphis, Tennessee, 3:00 and 8:00 p.m.,.

November 14, Monday,: Forrest City High School Auditorium, Forrest City, Arkansas, 7:00 and 9:15 p.m.,.

November 15, Tuesday,: Community Center, Sheffield, Alabama, 7:00 and 9:30 p.m.,.

November 16, Wednesday,: Camden City Auditorium, Camden, Arkansas, 7:00 and 9:15 p.m.,.

November 17, Thursday,: Arkansas Municipal Auditorium, Texarkana, Arkansas, 7:00 and 9:15 p.m.,.

November 18, Friday,: Reo Palm Isle, Longview, Texas.

November 19, Saturday,: Louisiana Hayride, remote radio broadcast from Gladewater, Texas high school.

November 25, Friday,: Woodrow Wilson High School, Port Arthur, Texas.

November 26, Saturday,: Louisiana Hayride, Municipal Auditorium, Shreveport, Louisiana.

November 29, Tuesday,: The Mosque Theater, Richmond, Virginia, Philip Morris Employees Night,.

## December 1955

By the time December 1, 1955 arrives, Elvis Presley has already lived a full year inside headlights.

He has performed approximately 305 shows before December even begins. Not 305 nights. Three hundred and five separate times he walked out, faced a crowd, and did the work.

He has played on roughly 240 different calendar days. On 59 of those days he performed twice or more. A handful of times he reached three sets in a single day.

That kind of pace changes the meaning of ordinary things. Breakfast becomes uncertain. Towns begin to blur. The next venue feels like it is already pressing against the door before the current one empties.

The real story is not just the dates. It is what exists between them.

The year becomes a ribbon of highways, gas stations, roadside diners, and quick meals eaten standing up. One hand still dusty from moving equipment. The other reaching for the steering wheel.

If you begin in Memphis and trace the calendar forward the way the band would have driven it, Elvis has covered an estimated 57,000 miles by car before December begins. Nearly all of it by road. There was one flight to New York for the Arthur Godfrey opportunity. Apart from that, 1955 was measured in tires, motel keys, and long stretches of dark highway.

By December 1, the arithmetic is blunt.

Elvis has spent roughly 321 to 332 days away from home, leaving perhaps three to fourteen days physically in Memphis, depending on how the briefest gaps are counted. Even those days were rarely restful. Most were travel transitions between distant bookings.

At twenty years old, he must have felt both indestructible and worn down. The body keeps moving. The voice keeps answering. But there is very little space to reset.

Gladys would have measured that differently. Three hundred shows do not sound like triumph to a mother. They sound like strain.

Parker heard something else entirely.

He heard durability.

---

## Method Note

The performance totals referenced here are drawn from the confirmed show record in the appendix, including clearly labeled reported appearances. Mileage figures are rough point to point driving estimates between consecutive cities and should be read as approximations rather than exact odometer readings.

---

## Between Two Worlds

December 1955 finds Elvis caught between two realities.

On stage, he is still playing gyms, auditoriums, theaters, armories, and clubs across the South and lower Midwest.

Offstage, Colonel Tom Parker is arranging something larger.

Television contracts are forming. RCA paperwork is tightening. Meetings in New York are no longer exploratory.

The month reveals how close Elvis stands to national exposure, even before a single network broadcast airs.

---

## December 2, 1955

Sports Arena, Atlanta, Georgia

The month opens in Atlanta.

The turnout is smaller than anticipated. Elvis earns $300 for the evening. The crowd does not match the intensity found in Memphis or Richmond.

This unevenness matters.

At twenty, he must have felt the contrast sharply. Some cities ignite instantly. Others hesitate. Momentum is real, but it is not uniform.

Parker would not have read disappointment into this. He would have read geography. Markets mature at different speeds.

---

## December 3, 1955

State Coliseum, Montgomery, Alabama

Montgomery brings a package setting that includes Roy Acuff and Kitty Wells.

On the same day, Billboard refers to Elvis as "one of the most sought after warblers this year," noting his new contracts with RCA and Hill and Range publishing.

Industry language is changing even while the stage format remains familiar.

He is still appearing on shared bills. Yet the business press is beginning to classify him differently.

Elvis must have felt the distance between those two realities. On stage he is still part of the lineup. On paper he is already being repositioned.

---

## December 4–7, 1955

Lyric Theater, Indianapolis, Indiana

Beginning December 4, Elvis joins Hank Snow for a four day run at the Lyric Theater.

He is billed as an "extra added attraction."

The wording understates the reaction.

By December 5, he tours the RCA manufacturing plant in Indianapolis with Anita Carter. It is symbolic. Pressing plants. Assembly lines. The machinery of national distribution.

At twenty, walking through that plant must have felt surreal. Records stamped by the thousands. His name about to travel further than the car ever could.

Reports from Tom Diskin on December 6 and 7 note that Elvis improves nightly, though pacing remains a concern.

Improvement under fatigue is not automatic. It is discipline.

---

## December 8, 1955

Rialto Theater, Louisville, Kentucky

Louisville brings a special show for Philip Morris employees.

Executives reportedly express discomfort with Elvis's stage movement.

The reaction is not public outrage. It is private unease.

Even inside corporate walls, physical response unsettles authority.

Elvis must have sensed that tension. When adults stiffen, a performer notices.

---

## December 9, 1955

Swifton, Arkansas

The evening splits in two.

Earlier, Elvis appears at a local high school alongside Johnny Cash. Later he performs at the B and I Club.

Club owner Bob King later recalls Elvis introducing "Heartbreak Hotel" and saying, "It's gonna be my first hit."

The song has not yet been released.

Confidence like that at twenty could be instinct. It could also be hope spoken aloud before doubt can interfere.

---

## December 10, 1955

Louisiana Hayride
Municipal Auditorium, Shreveport

Shreveport remains the testing ground.

Songs are tried. Timing adjusted. Audience loyalty provides feedback without hesitation.

The Hayride records the night efficiently.

No commentary required.

---

## December 12, 1955

National Guard Armory, Amory, Mississippi

Elvis appears with Johnny Cash and Carl Perkins.

Even the documentation reflects density. Some listings debate whether the show occurred on the 12th or 13th.

When schedules compress this tightly, record keeping strains.

At twenty, dates may have blurred as much as towns.

---

## December 15, 1955

Catholic Club, Helena, Arkansas

Five hundred tickets sell out two days early.

Smaller markets accelerate quickly now.

Demand is no longer experimental.

Gladys would have heard numbers like this and worried about crowds pushing too close.

Parker would have heard expansion.

---

## December 17, 1955

Louisiana Hayride, Shreveport

Elvis performs six songs, including "Sixteen Tons," "Only You," and "Tutti Frutti."

The audience resists letting him leave the stage.

That same day, Parker forwards Bob Neal the contract for Elvis's upcoming appearances on CBS's Stage Show. Instructions are clear. No ad libs. No gestures beyond what producers approve.

The contrast is stark.

Live audiences demand more.

Television demands restraint.

Elvis must have felt that tightening boundary. What works in an armory may not be permitted in a studio.

---

## December 31, 1955

Louisiana Hayride

The year closes where much of it was forged.

Elvis appears once more on the Hayride.

For 1955, his reported income totals $25,240.15.

Two years earlier he was driving a truck.

Now the arithmetic tells a different story.

At twenty, that number must have felt unreal. Pride mixed with disbelief.

Gladys would have seen stability for the first time.

Parker would have seen projection.

---

## Parker Moves in December

While Elvis continues performing, Parker moves decisively.

On December 1, Elvis and Parker travel to New York to meet RCA executives including Larry Kanaga and Anne Fulchino. Promotional photographs are taken for the back of Elvis's first RCA album.

By December 13 and 14, CBS requests song lists for Stage Show. Compensation is set at $1,250 per appearance with options for extension at higher rates.

When agent Harry Kalcheim expresses frustration about negotiations, Parker responds firmly on December 16. Half measures are not acceptable.

He is no longer testing the market.

He is structuring it.

---

## End of 1955

December closes with Elvis still on the road.

Still entering halls that react before the first chorus settles.

Still leaving towns that stay awake after he departs.

But the boundaries are shifting.

Sun braces.

RCA prepares.

Television waits.

Elvis keeps singing.

When he steps onto national television in January 1956, it will not feel like introduction.

It will feel like release.

And he will walk into that moment carrying 305 shows, 57,000 miles, and a year that hardened him faster than anyone outside the car could fully see.

## FULL KNOWN DECEMBER 1955 PERFORMANCE RECORD

December 2 (Friday): Sports Arena, Atlanta, Georgia.

December 3 (Saturday): State Coliseum, Montgomery, Alabama.

December 4 (Sunday): Lyric Theater, Indianapolis, Indiana.

December 5 (Monday): Lyric Theater, Indianapolis, Indiana.

December 6 (Tuesday): Lyric Theater, Indianapolis, Indiana.

December 7 (Wednesday): Lyric Theater, Indianapolis, Indiana.

December 8 (Thursday): Rialto Theater, Louisville, Kentucky.

December 9, Friday,: High School, Swifton, Arkansas. B&I Club, Swifton, Arkansas, later in the evening,.

December 10, Saturday,: Louisiana Hayride, Municipal Auditorium, Shreveport, Louisiana.

December 12, Monday,: National Guard Armory, Amory, Mississippi, or Dec 13,.

December 15 (Thursday): Catholic Club, Helena, Arkansas.

December 17, Saturday,: Louisiana Hayride, Municipal Auditorium, Shreveport, Louisiana.

December 31, Saturday,: Louisiana Hayride, Municipal Auditorium, Shreveport, Louisiana.

## Parker Applies Pressure

By late 1955, Colonel Tom Parker is no longer watching from the perimeter. He is structuring the next phase.

His instinct is not artistic. It is logistical and financial. He reads crowds the way others read contracts. What he sees in Elvis by December is not simply talent. It is velocity. The touring calendar has demonstrated durability. It has demonstrated expansion. And expansion requires infrastructure.

Sun Records built the foundation. It shaped the sound. It provided the first environment where Elvis could develop.

What it cannot provide is national saturation.

Parker does not frame this as criticism. He frames it as arithmetic.

Crowds are growing. Geographic reach is widening. Revenue ceilings must rise accordingly. A regional operation cannot sustain national acceleration indefinitely.

The pressure Parker applies is steady rather than dramatic. He speaks in terms of opportunity cost. Every month Elvis remains within limited distribution is a month of unrealized exposure. Timing matters. Momentum must be converted while it is rising.

He does not wait for exhaustion. He moves during ascent.

By late November and into December, Sun's role begins to shift in Parker's calculations. Not as adversary. Not as failure. As limitation.

Talks do not begin as rupture. They begin as recalibration.

Parker controls touring access. He controls bookings. He influences calendar flow. Visibility becomes currency. Numbers become argument.

When RCA Victor enters discussion, the equation changes.

RCA does not promise creative reinvention. It promises national pressing capacity. Coordinated promotion. Established distribution networks. Broad retail penetration.

Parker understands this distinction clearly. He is not selling songs. He is selling expansion.

By December, the groundwork is laid. Once the Sun contract is secured, the Memphis recordings are positioned for national reintroduction. Early sides such as "Good Rockin' Tonight" and "I Don't Care If the Sun Don't Shine" begin circulating under expanded distribution.

For listeners, nothing feels recycled. It feels amplified.

Every jukebox becomes an advance signal. Every record rack carries anticipation.

The crowds do not soften. They intensify.

Parker pushes for terms that reflect evidence rather than speculation. Elvis is not being presented as potential. He is being presented as documented draw.

The touring year becomes exhibit A.

Every sold out auditorium strengthens Parker's negotiating posture. The calendar becomes data. Attendance becomes financial validation.

The contract discussion evolves into recognition of what is already happening.

Sun's contribution remains undeniable. The label captured something authentic. It allowed it to develop naturally. Parker does not erase that achievement.

He moves beyond its structural limits.

By December's end, the transfer feels less like betrayal and more like transition. Parker has not altered Elvis's sound. He has expanded the framework around it.

The move represents a shift from regional momentum to national deployment.

The engine remains the same.

The infrastructure changes.

---

## Other Sun Records Artists Rising

Sun Records in 1955 is not declining. It is creatively vibrant.

### Johnny Cash

By 1955, Johnny Cash has established himself as a distinct presence. "Cry! Cry! Cry!" and "Folsom Prison Blues" present a controlled, morally grounded voice. Cash demonstrates Sun's ability to cultivate identity driven artists rather than novelty acts.

His success reinforces Sun's strength in authenticity. It does not diminish Parker's argument. It clarifies it. Sun excels at discovery and definition. National distribution remains a separate challenge.

### Carl Perkins

Carl Perkins represents Sun's sharpest rockabilly expression. By late 1955 his trajectory is accelerating toward "Blue Suede Shoes."

Perkins proves that Sun can generate national attention with the right song at the right moment. Yet even in his case, broader commercial expansion depends on outside channels capable of sustained national promotion.

### Jerry Lee Lewis

Jerry Lee Lewis arrives just beyond this moment, but his emergence confirms Sun's role as ignition point. His style extends performance intensity into even more physical territory.

Sun is not a one artist anomaly. It is a pressure zone for new stage language.

## Roy Orbison

Roy Orbison's early Sun recordings do not yet bring widespread commercial success. They matter artistically. His later prominence elsewhere reflects a pattern. Sun develops talent. Larger operations often carry it further.

## Charlie Rich

Charlie Rich's time at Sun broadens the label's stylistic reach into country, blues, and jazz tones. His career reinforces Sun's creative range, even if mainstream breakthrough arrives later.

---

## Why This Matters

Sun Records in 1955 is thriving creatively.

That strength supports Parker's position rather than undermines it.

Sun is a launchpad.

Elvis's trajectory requires broader infrastructure.

Other artists can develop gradually within a regional framework. Elvis cannot. His touring pattern, attendance numbers, and geographic response indicate acceleration that exceeds regional containment.

Seen from that angle, the RCA negotiations represent expansion rather than extraction.

Sun fulfills its function. It discovers. It records. It develops.

Parker's responsibility is different. He converts momentum into national reach.

RCA provides the mechanism.

By the end of December 1955, the transition is nearly complete.

The sound remains Memphis born.

The distribution becomes national.

In the next chapter Elvis In 56, we will examine how the contract transfer reshaped Sun's finances, identity, and long term positioning, and how it positioned Elvis for the eruption that followed in 1956.

# FULL KNOWN RECORD OF ALL 1955 PERFORMANCE DATES

January 1, Saturday,: Grand Prize Saturday Night, Jamboree, Eagles Hall, Houston, Texas.

January 2-4, Sunday-Tuesday,: Houston area, reported. period coverage suggests Elvis may have remained and performed in the Houston area through Tuesday, January 4,.

January 5, Wednesday,: City Auditorium, San Angelo, Texas.

January 6 (Thursday): Fair Park, Lubbock, Texas.

January 7, Friday,: High School Auditorium, Midland, Texas.

January 8, Saturday,: Louisiana Hayride, Municipal Auditorium, Shreveport, Louisiana.

January 11, Tuesday,: High School Gym, New Boston, Texas.

January 12 (Wednesday): City Auditorium, Clarksdale, Mississippi.

January 13 (Thursday): Catholic Club, Helena, Arkansas.

January 14, Friday,: Futrell High School Gym, Marianna, Arkansas.

January 15, Saturday,: Louisiana Hayride, Municipal Auditorium, Shreveport, Louisiana.

January 17, Monday,: Junior College Auditorium, Booneville, Mississippi.

January 18, Tuesday,: Alcorn County Courthouse, Corinth, Mississippi.

353

January 19 (Wednesday): Community Center, Sheffield, Alabama.

January 20, Thursday,: Leachville High School Gym, Leachville, Arkansas.

January 21, Friday,: National Guard Armory, Sikeston, Missouri.

January 22, Saturday,: Louisiana Hayride, Municipal Auditorium, Shreveport, Louisiana.

January 24, Monday,: Humble Oil Company Camp, Hawkins, Texas.

January 25 (Tuesday): Mayfair Building, Tyler, Texas.

January 26, Wednesday,: REA, Rural Electric Administration, Building, Gilmer, Texas.

January 27, Thursday,: Reo Palm Isle Club, Longview, Texas.

January 28 (Friday): High School, Gaston, Texas.

January 29, Saturday,: Louisiana Hayride, Municipal Auditorium, Shreveport, Louisiana.


## February

February 1 (Tuesday): High School, Randolph, Mississippi.

February 2 (Wednesday): High School, Augusta, Arkansas.

February 4, Friday,: Jesuit High School, New Orleans, Louisiana.

February 5, Saturday,: Louisiana Hayride, Municipal Auditorium, Shreveport, Louisiana.

February 6, Sunday,: Ellis Auditorium, Memphis, Tennessee, 3:00 and 8:00 p.m.,.

February 7, Monday,: Ripley High School Gym, Ripley, Mississippi.

February 10 (Thursday): High School, Alpine, Texas.

February 11, Friday,: Sports Arena, Carlsbad, New Mexico, 4:00 p.m.,. Hobbs, New Mexico, evening,.

February 12, Saturday,: Legion Hut, Carlsbad, New Mexico.

February 13, Sunday,: Fair Park Coliseum, Lubbock, Texas, 4:00 p.m.,.

February 14, Monday,: North Junior High School Auditorium, Roswell, New Mexico, 7:30 and 9:30 p.m.,.

February 15, Tuesday,: Fairpark Auditorium, Abilene, Texas, 7:00 and 9:00 p.m.,.

February 16, Wednesday,: Odessa Senior High School Field House, Odessa, Texas, 7:30 and 9:30 p.m.,.

February 17, Thursday,: City Auditorium, San Angelo, Texas, 7:30 and 9:30 p.m.,.

February 18, Friday,: West Monroe High School Auditorium, Monroe, Louisiana, 7:30 and 9:30 p.m.,.

February 19, Saturday,: Louisiana Hayride, Municipal Auditorium, Shreveport, Louisiana.

February 20, Sunday,: Robinson Auditorium, Little Rock, Arkansas, 3:00 and 8:15 p.m.,.

February 21 (Monday): City Auditorium, Camden, Arkansas.

February 22 (Tuesday): City Hall, Hope, Arkansas.

February 23, Wednesday,: High School Auditorium, Pine Bluff, Arkansas, 7:30 and 9:30 p.m.,.

February 24, Thursday,: South Side Elementary School, Bastrop, Louisiana, 7:30 and 9:30 p.m.,.

February 26, Saturday,: Hillbilly Jamboree, Circle Theater, Cleveland, Ohio, 7:30 and 10:30 p.m.,.


## March

March 2, Wednesday,: U.S. Armory, Newport, Arkansas, 8:00 p.m.,. Porky's Rooftop Club, Newport, Arkansas, 10:00 p.m.,.

March 4, Friday,: High School, De Kalb, Texas, unconfirmed,.

March 5, Saturday,: Louisiana Hayride, Municipal Auditorium, Shreveport, Louisiana.

March 7 (Monday): City Auditorium, Paris, Tennessee.

March 8 (Tuesday): Catholic Club, Helena, Arkansas.

March 9 (Wednesday): Armory, Poplar Bluff, Missouri.

March 11, Friday,: Jimmie Thompson's Arena, Alexandria, Louisiana.

March 12, Saturday,: Louisiana Hayride, Municipal Auditorium, Shreveport, Louisiana.

March 16 (Wednesday): Ruffin Theater, Covington, Tennessee.

March 17 (Thursday): Dessau Hall, Austin, Texas.

March 19, Saturday,: Grand Prize Jamboree, Eagles Hall, Houston, Texas.

March 25, Friday,: Dermott High School, Dermott, Arkansas.

March 26, Saturday,: Louisiana Hayride, Municipal Auditorium, Shreveport, Louisiana.

March 28, Monday,: Big Creek High School Gym, Big Creek, Mississippi.

March 29 (Tuesday): High School, Tocopola, Mississippi.

March 30, Wednesday,: El Dorado High School Auditorium, El Dorado, Arkansas.

March 31, Thursday,: Reo Palm Isle, Longview, Texas.


April

April 1, Friday,: Ector County Auditorium, Odessa, Texas.

April 2, Saturday,: Louisiana Hayride, City Auditorium, Houston, Texas.

April 7, Thursday,: Court House, Corinth, Mississippi, 2:30 and 8:00 p.m.,.

April 8 (Friday): B&B Club, Gobler, Missouri.

April 9, Saturday,: Louisiana Hayride, Municipal Auditorium, Shreveport, Louisiana.

April 13 (Wednesday): High School, Breckenridge, Texas.

April 14 (Thursday): Owl Park, Gainesville, Texas.

April 15 (Friday): High School, Stamford, Texas.

April 16, Saturday,: The Big "D" Jamboree, Sportatorium, Dallas, Texas.

April 20, Wednesday,: American Legion Hut, Grenada, Mississippi.

April 23, Saturday,: Louisiana Hayride, Heart O' Texas Arena, Waco, Texas.

April 24, Sunday,: Cook's Hoedown Club, Houston, Texas, evening,.

April 24, Sunday,: Magnolia Gardens, Houston, Texas, afternoon,.

April 25, Monday,: M-B Corral, Wichita Falls, Texas. Texas High School, Seymour, Texas.

April 26, Tuesday,: City Auditorium, Big Spring, Texas.

April 27, Wednesday,: American Legion Hall, Hobbs, New Mexico.

April 29, Friday,: The Cotton Club, Lubbock, Texas.

April 30, Saturday,: Louisiana Hayride, Gladewater High School, Gladewater, Texas.


**May**

May 1 (Sunday): Municipal Auditorium, New Orleans, Louisiana (2:00, 5:00, and 8:00 p.m.).

May 2 (Monday): High School, Baton Rouge, Louisiana (7:00 and 9:00 p.m.).

May 4 (Wednesday): Ladd Stadium, Mobile, Alabama.

May 5 (Thursday): Ladd Stadium, Mobile, Alabama.

May 7 (Saturday): Peabody Auditorium, Daytona Beach, Florida.

May 8 (Sunday): Fort Homer Hesterly Armory, Tampa, Florida (2:30 and 8:15 p.m.).

May 9 (Monday): City Auditorium, Fort Myers, Florida.

May 10 (Tuesday): Southeastern Pavilion, Ocala, Florida.

May 11 (Wednesday): Auditorium, Orlando, Florida (7:30 and 9:30 p.m.).

May 12 (Thursday): The new baseball park (eventually named the Gator Bowl), Jacksonville, Florida.

May 13 (Friday): The new baseball park, Jacksonville, Florida.

May 14 (Saturday): Shrine Auditorium, New Bern, North Carolina (7:00 and 9:00 p.m.).

May 15 (Sunday): Auditorium, Norfolk, Virginia (3:00 and 8:00 p.m.).

May 16 (Monday): Mosque Theater, Richmond, Virginia.

May 17 (Tuesday): City Auditorium, Asheville, North Carolina (7:00 and 9:00 p.m.).

May 18 (Wednesday): American Legion Auditorium, Roanoke, Virginia (7:00 and 9:00 p.m.).

May 19 (Thursday): Memorial Auditorium, Raleigh, North Carolina.

May 21 (Saturday): Louisiana Hayride, Municipal Auditorium, Shreveport, Louisiana.

May 22 (Sunday): Magnolia Gardens, Houston, Texas.

May 25 (Wednesday): American Legion Hall, Meridian, Mississippi.

May 26 (Thursday): Junior College Stadium, Meridian, Mississippi.

May 28 (Saturday): The Big "D" Jamboree, Sportatorium, Dallas, Texas.

May 29 (Sunday): North Side Coliseum, Fort Worth, Texas (4:00 p.m.); Sportatorium, Dallas, Texas (8:00 p.m.).

May 31 (Tuesday): High School Auditorium, Midland, Texas (7:30 p.m.); High School Field House, Odessa, Texas (8:30 p.m.).

## June

June 1, Wednesday,: High School Auditorium, Guymon, Oklahoma.

June 2 (Thursday): City Auditorium, Amarillo, Texas.

June 3, Friday,: Johnson-Connelley Pontiac Showroom, Lubbock, Texas. Fair Park Coliseum, Lubbock, Texas, 8:00 p.m.,.

June 4, Saturday,: Louisiana Hayride, Municipal Auditorium, Shreveport, Louisiana.

June 5, Sunday,: Hope Fair Park, Hope, Arkansas.

June 8 (Wednesday): Auditorium, Sweetwater, Texas.

June 10, Friday,: American Legion Hall, Breckenridge, Texas.

June 11, Saturday,: Louisiana Hayride, Municipal Auditorium, Shreveport, Louisiana.

June 14, Tuesday,: Bruce High School Gym, Bruce, Mississippi.

June 15, Wednesday,: Belden High School Gym, Belden, Mississippi.

June 17, Friday,: Roundup Hall, High School Gym, Stamford, Texas.

June 18, Saturday,: The Big "D" Jamboree, Sportatorium, Dallas, Texas.

June 19 (Sunday): Magnolia Gardens, Houston, Texas.

June 20, Monday,: City Auditorium, Beaumont, Texas, 7:00 and 9:00 p.m.,.

June 21, Tuesday,: City Auditorium, Beaumont, Texas, 2:30, 7:00, and 9:00 p.m.,.

June 23, Thursday,: McMahon Memorial Auditorium, Lawton, Oklahoma, 8:00 p.m.,. Southern Club, Lawton, Oklahoma, 11:00 p.m.,.

June 24 (Friday): Altus, Oklahoma.

June 25, Saturday,: Louisiana Hayride, Municipal Auditorium, Shreveport, Louisiana.

June 26 (Sunday): Slavonian Lodge, Biloxi, Mississippi.

June 27, Monday,: Airman's Club, Keesler Air Force Base, outside Biloxi, Mississippi.

June 28, Tuesday,: Airman's Club, Keesler Air Force Base, outside Biloxi, Mississippi.

June 29, Wednesday,: Curtis Gordon's Radio Ranch, Mobile, Alabama.

June 30, Thursday,: Curtis Gordon's Radio Ranch, Mobile, Alabama.


July

July 1, Friday,: Plaquemine Casino Club, Baton Rouge, Louisiana.

July 2, Saturday,: Louisiana Hayride, Municipal Auditorium, Shreveport, Louisiana.

July 3, Sunday,: Hoedown Club, Corpus Christi, Texas, 4:00 to 8:00 p.m.,.

July 4, Monday,: Hodges Park, De Leon, Texas. Recreation Hall, Stephenville, Texas. Memorial Hall, Brownwood, Texas, 8:00 p.m.,.

July 20, Wednesday,: Cape Arena Building, Cape Girardeau, Missouri.

July 21, Thursday,: Silver Moon Club, Newport, Arkansas.

July 23, Saturday,: The Big "D" Jamboree, Sportatorium, Dallas, Texas.

July 25, Monday,: New City Auditorium, Fort Myers, Florida.

July 26 (Tuesday): Municipal Auditorium, Orlando, Florida.

July 27 (Wednesday): Municipal Auditorium, Orlando, Florida.

July 28, Thursday,: The new baseball stadium, Jacksonville, Florida.

July 29, Friday,: The new baseball stadium, Jacksonville, Florida.

July 30, Saturday,: Peabody Auditorium, Daytona Beach, Florida, 7:30 and 9:30 p.m.,.

July 31, Sunday,: Fort Homer Hesterly Armory, Tampa, Florida, 2:15 and 8:15 p.m.,.


## August

August 1 (Monday): Fairgrounds, Tupelo, Mississippi.

August 2, Tuesday,: Community Center, Sheffield, Alabama, 7:00 and 9:30 p.m.,.

August 3, Wednesday,: Robinson Auditorium, Little Rock, Arkansas.

August 4, Thursday,: Municipal Auditorium, Camden, Arkansas, 7:00 and 9:30 p.m.,.

August 5, Friday,: Overton Park Shell, Memphis, Tennessee.

August 6 (Saturday): River Stadium, Batesville, Arkansas.

August 7, Sunday,: Magnolia Gardens, Houston, Texas, afternoon,. Cook's Hoedown, Houston, Texas, evening,.

August 8 (Monday): Mayfair Building, Tyler, Texas.

August 9 (Tuesday): Rodeo Arena, Henderson, Texas.

August 10 (Wednesday): Baseball Park, Gladewater, Texas.

August 11, Thursday,: Reo Palm Isle, Longview, Texas.

August 12 (Friday): Driller Park, Kilgore, Texas.

August 13, Saturday,: Louisiana Hayride, Municipal Auditorium, Shreveport, Louisiana.

August 20, Saturday,: Louisiana Hayride, Municipal Auditorium, Shreveport, Louisiana.

August 22, Monday,: Spudder Park, Wichita Falls, Texas.

August 23 (Tuesday): Bryan, Texas.

August 24, Wednesday,: Davy Crocket High School Football Stadium, Conroe, Texas.

August 25 (Thursday): The Sportcenter, Austin, Texas.

August 26 (Friday): Baseball Park, Gonzales, Texas.

August 27, Saturday,: Louisiana Hayride, Municipal Auditorium, Shreveport, Louisiana.


## September

September 1, Thursday,: Pontchartrain Beach Amusement Park, New Orleans, Louisiana.

September 2, Friday,: Arkansas Municipal Auditorium, Texarkana, Arkansas.

September 3, Saturday,: The Big "D" Jamboree, Sportatorium, Dallas, Texas. The Round-Up Club, Dallas, Texas, later in the evening,.

September 5, Monday,: St. Francis County Fair and Livestock Show Jamboree, Smith Stadium, Forrest City, Arkansas.

September 6, Tuesday,: High School Gym, Bono, Arkansas.

September 7, Wednesday,: National Guard Armory, Sikeston, Missouri.

September 8 (Thursday): City Auditorium, Clarksdale, Mississippi.

September 9, Friday,: McComb High School Auditorium, McComb, Mississippi.

September 10, Saturday,: Louisiana Hayride, Municipal Auditorium, Shreveport, Louisiana.

September 11, Sunday,: City Auditorium, Norfolk, Virginia, 3:00 and 8:00 p.m.,.

September 12 (Monday): City Auditorium, Norfolk, Virginia.

September 13, Tuesday,: Shrine Auditorium, New Bern, North Carolina.

September 14, Wednesday,: Fleming Stadium, Wilson, North Carolina.

September 15, Thursday,: American Legion Auditorium, Roanoke, Virginia.

September 16, Friday,: City Auditorium, Asheville, North Carolina.

September 17, Saturday,: High School Auditorium, Thomasville, North Carolina.

September 18, Sunday,: WRVA Theater, Richmond, Virginia, 2:30 and 8:30 p.m.,.

September 19 (Monday): WRVA Theater, Richmond, Virginia.

September 20 (Tuesday): Danville Fairgrounds, Danville, Virginia.

September 21, Wednesday,: Memorial Auditorium, Raleigh, North Carolina.

September 22 (Thursday): Civic Auditorium, Kingsport, Tennessee.

September 24, Saturday,: Louisiana Hayride, Municipal Auditorium, Shreveport, Louisiana.

September 26, Monday,: Junior High School Gym, Gilmer, Texas.

September 28 (Wednesday): B&B Club, Gobler, Missouri.


## October

October 1, Saturday,: Louisiana Hayride, Municipal Auditorium, Shreveport, Louisiana.

October 3, Monday,: G. Rolle White Coliseum, College Station, Texas.

October 4, Tuesday,: Boys Club Gymnasium, Paris, Texas, sponsored by the Optimist Club,.

October 5 (Wednesday): City Auditorium, Greenville, Texas.

October 6, Thursday,: Southwest Texas State University, San Marcos, Texas, afternoon,. Skyline Club, Austin, Texas, evening,.

October 8, Saturday,: Louisiana Hayride, Municipal Auditorium, Shreveport, Louisiana.

October 9, Sunday,: Cherry Springs Dance Hall, Cherryspring, Texas.

October 10, Monday,: Memorial Hall, Brownwood, Texas, sponsored by the Brownwood Volunteer Fire Department,.

October 11, Tuesday,: Fair Park Auditorium, Abilene, Texas, 7:00 and 9:15 p.m.,.

October 12, Wednesday,: Midland High School Auditorium, Midland, Texas.

October 13 (Thursday): Municipal Auditorium, Amarillo, Texas.

October 14, Friday,: High School Field House, Odessa, Texas.

October 15, Saturday,: Fair Park Auditorium, Lubbock, Texas. Cotton Club, Lubbock, Texas, later in the evening,.

October 16, Sunday,: Municipal Auditorium, Oklahoma City, Oklahoma, 3:30 and 8:00 p.m.,.

October 17, Monday,: Memorial Stadium, El Dorado, Arkansas.

October 19, Wednesday,: Circle Theater, Cleveland, Ohio, 7:30 and 10:00 p.m.,.

October 20, Thursday,: Brooklyn High School Auditorium, Cleveland, Ohio, 1:30 p.m.,. St. Michael's Hall, Cleveland, Ohio, 8:00 p.m.,.

October 21, Friday,: Missouri Theater, St. Louis, Missouri, 7:00 and 9:30 p.m.,.

October 22, Saturday,: Missouri Theater, St. Louis, Missouri, 7:00 and 9:30 p.m.,.

October 23, Sunday,: Missouri Theater, St. Louis, Missouri, 2:00, 5:00, and 8:00 p.m.,.

October 24, Monday,: Silver Moon Club, Newport, Arkansas.

October 26, Wednesday,: Vigor High School, Mobile, Alabama, 10:00 a.m.,. Greater Gulf States

Fair, Prichard, Alabama, 3:30 and 7:30 p.m.,.
National Guard Armory, Jackson, Alabama.

October 28, Friday,: Curtis Gordon's Ranch
Club, Mobile, Alabama.

October 29, Saturday,: Louisiana Hayride,
Municipal Auditorium, Shreveport, Louisiana.


## November

November 5, Saturday,: Louisiana Hayride,
Municipal Auditorium, Shreveport, Louisiana.

November 6, Sunday,: Biloxi Community
House, Biloxi, Mississippi, 2:00 and 8:00 p.m.,.

November 7, Monday,: Keesler Air Force Base,
outside Biloxi, Mississippi.

November 8, Tuesday,: Keesler Air Force Base,
outside Biloxi, Mississippi.

November 12, Saturday,: Carthage Milling
Company, Carthage, Texas, 2:00 p.m.,. Louisiana
Hayride, Municipal Auditorium, Shreveport,
Louisiana.

November 13, Sunday,: Ellis Auditorium,
Memphis, Tennessee, 3:00 and 8:00 p.m.,.

November 14, Monday,: Forrest City High
School Auditorium, Forrest City, Arkansas, 7:00
and 9:15 p.m.,.

November 15, Tuesday,: Community Center,
Sheffield, Alabama, 7:00 and 9:30 p.m.,.

November 16, Wednesday,: Camden City
Auditorium, Camden, Arkansas, 7:00 and 9:15
p.m.,.

November 17, Thursday,: Arkansas Municipal
Auditorium, Texarkana, Arkansas, 7:00 and 9:15
p.m.,.

November 18, Friday,: Reo Palm Isle, Longview, Texas.

November 19, Saturday,: Louisiana Hayride, remote radio broadcast from Gladewater, Texas high school.

November 25, Friday,: Woodrow Wilson High School, Port Arthur, Texas.

November 26, Saturday,: Louisiana Hayride, Municipal Auditorium, Shreveport, Louisiana.

November 29, Tuesday,: The Mosque Theater, Richmond, Virginia, Philip Morris Employees Night,.


## December

December 2 (Friday): Sports Arena, Atlanta, Georgia.

December 3 (Saturday): State Coliseum, Montgomery, Alabama.

December 4 (Sunday): Lyric Theater, Indianapolis, Indiana.

December 5 (Monday): Lyric Theater, Indianapolis, Indiana.

December 6 (Tuesday): Lyric Theater, Indianapolis, Indiana.

December 7 (Wednesday): Lyric Theater, Indianapolis, Indiana.

December 8 (Thursday): Rialto Theater, Louisville, Kentucky.

December 9, Friday,: High School, Swifton, Arkansas. B&I Club, Swifton, Arkansas, later in the evening,.

December 10, Saturday,: Louisiana Hayride, Municipal Auditorium, Shreveport, Louisiana.

December 12, Monday,: National Guard Armory, Amory, Mississippi, or Dec 13,.

December 15 (Thursday): Catholic Club, Helena, Arkansas.

December 17, Saturday,: Louisiana Hayride, Municipal Auditorium, Shreveport, Louisiana.

December 31, Saturday,: Louisiana Hayride, Municipal Auditorium, Shreveport, Louisiana.

## Sources & Notes

General References

Sourcing priority: when accounts differ, I
privilege dated from that time documentation, trade
press, local papers, ads, and session logs, and the
major Elvis chronologies over later recollections
and web summaries.

Texas State Historical Association, Handbook of
Texas Online: San Angelo. Lubbock. Midland. Tyler.
Longview. New Boston. Hawkins. Gilmer.

Louisiana Endowment for the Humanities, 64
Parishes: Louisiana Hayride. Shreveport.

Mississippi Encyclopedia: Coahoma County.
Alcorn County. Prentiss County.

Encyclopedia of Arkansas History and Culture:
Helena-West Helena. Marianna. Leachville.

Encyclopedia of Alabama: Sheffield.

Missouri State Archives, Office of the Secretary
of State,: Missouri Bootheel history. Little River
Drainage background.

Major Elvis reference works for chronology and
context: Ernst Jorgensen, Elvis Presley: A Life in
Music. Peter Guralnick and Ernst Jorgensen, Elvis
day-by-day. Peter Guralnick, Last Train to
Memphis.

Elvis day-by-day: The Early Years, 1935-1959,
Random House, entries for February 1955 schedule,
including Shreveport, Memphis shows, and the
Hank Snow tour routing.

Supplemental online references, orientation only. not treated as primary evidence,:

LiveAbout, "Elvis Presley Timeline: 1955", entry for Jan. 11, 1955: Parker first takes notice after Texarkana DJ "Uncle Dudley" reports crowd frenzy,.

PopHistoryDig, "Elvis Presley & Colonel Parker", notes Parker first takes notice after Jan. 11, 1955, Texarkana report,.

Graceland Blog: 'Memphis Stages', Graceland. Com, context on Memphis venues, and the Feb. 6, 1955, Ellis Auditorium/Messick shows.

Graceland Blog: 'Louisiana Hayride', Graceland. Com, background on the Hayride as a radio broadcast platform in the 1950s.

Texas State Historical Association, Handbook of Texas Online, entries for Alpine, Brewster County, Abilene, San Angelo, and Odessa, town background, and local context.

Encyclopedia of Arkansas, Central Arkansas Library System, entries for Camden, Hope, and Pine Bluff, town background, and historical setting.

Encyclopaedia Britannica, Pine Bluff, Arkansas, geographic, and historical overview.

Country Living, 2017, overview of Elvis' early relationship with Dixie Locke and the pre-fame Memphis years.

Peter Guralnick, Last Train to Memphis. Ernst Jorgensen, Elvis Presley: A Life in Music. Alanna Nash, The Colonel. Billboard Magazine, 1955. from that time Southern newspaper advertisements.

For the recurring radio snapshots, I leaned on Billboard's 1955 charts, including the year-end Top R&B 45s lists and the 1955 singles rankings, alongside Library of Congress commentary on key crossover records such as Little Richard's "Tutti Frutti."

American Songwriter, "On This Day in 1955, Elvis Presley Incites His First Riot at a Florida Concert", May 13, 1955, Jacksonville crowd incident,.

Florida History Network, "May 13, 1955: Jax fans chase Elvis after show, tear off his clothes", Jacksonville riot account,.

Peter Guralnick, Last Train to Memphis, Richmond RCA Reps, McCuen/Crumpacker, and Meridian/Jimmie Rodgers Memorial Celebration context.

Ernst Jorgensen, Elvis Presley: A Life in Music / Elvis day-by-day, routing, and date confirmations for the Hank Snow package tour.

ElvisRecords. Com, Sun 223 "Mystery Train / I Forgot to Remember to Forget" discography entry, Sun single details,.

Billboard country chart histories, 1955-56 issues, "I Forgot to Remember to Forget" peaked at No. 1, Feb. 1956,.

ScottyMoore. Net, "First RCA Contract for Elvis", Sun contract price: $35,000 plus $5,000 back royalties,.

Major Elvis chronologies, Jorgensen. Guralnick, and RCA-era documentation, Mae Axton demo /

Nashville meeting, Nov. 10, 1955, and RCA signing, Nov. 21, 1955,.

Major Elvis discographies/chronologies, Jorgensen. sessionography sources, Sun attempt of "When It Rains, It Really Pours", Nov. 1955, and subsequent release history.

Inflation note, publisher standard,: Using BLS CPI-U annual averages, 1955 CPI = 26.8. 2024 CPI = 313.689, the multiplier is about 11.7048×. Approximate 1955→2024 equivalents: \$35,000 ≈ \$410,000. \$5,000 ≈ \$58,500. \$425 ≈ \$4,975. \$2,083.63 ≈ \$24,389.

ElvisRecords. Com, "Good Rockin' Tonight / I Don't Care If the Sun Don't Shine" discography entry, Sun original release and later RCA reissue listing,.

This document outlines additional historical sources beyond Peter Guralnick and Ernst Jørgensen, that document Colonel Tom Parker's actions in November and December 1955 to secure Elvis Presley's national television exposure in 1956. These sources predate or operate independently from later modern syntheses and demonstrate a broad, multi-source foundation for this interpretation.

Albert Goldman, Elvis, 1981,
Albert Goldman provides one of the clearest early accounts of Parker's deliberate decision to withhold Elvis from television until maximum power could be achieved. Goldman describes Parker's belief that television was a weapon rather than a mere promotional outlet, and that Elvis's debut needed to

be explosive and national in scope. Goldman emphasizes Parker's manipulation of controversy and his refusal to accept minor or local television appearances in late 1955.

Bob Neal, Interviews, and Memoirs
Bob Neal, Elvis's original manager, later acknowledged in interviews and memoir material that Colonel Parker assumed control of television talks in November 1955. Neal confirmed that Parker was already communicating directly with New York-based recording and television executives by Thanksgiving 1955, effectively removing Neal from national-level decision making. Neal's recollections are cited in early biographies and oral histories that predate modern syntheses.

Alanna Nash, Elvis Aaron Presley: Revelations from the Memphis Mafia, 1995,
Alanna Nash documents firsthand recollections from Elvis's inner circle indicating that Parker spoke openly in late 1955 about television being the decisive factor in Elvis's rise. Interviews with Red West and other early associates recall Parker's insistence that Elvis's television debut be live, national, and unavoidable. These oral histories were recorded independently of later scholarly interpretations.

Stanley Oberst, Early Biographical Research
Stanley Oberst's early Elvis research preserves first-generation accounts of Parker's maneuvering during the transition from Sun Records to RCA. Oberst documents Parker's courtship of New York media figures and his planning of television exposure prior

to the finalization of the RCA contract, a claim later corroborated by archival findings.

Jerry Hopkins, Elvis: A Biography, 1971, Jerry Hopkins situates Parker's television strategy within the broader context of 1950s media economics. Hopkins notes that Parker understood television's unmatched power to create instant national stardom and that he deliberately leveraged Elvis's controversial reputation to entice producers. Hopkins' work predates later biographies and served as a foundational source for subsequent scholarship.

Trade Press and Corporate Records, 1955, Contemporaneous reporting in Billboard, Variety, and Cash Box from late 1955 documents increasing industry attention to Elvis as a television-ready performer. RCA Victor corporate discussions referenced in these publications show that national television exposure was already part of Elvis's promotional strategy prior to his first RCA recording session. These sources provide independent, contemporaneous confirmation of Parker's actions.

Chapter-by-Chapter Sources

January 1955

Texas State Historical Association, Handbook of Texas Online: San Angelo. Lubbock. Midland. Tyler. Longview. New Boston. Hawkins. Gilmer.

Louisiana Endowment for the Humanities, 64 Parishes: Louisiana Hayride. Shreveport.

Mississippi Encyclopedia: Coahoma County. Alcorn County. Prentiss County.

Encyclopedia of Arkansas History and Culture: Helena-West Helena. Marianna. Leachville.

Encyclopedia of Alabama: Sheffield.

Missouri State Archives, Office of the Secretary of State,: Missouri Bootheel history. Little River Drainage background.

Major Elvis reference works for chronology and context: Ernst Jorgensen, Elvis Presley: A Life in Music. Peter Guralnick and Ernst Jorgensen, Elvis day-by-day. Peter Guralnick, Last Train to Memphis.

**Supplemental online references (orientation only):**

LiveAbout, "Elvis Presley Timeline: 1955", entry for Jan. 11, 1955: Parker first takes notice after Texarkana DJ "Uncle Dudley" reports crowd frenzy,.

PopHistoryDig, "Elvis Presley & Colonel Parker", notes Parker first takes notice after Jan. 11, 1955, Texarkana report,.


February 1955

Elvis day-by-day: The Early Years, 1935-1959, Random House, entries for February 1955 schedule, including Shreveport, Memphis shows, and the Hank Snow tour routing.

Memphis Press-Scimitar, Feb. 5, 1955, photo/feature inside Sun Studios, commonly referenced in day-by-day chronologies,.

Cash Box, Feb. 1955 trade-press report, Bob Neal's booking office noted at 160 Union Avenue, Memphis.

William Morris Agency correspondence, Harry Kalcheim to Bob Neal, Feb. 10, 1955, early agency interest noted in touring summaries.

RCA correspondence, Steve Sholes, Feb. 1955, internal notes on Elvis's Sun status and Parker's positioning, summarized in early-career chronologies,.

Graceland Blog: 'Memphis Stages', Graceland. Com, context on Memphis venues, and the Feb. 6, 1955, Ellis Auditorium/Messick shows.

Graceland Blog: 'Louisiana Hayride', Graceland. Com, background on the Hayride as a radio broadcast platform in the 1950s.

Texas State Historical Association, Handbook of Texas Online, entries for Alpine, Brewster County, Abilene, San Angelo, and Odessa, town background, and local context.

Encyclopedia of Arkansas, Central Arkansas Library System, entries for Camden, Hope, and Pine Bluff, town background, and historical setting.

Encyclopaedia Britannica, Pine Bluff, Arkansas, geographic, and historical overview.

Country Living, 2017, overview of Elvis' early relationship with Dixie Locke and the pre-fame Memphis years.

March 1955

See General References.

Ernst Jorgensen, Elvis: A Life in Music: Sun sessionography for March 1955, "I'm Left, You're Right, She's Gone". use of drums by Jimmie Lott,.

Peter Guralnick & Ernst Jorgensen, Elvis day-by-day: The Early Years, 1935-1959: March 1955 tour stops, timing notes, and the Arthur Godfrey Talent Scouts audition, March 23,.

Alanna Nash, The Colonel: The Extraordinary Story of Colonel Tom Parker and Elvis Presley, Parker/Kalcheim/Diskin correspondence and management power around the Godfrey audition.

from that time press/tour advertisements and surviving live tapes, Grand Prize Jamboree, Houston, bill details and circulating recordings, as compiled in major Elvis chronologies,.

April 1955

Peter Guralnick, Last Train to Memphis. Ernst Jorgensen, Elvis Presley: A Life in Music. Alanna Nash, The Colonel. Billboard Magazine, 1955. from that time Southern newspaper advertisements.

Billboard Magazine, June 4, 1955, Odessa, Texas item referencing Cecil Holifield and 850 admissions for the April 1 Ector County Auditorium show.

from that time local newspaper coverage and advertisements for Louisiana Hayride remotes, Houston, April 2. Waco, April 23. Gladewater, April 30, and TNT Records tour dates, April 25-29, supporting hall routing, overflow crowd reports, and touring context.

May 1955

American Songwriter, "On This Day in 1955, Elvis Presley Incites His First Riot at a Florida Concert", May 13, 1955, Jacksonville crowd incident,.

Florida History Network, "May 13, 1955: Jax fans chase Elvis after show, tear off his clothes", Jacksonville riot account,.

Meridian Star, May 1955, Jimmie Rodgers Memorial Celebration listings and local coverage, American Legion Hall note: "Music will be provided by Elvis Pressley and his orchestra",.

Country Song Roundup, 1955,: report on Presley's Meridian appearance, encores, song titles, and publishing/folio mentions,.

Peter Guralnick, Last Train to Memphis. Ernst Jorgensen, Elvis Presley: A Life in Music: touring context for the Hank Snow package, Florida routing, promotion days, radio interviews, and the Memphis prom interlude.

June 1955

See General References.

Peter Guralnick & Ernst Jorgensen, Elvis day-by-day: The Early Years, 1935-1959: June 1955 routing, Texas/Oklahoma/Mississippi/Gulf Coast, club openings, and multi-show runs, Beaumont/Lawton/Biloxi/Mobile,.

Billboard, June 1955 trade reporting, Cecil Holifield's report on Sun single sales velocity and local demand, as cited in major Elvis chronologies,.

Alanna Nash, The Colonel: The Extraordinary Story of Colonel Tom Parker and Elvis Presley, Parker correspondence with Tom Diskin and pressure dynamics with Bob Neal during June 1955.

Sun Records / Elvis discography & label-business timelines, as compiled in major discographies, contract inquiries, and growing major-label attention in mid-1955.

June Juanico recollections/interviews, as compiled in reputable Elvis biographies/chronologies, Keesler Air Force Base / Biloxi encounters in late June 1955.

Mac Davis recollections, later interviews/biographical accounts, attendance at the June 3, 1955, Lubbock car-dealer appearance. later songwriting connection to Elvis recordings.


July 1955

See General References.


August 1955

ElvisRecords. Com, Sun 223 "Mystery Train / I Forgot to Remember to Forget" discography entry, Sun single details,.

See General References: Billboard country chart histories, 1955-56, for "I Forgot to Remember to Forget" peak, Feb. 1956,.


September 1955

See General References.


October 1955

See General References.

Peter Guralnick, Last Train to Memphis, Parker's October telegrams, and the structure/timing of late-1955 contract-option talks.

Alanna Nash, The Colonel, business pressure, and negotiation context around the Sun contract purchase push.

November 1955

ScottyMoore. Net, "First RCA Contract for Elvis", Sun contract price: $35,000 plus $5,000 back royalties,.

Billboard Magazine, 1955, Annual DJ Poll, "Most Promising C&W Artist",.

See General References: major Elvis chronologies, Jorgensen. Guralnick, for Mae Axton demo / RCA signing timeline, Nov. 1955,.

See General References: major Elvis discographies/chronologies, Jorgensen.

sessionography sources, for "When It Rains, It Really Pours", Sun attempt, Nov. 1955, and later release history.

December 1955

See General References,

Stay Tuned For "ELVIS IN 56"

Thanks For LOVING ELVIS!

Joe Sins

www.ingramcontent.com/pod-product-compliance
Lightning Source LLC
Chambersburg PA
CBHW030906120626
46554CB00001B/25